AF697776

SPECTACULAR DISAPPEARANCES

Spectacular Disappearances

CELEBRITY AND PRIVACY, 1696–1801

Julia H. Fawcett

To Dennis + Morgan— Thanks for being such supportive friends!
Julia

University of Michigan Press
Ann Arbor

Copyright © 2016 by Julia H. Fawcett
All rights reserved

This book may not be reproduced, in whole or in part, including illustrations, in any form (beyond that copying permitted by Sections 107 and 108 of the U.S. Copyright Law and except by reviewers for the public press), without written permission from the publisher.

Published in the United States of America by the
University of Michigan Press
Manufactured in the United States of America
♾ Printed on acid-free paper

2019 2018 2017 2016 4 3 2 1

A CIP catalog record for this book is available from the British Library.

ISBN 978-0-472-11980-6 (hardcover : alk. paper)
ISBN 978-0-472-12180-9 (e-book)

ACKNOWLEDGMENTS

I have often wondered if my interest in authors who wrote themselves in order to obscure themselves stems from my own anxieties about the permanence of the printed word—my own longing (that I imagine everyone shares?) for words that linger on the page for a moment only and then—miraculously, mercifully—disappear before their inadequacies can be exposed. I think I will always harbor this anxiety, but I have been blessed with mentors, colleagues, friends, and family members who have known how to couch their criticism in kindness and without whom I could never have summoned the courage to keep this work up or to set these words down.

The germs for this book's ideas began many years ago, when, as an undergraduate at Harvard, I stumbled somewhat accidentally (to fulfill a requirement) into Lynn Festa's course on "Sex and Sensibility during the Enlightenment." Thank goodness for requirements. That course is one of the reasons I decided, years later, to study the eighteenth century. I owe a debt, too, to Beth Lyman, my undergraduate thesis advisor and the first to introduce me to performance theory.

I arrived at Yale believing I would study Gertrude Stein, and I often joke that I decided to study the eighteenth century because that's what all the cool kids at Yale were doing. People who knew those kids know how infectious their enthusiasm for their subject can be, and how much truth there is in the joke. My advisors, Joe Roach and Jill Campbell, reminded me of the kind of scholar I wanted to be. By asking generative questions, Jill helped me to write the book I was trying to write, and everything I was struggling to say in early drafts she has helped me to say better. Joe's ebullient personality, sense of humor, and limitless generosity constantly remind me why I got into this profession in the first place. His love for the literature he reads, the performances he watches, and the job he does (not to mention the Marlon Brando impression with which he lightened the mood at my prospectus defense) is infectious and has sustained me even when the obstacles seem insurmountable and the rewards small.

My professors Ala Alryyes, Wendy Lee, Claude Rawson, Katie Trumpener, and Elliott Visconsi offered me advice and support in the classroom and outside of it, on the dissertation and beyond. My fellow graduate students Dan Gustafson, James Horowitz, Daniel Jump, Heather Klemann, Hilary Menges, Lina Moe, Nichole Wright, and especially Andy Heisel provided a supportive community at and between our Eighteenth-Century Working Group sessions. I had the good fortune in graduate school to feel welcome within not one field, but two; I owe gratitude as well to the Performance Studies Working Group and especially to Joe Cermatori, Emily Coates, Miriam Felton-Dansky, Jason Fitzgerald, Jacob Gallagher-Ross, Chris Grobe, Dominika Laster, Paige McGinley, Madison Moore, John Muse, Alex Ripp, and Ariel Watson. Marc Robinson, Katie Trumpener, and Brian Walsh went above and beyond the call of duty by reading and commenting on substantial portions of the dissertation-in-progress. So, too, did Linda Peterson, whose scholarship on Mary Robinson and whose cheerful support undoubtedly helped to make this project what it is. Sadly, Linda passed away as this book was in production; she will be greatly missed.

My original cohort at Yale could not have been more supportive: a special thank you to Liz Appel, Sam Cross, David Currell, Mahni Ghorashi, Laura Miles, Fiona Robinson, Jesse Schotter, and Steve Tedeschi. When they weren't available, I found an extremely welcoming (and hilarious) adoptive cohort in Sam Fallon, Len Gutkin, Matt Hunter, Andrew Karas, Tom Koenigs, Sebastian Lecourt, Sarah Mahurin, Tessie Prakas, Natalie Prizel, Aaron Ritzenberg, Justin Sider, and Joe Stadolnik, Thanks, too, to Erica Sayers and Ruben Roman, who never ran out of Hershey's kisses.

The intellectual communities that have supported this project extend far beyond Yale. At Stanford, where I spent a year as a visiting student, John Bender, Blakey Vermuele, and Peggy Phelan welcomed me into their classrooms, their colloquia, and their conversations. Nathalie Phillips, James Wood, and especially Doug Jones and Derek Miller were generous with their thoughts, their time, and their friendship.

These communities include, too, those that cross institutional boundaries but are sustained by Joe Roach's influence and by the shared strangeness of studying performance within literature departments. I am especially grateful to Emily Anderson, Misty Anderson, Paula Backscheider, Jason Shaffer, and Stuart Sherman for their thoughtful comments on the work in progress. Conversations with and talks by Robin Bernstein, Laura Engel, Elaine McGirr, Felicity Nussbaum, Nick Salvato, and Sharon Setzer added greatly to my understanding of my topic in particular and literary and performance studies in general. Joe's dedication in using a Mellon Foundation grant to fund Interdisciplinary Performance Studies at Yale gave performance studies scholars in New Haven a community within and outside of our home departments. The program also gave me a postdoctoral fellowship that allowed me to continue my research after graduating, and for that, too, I am extremely grateful.

I have been fortunate to discover a wonderful institutional home at Ryerson University in Toronto, and I owe a deep gratitude to my colleagues in the English Department—especially Jason Boyd, Jennifer Burwell, Dennis Denisoff, Wendy Francis, Irene Gammel, Morgan Holmes, Lorraine Janzen Kooistra, Nima Naghibi, Luanne MacDonnell, Andrew O'Malley, Dale Smith, Sophie Thomas, and Monique Tschofen—as well as beyond the English Department—especially Ben Barry and Peggy Shannon. Colleen Derkatch and Laura Fisher deserve special thanks for their support, their humor, their fashion advice, and their wide-ranging knowledge of Toronto cocktail bars. In addition, I have benefitted from my proximity, in Toronto, to several other great universities and their faculty members' and graduate students' generosity and time. Special thanks to Brian Corman, Simon Dickie, Alex Hernandez, Tom Keymer, Laura Levin, Danny O'Quinn, Fiona Ritchie, Terry Robinson, David Francis Taylor, Marlis Schweitzer, and Katie Zien. Thanks, also, to the members of the Toronto Performance Studies Working Group and the Eighteenth-Century Working Group, both of which have provided a rich intellectual community for me in Toronto.

A two-week stint at the Mellon School for Theater and Performance at Harvard University at a critical moment allowed me better to put the issues I address in this book into context. The members of my cohort that year were insightful and inspiring. I owe a special thanks to Martin Puchner for founding the School, to Rebecca Kastleman for making sure it ran so smoothly, and to Andrew Sofer for his invaluable comments on my manuscript.

LeAnn Fields, my editor at Michigan, has provided a home not only for this book but for so many like it that don't fit neatly into categories of performance studies, theater history, or literary studies. The field wouldn't be what it is today without her vision and support. I am grateful, as well, to my anonymous readers, and to Christopher Dreyer, Marcia LaBrenz, and the entire staff of the University of Michigan Press. My fabulous research assistant, Kate Jefford, worked diligently and quickly to prepare the manuscript for publication; and my indexer, Daniel Gundlach, approached his task with endless patience and admirable diligence. An essay based on parts of Chapter 1 appeared as "The Over-Expressive Celebrity and the Deformed King: Recasting the Spectacle as Subject in Colley Cibber's *Richard III*," *PMLA*, 126.4 (October 2011): 950-965. Parts of Chapter 3 were published as "Creating Character in '*Chiaro Oscuro*': Sterne's Celebrity, Cibber's *Apology*, and the

Life of *Tristram Shandy*," *The Eighteenth Century: Theory and Interpretation* 53.2 (Summer 2012): 141-162. I appreciate the thoughtful comments and careful attentions of both journals' readers and editors, particularly Jean Howard, Patricia Yaeger, and Nancy Vickers. Fellow members of the Yale Eighteenth-/Nineteenth Century Colloquium and the Yale British Studies Colloquium as well as of the American Society for Eighteenth-Century Studies, the American Society for Theater Research, American Theater in Higher Education, and Performance Studies International commented on and influenced this work in its early stages.

I am grateful to the archivists, curators, and staffs of the libraries where I conducted much of the research for this project: the Beinecke Library at Yale University, the Lewis Walpole Library at Yale University (especially Susan Odell Walker and Cynthia Roman), Yale University Libraries, Stanford University Libraries, Belmont Public Libraries, the New York Public Library, Ryerson University Libraries, and the Thomas Fisher Rare Books Library at the University of Toronto. Thanks, also, to the staffs of the coffee shops that allowed me to sit for long hours with laptop and library books: Blue State and Booktraders (New Haven), Vineapple (Brooklyn), and Seven Grams and Ezra's Pound (Toronto).

All of these places and crossings have introduced me to countless friends and confidantes whose influence over this work is indirect but no less important for being so. In Toronto and beyond: Tushar Arora, Jo Baron, Teresa Bejan, Amanda Hollingworth, Sameer Farooq, Mandy Goodwin, Jess Prince, Ali Qadeer, Belinda Schubert, Lee Slinger, Penny Smith, Morgan Sonderegger, Nick Stang, Heather Stewart, Erin Stropes, Anna Treusch, David Weinfeld, Isla Whitford, Nathan Whitford, Brad Wong, my Y Ladies and my friends at the Ramsden dog park; and especially the Cesare-Schotzko family (Nikki, David, Leo, and Duncan), Kavitha Krishnamurthy, Ronit Rubinstein, and Larry Switzky. In New York: Alison Cherry, Colleen Clark, Josh DeFlorio, Colleen Egan, Mike Hines, Wally Novacich-DeFlorio, and the Novacich family. In New Haven: Priyanka Anand, Cynthia Chang, Lucy Currell, Ben Siracusa Hillman and Betty Luther Hillman, Jamie O'Leary, Francis Song, Nikki Strong, and Owen Wolfram. In the Bay area: Davey Hathorn and Kathy Lee, the Ghorashi family, and especially Jeff Lamont. And in Cambridge: Laura Perry, Tess Mullen, Julia Reischel, and Heather Thomason for realizing women could run a theater company (imagine!) and the Six-Headed Monster (Ellen Ching, Candice Cho, Christine Mulvey, Lauren Sirois, and Laura Yilmaz) for pretty much everything. Thank you.

Finally, there are a few friends missing from the lists above because they transcend all categories and have been instrumental to this project at multiple stages of its development. Sarah Novacich, Nathalie Wolfram, and Molly Farrell: thanks for lunches, for laughter, and for flowers; for reading everything from prospectus to page proofs and from edits to emails; for THE VOICE, for takeout, for early mornings and late nights, and for Thursdays. And then, of course, to my family: Robert and Christy Fawcett, Claire Fawcett, and Scout Fawcett: thanks for teaching me the words to everything (and for forgiving me even when I got them wrong).

CONTENTS

Introduction

How can the modern individual maintain control over his or her self-representation when the whole world seems to be watching?

This question is a familiar one amid the early twenty-first century's elaborate architecture of twenty-four-hour newsrooms, chat rooms, and interrogation rooms. But in the pages that follow I argue that the question first emerged in the streets and on the stages of Restoration and eighteenth-century London, a city with its own elaborate architecture of playhouses, coffeehouses, clubs, pubs, and print shops—and its own anxieties about privacy and the modern subject. It was, after all, in the years following the English Civil War that newspapers sprang up to document and to direct the daily life of urbanites, that the criminal justice system was reconceived as an institution not to punish but to monitor the nation's subjects, and that mere actors and actresses—people with nothing to their names but the willingness to submit themselves to an ever-hungrier public gaze—began to live like kings and queens. And as this question began to circulate with more urgency, I will argue, it was England's early celebrities—the comedian Colley Cibber; his cross-dressing daughter Charlotte Charke; the preacher-turned-novelist Laurence Sterne; the pioneering actor David Garrick; his protégée George Anne Bellamy; and the actress, poet, and royal courtesan Mary Robinson—who first proposed an answer.

The answer that they proposed and that the rest of this book will elucidate suggests a new way of approaching and understanding eighteenth-century descriptions and performances of the self—specifically, those descriptions and performances that resist the well-known narrative of how the self was made modern. These include *The Life and Opinions of Tristram Shandy, Gentleman*, which Ian Watt famously excluded from his seminal work *The Rise of the Novel* (1957) by dismissing it as "not so much a novel as the parody of a novel."[1] They include, also, the actor's autobiographies (as well as the autobiographical performances surrounding them) that take the form of a novel but assume the reader's knowledge of the stage, thereby disturbing the otherwise neat division that previous scholarship has recognized between novelistic and theatrical selves. Since Watt, much of this scholarship has been concerned with tracing the individual's emergence as "essentially the proprietor of his own person or capacities," in C. B. Macpherson's words[2]—or, in Dror Wahrman's, with tracking precisely when and how England's writers, readers, and spectators first began to construe and to create the modern subject in terms of "a very particular understanding of personal identity, one that presupposes an essential core of selfhood characterized by psychological depth, or interiority, which is the bedrock of unique, expressive identity."[3] Implicit in this definition, as Wahrman and others have pointed out, is the assumption that this "unique, expressive identity" is a consummation devoutly to be wished—a mark of modernity that, sometime between the Renaissance and Romanticism, all Britons began to strive for but only certain characters (and certain literary genres) could achieve.[4]

Yet it is striking how many writers during the long eighteenth century evince a deep anxiety about the vulnerability and even the dispossession facing anyone who displayed a "unique, expressive identity" to a reading or viewing public. Pamela's epistolary self comes into being only when her defining trait—her virtue—is threatened by Mr. B's advances; Alexander Pope's declarations of himself as the author and the owner of his poetry betray his awareness of the price of owning up to his words and bearing the criticism that ownership entails;[5] Mr. Spectator introduces himself to his readers in his first issue by warning them not to inquire too much into his identity, "for the greatest Pain I can suffer, is the being talked to, and being stared at."[6] Whether fictional (like Pamela), historical (like Pope) or pseudonymous (like Mr. Spectator), these characters declare the desire to be known at the same time that they betray their or their authors' apprehensions about the loss of control over self-definition to which knowability subjects them.

The celebrities whose stories fill the chapters of this book lament this loss most keenly. Consider, for instance, the actor Colley Cibber, who rose to national prominence after his comedy *Love's Last Shift* became the runaway hit of 1696. Cibber went on to publish the first secular autobiography in English, *An Apology for the Life of Colley Cibber*, in 1740—only to admit within its pages his discomfort at the attention his fame had garnered him: "Against blind Malice, and staring Inhumanity, whatever is upon the Stage, has no

Defence!" he writes. "There . . . I stood helpless, and expos'd, to whatever they might please to load, or asperse me with."[7] Cibber's complaint articulates a paradox that the other examples merely suggest: by defining himself clearly and legibly, as this new ideology of selfhood seemed to require and as his career onstage demanded, Cibber left himself "helpless, and expos'd" to his spectators' and readers' opinions, misinterpretations, and manipulations of the identity he had made known. This paradox suggests, contrary to the prevailing narrative of the individual's emergence, that eighteenth-century writers, performers, and citizens had as much to gain from unmaking as they did from making the modern self.

But how might a modern self be unmade? How might an eighteenth-century man or woman perform the legibility that guaranteed his or her citizenship within the ideology of "unique, expressive identity" while shielding himself or herself from the public gaze that threatened his or her control over that identity's expression? Though pressing for Pamela, Pope, and Mr. Spectator, such questions were even more pressing for celebrities like Cibber, whose careers demanded that they live their lives in the public eye. In this book, I chart these celebrities' responses to such questions by exploring the unique but related strategies each developed to paralyze their publics' attempts to decipher their private selves. By understanding why and how celebrities deployed these strategies, we can better understand not only the threats that the ideology of modern selfhood posed for those engaged in it, but also why characters who seemed to break all the rules of this ideology nonetheless enjoyed such popularity in eighteenth-century culture. And we can understand, too, the possibilities for self-representation within a modern world where someone always seems to be watching.

Though there are important differences between the self-representations I will examine here, my contention is that all have a common ancestor in a strategy of performance that I am calling *overexpression*. This strategy allows its practitioners at once to invite and to disrupt the public gaze, paradoxically, by enhancing or exaggerating the features through which they might be recognized and evaluated by their spectators. An overexpressive performance appears at first glance to be an unskilled or overwrought attempt at self-definition. It employs the same signifiers that eighteenth-century audiences had already begun to regard as clear indications of selfhood, as modern assumptions about disability, gender, sexuality, nationality, and identity were taking shape to sort the nation's bodies and characters into increasingly rigid taxonomies.[8] Employing this established vocabulary, an overexpressive performance secures the spectator's interest by seducing him or her into believing that the celebrity's true identity will be legible to anyone attempting to interpret it.[9]

Upon closer examination, however, an overexpressive self-representation seems impossibly excessive and spectacular. It employs costumes, gestures, or vocabularies that draw attention to themselves: misspelled words or ungrammatical sentences; wigs, hats, and suits so large they seem to dwarf their wearers—or the famous black page of *Tristram Shandy*, which, as Thomas Keymer has written, might represent not the absence of words but an abundance of them, reproduced over and over until their meanings are no longer available to us.[10] As this last example suggests, the very excesses of the overexpressive performance transform it from a self-representation that invites to a self-representation that frustrates its spectators' attempts to interpret it. These excesses work not to obscure the self, but rather to exaggerate and thus destabilize the language through which the self is thought to be revealed.

Cibber's staging of his own celebrity and Sterne's "caperings around" his semiautobiographical *Tristram Shandy* offer the most straightforward examples of overexpression, presenting subjects so comprehensively as to make them incomprehensible.[11] I begin with Cibber as the first celebrity to have produced his own autobiography; and I have chosen the five celebrities who follow him in this study based on the availability of their autobiographical materials, whether printed books or the printed pages of the periodicals they so carefully manipulated, and on the relationship of these autobiographical materials to each other.[12] Celebrities with fewer extant autobiographical materials—such as Thomas Betterton or Anne Bracegirdle—or those with a more tenuous connection to those studied here—such as the preacher and autobiographer George Whitefield—I leave to other studies.[13] I focus instead on the autobiographical performances of Cibber and Sterne and those who directly follow them and who, as I argue in subsequent chapters of this book, pay tribute to their earlier brand of overexpression without reproducing it exactly.

For David Garrick, this means dismantling the sentimental signs through which his audience distinguished between the sincere self and the exaggerated one, between true emotion and the actor's performance of it. For the women of my study—Charlotte Charke, George Anne Bellamy, and Mary Robinson—adapting overexpression is even more complicated. Charke and Bellamy, I argue, attempt to adapt their male predecessors' strategies of overexpression—quite pointedly, in the case of Charke, who situates her 1755 autobiography as a response to her father's. Time and again, however, their overexpressions fail to disrupt the judgments of their spectators, who read even their most exaggerated performances as earnest (if ineffective) attempts to express themselves, where these same spectators had read their male colleagues' performances as deliberately perplexing. Mary Robinson, the final celebrity of my study, addresses this tendency by turning overexpression on its head, exaggerating not a certain aspect of her persona but rather that persona's conspicuous absence from the poems, portraits, and performances that promise to reveal it. In this her autobiographical performances resemble less the black page of *Tristram Shandy* than its white page, which, like Robinson's self-representations, invites the reader to fill in its blanks and thus transforms that reader from critic to collaborator. If we cannot read Robinson's performances as reproductions of Cibber's and Sterne's overexpressive strategy, then, we might read them as responses to this strategy.

Despite their differences, all of these performances share the tendency to break—in the very same breath that they make—elaborate promises to reveal their subjects' secrets. By describing them as part of a single narrative, I mean not to elide their particularities but rather to emphasize the ways in which they all emerge out of a single question: that is, how might a public figure protect his or her privacy? It is a question that few studies have asked, despite a growing interest in celebrity studies in recent years. The notable exceptions are Kristina Straub's *Sexual Suspects*, which illuminates how the conventions and discourse of the theater conflicted with emerging ideologies of gender and sexuality, forcing celebrities into the roles of "sexual suspects"; and Catherine Gallagher's *Nobody's Story*, which explores the print strategies that women writers developed to protect their personae while selling their stories. Both works offer important insights into how the public exposure demanded of literary and theatrical careers clashed with eighteenth-century gender norms, particularly those that limited women to the private sphere. Yet by focusing their discussions on gender, these scholars do not touch on the extent to which female celebrities adopted, adapted, and responded to the strategies of their male predecessors (in Gallagher's case) or the many aspects of identity beyond gender and sexuality that these performances explored (in Straub's). Studying these strategies in concert with each other, while paying close attention to their particularities, allows us to understand the development of such autobiographical performances as a literary/theatrical tradition—and one that runs counter to the rise of the novel as instilling the desire for a publicly known and publicly knowable self. Like a spotlight so brilliant it is blinding—or like *Tristram Shandy*'s black page, so full of ink it cannot be read—the self-representations that these six celebrities developed over the course of the long eighteenth century met their public's demands to stare while paralyzing that public's power to interpret.

The "expression" implied by the term *overexpression* is a mere illusion, of course; overexpressive performers don't reveal onstage a stable, interior self expressed from the inside out. Instead, they adopt the vocabulary that modernity has come to associate with that interior self to deploy what Felicity Nussbaum calls an "Interiority Effect"—the illusion of interiority through the clever manipulation of surfaces.[14] But unlike the performances that Nussbaum discusses, overexpressive performances present the illusion of interiority only to expose it as an illusion. When the spectator heeds the performer's invitation to investigate the private self supposedly lurking beneath the public performance, overexpression prevents him or her from discovering anything but another layer of clothing, another page of preamble, another surface passing for self.

The term *overexpression* also evokes *overwriting*—a word that implies excess at the same time that it suggests erasure: to overwrite a text is to include too many details or words or obnoxiously obvious statements of argumentation, but to overwrite a file is to erase it.[15] I use the term *overexpression* instead of *overwriting*, however, to emphasize that the celebrities I discuss deployed this strategy far beyond the confines of the printed page. Crucially, the autobiographical performances I examine are not limited to books; they include several forms and genres that traditional studies tend to segregate or to disregard altogether—from performances in print (playscripts, poems, portraits and novels as well as autobiographies) to printed ephemera (puffs, prologues, caricatures, and other publicity stunts) to the ephemeral performances of self staged on the streets of London before whatever impromptu audience happened to wander by. In this way they mirror and manipulate celebrity culture itself, which similarly depends upon an audience's willingness to read across multiple forms of self-creation. The encomiums and epistles to unnamed lovers scattered throughout Mary Robinson's poems, for instance, assume the readers' familiarity with the roles she made famous onstage and with the part she acted in life; and David Garrick's 1749 performance as Benedick in *Much Ado about Nothing* held special meaning for spectators who had read in the gossip columns of his recent marriage to the German singer Eva Marie Veigel.

When I refer to these self-stagings and life-writings as autobiographical *performances*, I am relying on the broadened definition of this word that performance studies has introduced: performance is not only a fiction presented on a stage but also an action executed on the street or even within the home.

I use it not as an antonym to print but rather as a term that refers to the interactions between a variety of media, as a theatrical performance consists of printed scripts and playbills, material props and costumes, and built sets and auditoriums as well as the live bodies and contingent reactions of actors and audience members. As performance studies reminds us, however, such performances are difficult to access or arrest in their own time—and even more difficult to recover three hundred years after the event.[16] The ephemeral nature of the performances I most want to examine complicates my methodology; since I can't hear the drawled accent that Colley Cibber adopted as the fop or witness the swagger of Laurence Sterne on his first entrance into London, I must piece together what I can from the prints, letters, reviews, playbills, puffs, autobiographies, and fictions that these performers left behind.

Though I am painfully aware of the limitations of this approach, I am also eager to resist the tendency in eighteenth-century scholarship to segregate cultural production by genre, so that those who study fiction rarely examine drama, and those who study theater and performance must apologize for their subjects in a field so dominated, in the past fifty years, by debates over the rise of the novel. Such divisions in eighteenth-century studies replicate the divisions affecting cultural studies in general, in which those who study the "live arts" in performance reject the conservatism of those who study what they describe (by implication) to be a dead or dying discipline, and those who describe themselves as literary historians reject what they see as the ahistoricism of performance studies. This segregation seems especially limited within eighteenth-century studies since it diverges from how people experienced the era, often spending their mornings reading letters and novels only to find themselves at the theater by the late afternoon. Recently, several scholars (including Joseph Roach, Felicity Nussbaum, Stuart Sherman, Emily Hodgson Anderson, and Misty Anderson) have demonstrated the important insights we might gain when we study eighteenth-century theater in dialogue with other forms. In following their examples, I share Peggy Phelan's belief: "If we lose the intimacy of the connection between literature and performance, we diminish something vital in and between them."[17]

In addition to an exploration of the paradox of modern selfhood, this study is also an attempt to answer Phelan's plea that we resuture the connections between literature and performance, despite the methodological difficulties of doing so. By combining the close-reading methods at the heart of literary studies and theater history with performance theory's attention to the contingencies of the live event, I hope to explain how these six eighteenth-century celebrities used their spectacular performances and their overwritten pages to evade their spectators' attempts to interpret them—and, moreover, why they should want to. For although the vulnerability of the expressed identity was a problem shared by many of England's citizens in the eighteenth century, it was a problem identified most articulately by England's celebrities. I want to take a moment to discuss the characteristics and context that make the celebrities of the long eighteenth century such unique and useful case studies for understanding this paradox of modern selfhood, before turning to a passage from Cibber's *Apology* that deftly articulates the strategy I am calling overexpression and that will guide our explorations of autobiographical performance throughout this book.

THE RISE OF THE CELEBRITY IN EIGHTEENTH-CENTURY ENGLAND

Several related cultural trends emerged in the late seventeenth and early eighteenth centuries to produce the problems that overexpression attempted to solve for the modern celebrity. These include the rise of a celebrity industry, based around the creation, publicization, and consumption of a few "abnormally interesting people";[18] the reorientation of social and political authority around a public sphere; and the emergence of a professional class of literary and theatrical critics increasingly influential over how actors and authors regarded and practiced their craft.

Though scholars disagree about who might be crowned the *first* modern celebrity, few have disputed Leo Braudy's claim that "the roots of the urge to find the place of fame were particularly fertilized in the eighteenth century."[19] Early modern English speakers had long been familiar with "fame" as "reputation"—the gossip, good or ill, that spreads by word of mouth—or as "renown"—the deserved merit that immortalizes the writers of great poems or the doers of great deeds.[20] But starting at the end of the seventeenth century the language began to register a new sort of fame—a flash-in-the-pan phenomenon that recognized individuals not for what they had done but simply for who they were (or for what they represented) and that transformed ordinary men and women into media sensations. This new fame was not, as Alexander Pope notes in his allegorical poem *The Temple of Fame* (1715), a lasting merit enjoyed by "fabled Chiefs in darker Ages born, / Or Worthys old, whom Arms or Arts adorn"; it was instead a "doubtful Fame . . . Which o'er each Object casting various Dies, / Enlarges some, and others multiplies."[21]

The fact that Pope adapted his eighteenth-century *Temple of Fame* from

Geoffrey Chaucer's fourteenth-century *House of Fame* might make us suspicious of his suggestion that this "doubtful Fame" was an entirely new phenomenon. Nonetheless, new technologies of communication and new ideologies of self-creation were changing the way Britons discussed and circulated celebrity, if not how they conceived of it. Stella Tillyard has identified three factors that made the celebrity that arose in Pope's day qualitatively different from that which existed before the Restoration: "a limited monarchy, the lapse in 1695 of the Licensing Act which had controlled the numbers of printing presses and to some extent printing, and a public interested in new ways of thinking about other people and themselves."[22]

Previous studies have already examined how the second of these three factors—the lapse of the Licensing Act—led to an explosion in the number of printing presses and facilitated a dramatic increase not only of periodicals like *The Tatler* and *The Spectator*, but also of gossip columns, scandal sheets, and broadsides. These latter publications worked to disseminate both news and rumors about celebrities' adventures, along with images of those celebrities, far beyond the relatively small circle of Londoners who had seen those celebrities in the flesh. At the same time, they whetted the public's appetite for "'secret histories,' which told scandalous stories of immorality at court and in other high places" as well as "biographies of notorious and famous individuals."[23] These biographies and secret histories contributed to the trend to which I have already alluded—and with which scholars of eighteenth-century culture will be quite familiar—that established the private, interior self both as the basis of citizenship and also as a topic of increasing fascination to biographers, spectators, and gossips alike. "The notion of fixed character that could be written as a literary construct and then used in a plot [was] becoming commonplace," Tillyard explains. "Celebrity was born," in other words, "at the moment private life became a tradable public commodity."[24]

This public interest in private life arose in part to compensate for the third factor that Tillyard attributes to the growth of celebrity at the turn into the eighteenth century: an increasingly "limited monarchy" that failed to satisfy the public desire for spectacular display. The fascination that Britons had once shown for a few "spectacular politicians" and "public representatives," who had cemented their authority by performing it in great pageants of wealth and power, was declining with the ceding of monarchical power to parliamentary control and the ceding of the church's influence to that of the state.[25] This decline didn't curb Britons' enthusiasm for spectacles of glitz and glamour, however. Instead, actors, actresses, rogues, and socialites arose from relatively humble origins, according to sociologist Chris Rojek, "to fill the absence created by the decay in the popular belief in the divine right of kings, and the death of God."[26]

What Pope denigrates as "doubtful Fame," then, most recent scholars have celebrated as fame's democratization. Men and women no longer had to commit "heroic actions" or prove their belonging within "a noble or royal class in which such regard naturally accompanies station," as Cheryl Wanko points out, in order to earn the "roles of authority" that fame offered them.[27] They could become celebrities simply by being themselves—or, rather, by being the selves that popular gossip and publicity periodicals had created for them and would keep alive as long as they continued to sell papers. Their development helps to explain why, despite Cibber's complaints at being "helpless, and expos'd" to his public's interpretations of his private life, he should nonetheless publicize that life in a lengthy autobiography—or why, despite the vulnerabilities famous figures must suffer, none of the celebrities I examine here elected simply to cover up or hide out until their public's attention strayed elsewhere. To eschew such attention because of the loss of self-possession it entailed was to eschew also the lifestyle on which they had come to depend. To embrace it was to enjoy a power and a status that would have been inconceivable to lower- or middle-class men and women only a generation before.

At the same time, Pope's description of this new fame as "doubtful" suggests that celebrities didn't simply usurp the places once held by kings and gods, as several recent studies of celebrity have implied. In their focus on the new power that the commodification of private life allowed the modern celebrity, works such as Nussbaum's *Rival Queens* or Cheryl Wanko's *Roles of Authority* have paid less attention to the violations and humiliations to which the star who sells himself or herself on the open market is so often prone. Yet throughout their autobiographies and performances, eighteenth-century celebrities from Cibber to Robinson repeatedly express anxieties about publicity that stem from (and might be read against) ideologies of the modern subject more generally.

Jürgen Habermas has theorized these ideologies as arising from the separation of society into public and private spheres.[28] In order to be recognized as a legal subject, as I noted earlier, the early modern Briton had to demonstrate his or her plausibility as a coherent subject—as a possessive individual whose word could be depended upon and whose character could be known. But in order to participate in the sphere of public opinion that controlled the invisible hand of commerce, the artistic leanings of a growing popular culture, and the political decisions of an increasingly republican state, Habermas contends, the eighteenth-century Briton also had to demonstrate his or her plausibility as a rational subject—one informed but not blinded by his or her private experience. And in order to demonstrate such rationality one had to divest oneself of the obvious markings of particularized identity and blend in to the crowd. One had to appear, in Michael McKeon's recent reformulation of Habermas's ideas, "disembodi[ed]" and "depersonaliz[ed]."[29]

McKeon's words hint at the ways that the public sphere might be seen to exclude celebrities, who make their names displaying their bodies and marketing their personalities for public consumption. If all the world's a stage, those who rule it aren't the players. Instead, political power, social status, and even cultural capital belong to the spectators who watch, interpret, and critique from the pit, only to blend back into the crowd before their own performances can be seen, interpreted, or critiqued. (Consider Pope's denigration of the celebrity's "doubtful" and undeserved fame as opposed to the fame of the truly virtuous, who "Would die unheard of, as [they] liv'd unseen.")[30]

The representative of these spectators, for Habermas as well as for the celebrities that interest me, is Joseph Addison and Richard Steele's enormously popular creation and arbiter of English taste, Mr. Spectator. As Habermas and others have pointed out, Mr. Spectator guarantees his authority as the unobserved observer of London society by insisting on his anonymity, pointedly refusing to reveal "an Account of my Name, my Age, and my Lodgings" in his first issue.[31] Scott Paul Gordon argues that "it is only by emptying himself out, becoming passionless, friendless, and, above all, formless, that Mr. Spectator can subject readers to constant surveillance."[32] In this way, Mr. Spectator's printed and disembodied persona serves as antonym and antidote to the eighteenth-century celebrity's theatrical and personality-driven presence, and it is striking how often his image (or lack of an image) haunts eighteenth-century celebrities' self-representations as an ideal valuable to pursue but impossible to attain. The "disinterestedness" that makes Mr. Spectator such an exemplary representative of the public sphere depends on his refusal to locate himself in a particular place or to inhabit a particular body—his refusal, in other words, to appear as a performer rather than to circulate as a printed text. "To be seen" in eighteenth-century society, as Gordon explains, "is to be vulnerable, to be positioned in another's field of vision and to be enlisted in another's plot."[33]

Mr. Spectator's example suggests that what was at stake for these celebrities was more than just the indulgence of vanity or the ability to walk through the streets of London without being accosted by adoring fans. It was, on the one hand, access to the fortune and social status that their publicity allowed them; and, on the other, access to the political, social, and literary authority reserved for those who made their private lives impregnable. In short, it was their right to define themselves rather than being "enlisted in another's plot."

Such stakes become viscerally and viciously clear when we consider an amazing but not atypical artifact from eighteenth-century celebrity culture: Benjamin Victor's 1733 biography of Colley Cibber's friend, fellow actor, and longtime managing partner at Drury Lane theater, Barton Booth. Victor's volume provides a fascinating insight not only into celebrity culture but also into eighteenth-century assumptions about literary and theatrical criticism—and, indeed, it might stand alone as the impetus for overexpression in Cibber's self-performances. Not content simply to strip Booth down to his street clothes or even to his underclothes within the pages of his biography, Victor includes in his text a copy of Booth's autopsy report. Literalizing the eighteenth-century spectator's desire to glimpse the celebrity's interior self, the report details how, upon his death, Booth's "*Rectum*, with the other Intestines, were ript up with a Pair of Scissars, in which was found very little Excrement, but the whole Tract on the inside, lin'd with *Crude Mercury* divided in Globules, about the Bigness of Pins Heads."[34] (The biography continues in this vein for several pages.)

The posthumous airing of Booth's interior self might seem an extreme example of the sorts of revelations compelled by the emerging cult of celebrity, but it was not uncommon to find autopsy reports among the pages of the era's most popular celebrity biographies. Arthur Murphy's 1801 biography of David Garrick concludes with the actor's autopsy report—a fact that Garrick seemed to have anticipated when, in a 1769 letter, he praised his friend Sturz's critique of French actress Madame Clairon's performance as "your desection of her, . . . as accurate as if you had opened her alive."[35] Sterne alludes to such practices in *Tristram Shandy* when he declaims against those writers "who will draw a man's character from no other helps in the world, but merely from his evacuations."[36] Both statements draw an implicit comparison between the job of the coroner and the job of the theater critic—a job that, like that of the celebrity, was a relatively new one in eighteenth-century England.[37] In an era when every pit seemed suddenly filled with professional hecklers, every newspaper overcrowded with theater reviews, and every review littered with bits of gossip dissecting players' private lives and social performances, everyone who appeared upon a stage or published himself in print exposed himself to the scrutiny and the censure of such reviewers.

The articulate targets of Grub Street's jibes (including Pope himself) have taught us to disregard these early critics as hacks, and yet it isn't difficult to see the ways in which their preoccupations with exposing the innards of a text or a character have continued to structure literary, theatrical, and cultural criticism, even today. Consider the words we often use to describe how we work on a text: we *penetrate*, we *exfoliate*, we *unpack*. Or consider Joseph Roach's decision to arrange the chapters of his recent book, *It*—one of the most insightful and influential analyses of modern celebrity—according to the attributes that Pygmalion layers onto his statue in Dryden's translation of the *Metamorphoses*. Roach claims to construct his own celebrity-statue piece by piece, beginning with accessories and clothes and bringing it to life through the final addition of flesh and bone.[38] But we might view this structure less as a building up than as a stripping down—a dissection that lays open the body and the identity of the celebrity for the consumption of his or her culture in much the same way that Victor's reproduced autopsy report lays open the body of Barton Booth. No wonder eighteenth-century icons like Cibber seemed so wary of public attention.

Studying overexpression and its discontents allows us to examine celebrity culture not from the perspective of a society creating celebrities the way that Pygmalion created his living statue, as so many previous studies have done, but rather from the perspective of the celebrities themselves, asking what part they might have played in developing and directing the cult of personality that we have inherited from eighteenth-century England. In other words, it allows us to understand these celebrities as authors in their own right, and to delve into the ways that their autobiographical performances not only reflected but also manipulated the eighteenth century's celebrity culture as well as emerging ideologies of subjectivity. Such a perspective influences how we regard the individual characters in this study, so that Colley Cibber becomes not only the victim of history and the King of the Dunces in Pope's *Dunciad*, but, like the deformed king he plays in his version of *Richard III*, a man manipulating how he will be remembered; Charlotte Charke becomes not only a sexual misfit weighed down by her culture's oppressive ideologies of gender and sexuality but an actress trying on, only to critique, the languages through which those ideologies operate; and David Garrick becomes not a professional performer protecting his private life by refusing to reveal it but a highly articulate innovator in celebrity culture who curries his public's attentions at the same time that he deflects its attempts to discover his secrets.

In addition to influencing how we understand these individuals, such a narrative also influences how we understand the theater history for which their autobiographical works often serve as sources. Many of the texts I examine here—most notably Cibber's *Apology* but also several (possibly apocryphal) stories surrounding David Garrick's performances as well as George Anne Bellamy's autobiography and Mary Robinson's *Memoirs*—have been taken by generations of theater historians as fact. As such, they have influenced how we understand the conventions and traditions of the eighteenth-century stage.[39] To read these works not as history but as literature, however, is to raise important questions about the ways we have understood Garrick's "natural" acting style as a foil to Cibber's declamations, or the ways we have understood *Tristram Shandy* within the tradition of novels rather than within the tradition of theatrical autobiography. Before defining more precisely the particular shape that this book will take, I want to turn to a specific instance of overexpression in Colley Cibber's *Apology* to demonstrate both how it works and how it might contribute to our understanding of the eighteenth-century theater and the eighteenth-century subject.

OVEREXPRESSION AS "THIS *CHIARO OSCURO* OF MY MIND"

In the early pages of his autobiography, Colley Cibber offers one of the pithiest justifications for and one of the most articulate definitions of overexpression—one that might serve as a key to the strategy of autobiographical performance that the rest of this book will theorize. He begins, significantly, with a direct allusion to Benjamin Victor's biography of Barton Booth as an example of eighteenth-century spectators' impertinent desire "to know" what an actor "really was."[40] "It was, doubtless, from a Supposition that this sort of Curiosity would compensate their Labours," Cibber writes, "that so many hasty Writers have been encourag'd to publish the Lives of the late [actors] Mrs. [Anne] *Oldfield*, Mr. [Robert] *Wilks*, and Mr. [Barton] *Booth*, in less time after their Deaths than one cou'd suppose it cost to transcribe them."[41] Cibber explains his composition of the lengthy autobiography as an attempt to avoid the gaze of the same critics who memorialized and anatomized the unfortunate "Mr. *Booth*." "Now, Sir, when my Time comes," he addresses his dedicatee only a page later, "lest they shou'd think it worth while to handle my Memory with the same Freedom, I am willing to prevent its being so odly besmear'd (or at best but flatly white-wash'd) by taking upon me to give the Publick This": that is, the meandering memoir that he characterizes a few lines later as "this *Chiaro Oscuro* of my mind."[42]

Cibber's vocabulary here exemplifies the play of interiority and exteriority that characterizes overexpression and that complicates eighteenth-century scholars' strict divisions between the novelistic self and the staged self. Cibber first declares his dread of a memory "besmear'd"—a word whose etymology (particularly given its juxtaposition to Cibber's complaint against invasive memoirs like Victor's) suggests excrement, something from inside the body being wiped across the page as a representation of character.[43] But no less a threat to Cibber is a memorial that has been "but flatly white-wash'd"—one as superficial and "flat" as the "besmear'd" page is invasive. To make himself visible is to make himself vulnerable to smears by his spectators, Cibber suggests, but to disguise or to conceal his flaws is to deny himself the status of a star.

Recoiling at both possibilities, Cibber declares his wish to be remembered instead in "*Chiaro Oscuro.*" A visual art term that refers to the contrasting juxtaposition of lights (or *chiaro* in Italian) and darks (*oscuro*) in a painter's palette, "*Chiaro Oscuro*" seems to imply here either the balance of virtues and faults that attests to the veracity of Cibber's self-portrait or the collection of black letters that grace the white pages of his *Apology*. More complexly, however, it suggests that the picture he will paint of himself doesn't reject either the "odly besmear'd" and blackened page exposing his interior or the "flatly white-wash'd" page recording only his superficial persona, but rather incorporates both. It includes, in other words, both the gruesomely embodied self of the scatological "smear"—a detail that, counter to eighteenth-century scholarship's usual division between print and performance, associates the embodied self with interiority—and the disembodied and nonspecific self "flatly white-wash'd" onto a blank canvas or a printed page. Cibber's *Chiaro Oscuro* self-portrait promises to plunge the reader into what seems to be the inner recess of the celebrity's selfhood, while in fact limiting the reader to the flattened surfaces of his public persona. It offers an understanding of Cibber's life that is so apparently profound as to be profoundly apparent; and it delineates a character in language that is (as the English cognates of *Chiaro Oscuro* suggest) so clear it is obscure.

The image of a self-portrait so clear it is obscure, so overwrought it is unreadable, seems a particularly apt characterization not only of Cibber's verbose and voluminous *Apology* but also of so many of the autobiographical performances of eighteenth-century England's biggest stars: from Sterne's *Chiaro Oscuro* pairing of the black page that says too much about the parson Yorick with the white page that says nothing at all about the Widow Wadman, to George Anne Bellamy's adoption of the overwrought, epistolary style of the sentimental novel to suggest her sentimental self's inaccessibility; from Charlotte Charke's decision to evade her spectators by donning her father's oversized wig, to the self-stylings that, as Pope wrote about Cibber's poetry, "explain a thing till all men doubt it."[44] Displaying bodies so spectacular that they become unreadable, adopting masculine costumes so exaggerated that they become feminine, and declaring their sincerity so assiduously that it becomes theatrical, these celebrities secured their fame and destabilized their identities at once. Studying their strategies allows us not only to reexamine our assumptions about how eighteenth-century celebrities contributed to the making—and to the unmaking—of the modern self; it also allows us to examine the ways that selves staged in performance seem sometimes to accrue the revelatory power that literary historians often attribute to the interiorized selves of the novel—and the way that selves printed on static pages might defy readers' and critics' assumptions about their stability and seem, through their very spectacle, to disappear.

STAGING PROPERTIES AS STAGE PROPERTIES: THE STRUCTURES OF OVEREXPRESSION

The disappearances and instabilities of the overexpressed self return us to C. B. Macpherson's description of the modern subject as the "proprietor of his own person or capacities" and complicate the classic theorizations of the printed autobiography as a way of proving one's proprietorship over his or her person.[45] In *The Autobiographical Subject*, Felicity Nussbaum explains that eighteenth-century autobiographies, journals, and diaries "allowed a literate class to define its supposed superiority to an illiterate one. . . . 'Knowing oneself' allowed an individual subject to exercise privilege [over], as well as discipline and regulate, the behavior of those who did not 'know' themselves."[46] The autobiographer's proprietorship over "his [or her] own person or capacities" becomes more complicated, however, when he or she publishes and sells his or her autobiography to readers, who purchase not only the material book but also the right to interpret, discuss, and judge the "person or capacities" that that book describes. The predicament of the eighteenth-century autobiographer mirrors that of the eighteenth-century celebrity (and as we have seen, these categories often overlap): owning oneself means writing oneself down, but writing oneself down means offering oneself up to consumption by, circulation between, and misinterpretations of one's readers. It is this paradox, as Phelan argues in a book on several autobiographical performances of the late twentieth century, that performance's ephemerality resists. By disappearing in the very moment that it is staged, she contends, performance cannot be commodified; it "clogs the smooth machinery of reproductive representation necessary to the circulation of capital."[47]

Despite its influence as a foundational work in performance studies, Phelan's argument has drawn criticism from scholars who point out that performance can be and often is commodified—and who brandish the price lists for a seat at a Broadway show or a play in London's West End as proof. The performers that I examine here share with Phelan's twentieth-century artists a penchant for spectacular disappearance, employing the conventions of autobiography and celebrity and the vocabularies of self-revelation only to exaggerate and deform those conventions, those vocabularies, and dissolve the selves they've promised to reveal. While these performers don't exactly prevent the commodification of their lives or their performances—many of which, like Broadway hits, yielded substantial profits—they do challenge traditional theorizations of autobiography as either the private property of the autobiographer or the public property of its readers and point to the difficulties of commodifying overexpressive narratives in the ways that more traditional properties might be commodified.

Jean Baptiste Suard demonstrates precisely these difficulties in his 1765 *London Chronicle* review of *Tristram Shandy*, Volumes VII and VIII. "This adventure," he writes of Sterne's narrative, "is not unlike the famous story of the *man* who, some years ago, informed the public, that he would put himself in a *bottle* before their eyes." But after the "credulous multitude" had paid for their tickets to see such a sight, the man "carried away their money and left the bottle empty."[48] The performance to which Suard compares Sterne's narrative is certainly commodifiable and commodified here. Yet Suard's description points to an important anxiety that we shall see recurring in the reviews of and commentaries on a number of the autobiographical performances I examine—an essential confusion, when these autobiographical performances and the abnormally interesting personalities they represent are offered up for sale, over precisely what is being sold. Such anxieties complicate traditional descriptions of printed autobiographies and the life stories they narrate as either the private properties of their writers or the public properties of their readers. Instead, I want to think about these autobiographical performances in terms of stage properties.

Rather than chattel that can be valued and evaluated even if it changes hands, stage properties are material objects that take on a variety of constantly shifting meanings through their transferability to multiple contexts, multiple plays. It is this transferability that distinguishes a prop from a costume or a set piece, according to theater practitioners: if an onstage object stays in one place on the stage or adorns one actor's body in particular, it falls under the purview of the set designer or the costume designer; if it is used, moved, or manipulated by multiple actors, it becomes the responsibility of the props master. In the law something becomes property when its owner can be established and documented—when its history of ownership, like the life story narrated by a printed autobiography, can be written down. In the theater it is just the opposite: something becomes a stage property when it cannot be identified with a single performer or fixed to a single space. By discussing these autobiographical performances not in terms of legal properties but in terms of stage properties, I mean to highlight the difficulty of commodifying them or of fixing them as the signifier of singular meanings or singular selves.

I mean also to emphasize the way that these performances, like the props they utilize, seem at once to invite and to frustrate their spectators' attempts to reduce them to simple or stable indicators of a single, identifiable quality. Stage props are, after all, tangible objects given special provenance within the semiotic world of the stage, and as such they seem to invite their spectators to read them as symbols. And yet, as Andrew Sofer explains in his history of the stage prop, this symbolism is never quite so simple as the tangibility of these objects might lead us to expect. Sofer describes the "unstable signifying excess" that objects assume when onstage, their tendency to suggest several contradictory interpretations at once and thus to frustrate their spectators' efforts to cement their meanings.[49] I want to suggest that the overexpressive performances I examine throughout this book strive for and in many cases achieve a similar "signifying excess," a capacity at once to magnify and to blur—indeed, to blur by magnifying—the identities they describe.

To this end, I have structured each chapter of this book around a particular prop that was central to the autobiographical performances of each celebrity I examine and that exemplifies the "signifying excess" that Sofer theorizes. In each case, the prop I choose begins as a fixed symbol of some aspect of identity—nationality, masculinity, or sincerity, for instance—and thus promises to stabilize the celebrity's identity by translating it into an object, a readable signifier that can be located, interpreted, and exchanged. In each case, however, the celebrity's manipulation of the prop makes its significations so excessive as to become uninterpretable or so obvious as to become undone.

Chapter 1 revolves around the royal crown—a prop that, when we spot it on the stages of Restoration and eighteenth-century Britain, might remind us of the modern celebrity's similarities to the early modern king, or of both public figures' roles as "effigies" of their nation.[50] The crown's legibility as a symbol of Englishness becomes more complicated, however, when we consider Colley Cibber's appearance as the deformed king in two related works: Cibber's 1699 adaptation of Shakespeare's *Richard III*, in which he stars as the hunchbacked monarch, and Alexander Pope's 1743 *Dunciad in Four Books*, which crowns Cibber King of the Dunces. I argue that Cibber's portrayal of and pointed identification with Richard III frustrated his spectators' critical gaze by exaggerating into illegible deformities his most recognizable physical features. My discussion of these deformities as overexpressions sheds new light on the deformities of Cibber's printed works as well—and the chapter concludes with a reexamination of the misspellings and malapropisms that Pope deplored as the height of Dulness but that I interpret as Cibber's strategy to render himself unreadable.

While chapter 1 focuses on the king's crown to interpret Pope's mock-epic hero and Cibber's deformed king as overexpressions of Englishness, chapter 2 describes another of Cibber's magnificent headpieces—the great white wig he wore as the fop—to explore his comic roles as overexpressions of gender and sexuality. Originally a symbol of masculinity, the wig in the exaggerated proportions it takes on in Cibber's performances becomes instead a mark of femininity. Its significations become even more complicated when it reappears on the head of Cibber's daughter, Charlotte Charke. Unlike scholars who mine Charke's transvestite performances and her 1755 *Narrative* for examples of queerness, I argue that Charke's ambivalent descriptions of her gender and sexuality arise not from her frustrated attempts to define herself as one identity or the other. Instead, they stem from her deliberate attempts to avoid defining herself at all. Such attempts were not always successful, and in the second half of the chapter I ask what about Charke's performances made them so much more vulnerable to her audiences' appropriations and misinterpretations—a question that will introduce some of the alternatives to overexpression that I explore in subsequent chapters.

In the subtitle of chapter 3, "the Overexpression of Character," might refer to any of the chapters in this study, all of which examine how a celebrity or group of celebrities emphasized in order to erase the features by which their spectators might attempt to interpret their characters. By lending this title to a chapter that examines Laurence Sterne's pseudoautobiography *Tristram Shandy* and Sterne's public appearances as two of the book's most popular characters, I mean to emphasize Sterne's centrality as the most perceptive theorist as well as the most influential practitioner of the strategy I am attempting here to define. I mean also to evoke the multiple meanings of the word "character" as a term that refers not only to the personality that distinguishes one individual from another or to the personae that populate a fictional work but also to the letters on a printed page. Sterne's radical experimentations with the printed page—the prop around which this chapter revolves—have defined his most famous work for generations of readers but strike me, as I will elaborate, as some of the most sophisticated musings on how these celebrities used overexpression to lend their printed works the instability of performance. Though it might seem an anomaly to the autobiographical performances in the surrounding chapters, I argue that *Tristram Shandy* is actually their epitome. The linchpin around which much of this project revolves, Sterne's pseudoautobiography includes several pointed allusions that its contemporary readers identified as linking it explicitly to Cibber's *Apology*; and its popularity introduced Cibber's strategies to later figures, who adopted and adapted them as the celebrity autobiography began to emerge as a genre.

In chapter 4, I analyze the self-representations of two such figures: Sterne's friend David Garrick, celebrated for the supposedly natural acting style that he introduced to the stage in the mid-eighteenth century, and Garrick's protégé George Anne Bellamy, who evokes Sterne explicitly throughout her 1785 *Apology for the Life of George Anne Bellamy*. Beginning with a famous wig that Garrick wore as Hamlet (a wig rigged to stand on end at the appearance of the ghost), I explore how Garrick's performances challenged his spectators' assumptions about the boundaries between natural and unnatural and between corpus and costume in an age of sentimentality. If early eighteenth-century celebrities developed overexpression to avoid exposing their private lives and personal emotions to public scrutiny, I ask, what happens to this strategy within a literary style that seems to celebrate emotional vulnerability? After reading Garrick's performances beside Denis Diderot's *Paradoxe sur le Comedien* as successful examples of sentimental overexpression, I turn to the autobiographical excursions of George Anne Bellamy. Like Charlotte Charke in chapter 2, Bellamy adopts props and performance styles that seem identical to those of her male colleagues, only to find that these props and performance styles fail to protect her from her spectators' jibes. Haunting Bellamy's autobiography is the awareness of and anxiety about this failure, which seems to have much to do with Bellamy's femininity. In the second half of the chapter, I ask how eighteenth-century audiences approached men's and women's autobiographical performances differently, and what this might have had to do with Bellamy's fears that her autobiographical performances would fail to stave off her spectators' stares.

This question leads me into a discussion of the works of Mary Robinson in chapter 5—a celebrity who, I argue, addressed this failure by inventing an alternative to overexpression that was more suited to a female performer. Robinson rose to fame as an actress and mistress to the Prince of Wales, but her poetry, feminist writings, and 1801 *Memoirs* influenced and were influenced by such Romantic figures as Mary Wollstonecraft, William Godwin, Samuel Taylor Coleridge, and William Wordsworth. This final chapter thus propels my line of inquiry into the Romantic era by examining the preoccupations with fame and visibility no less apparent in Robinson's later life as a poet than they were in her early years as "Perdita"—"the lost one"—a nickname she borrowed from her celebrated role in Garrick's adaptation of *The Winter's Tale*. Reacting to the celebrities who preceded her and who employ exaggerated personae in their performances of self, Robinson presents an autobiography littered with ellipses and a persona that seems always to leave something out. Her poems and portraits work in much the same way. Accordingly, Robinson employs a strategy related but antipodal to overexpression: one that points out the absence of her self rather than exaggerating her presence. The incomplete records of a woman whose name was well known but whose identity was "lost," Robinson's works provide a fitting final act to a century of celebrities whose images were ubiquitous, whose words were overflowing, and yet whose identities were nowhere to be found.

Robinson's autobiography, which appeared at the beginning of the Romantic era and at the dawn of the nineteenth century, was not the last such work in Anglo-American celebrity culture, of course. Although later works lie outside the scope of this project, I speculate on some directions future research might take—as well as reiterating the centrality of overexpression to modern celebrity culture—in a coda that takes a case study from my own lifetime. In the 1980s and 1990s, Michael Jackson made his celebrity not only the side effect but also the subject of many of his most spectacular musical performances. His contemporaries described him, alternately, as an idol and as an aberration. Yet if we look closely, commentaries on the agonies and ecstasies of his own celebrity—as well as the spectacular costumes, performances, and personae he presents to his curious spectators—start to seem eerily familiar. In tracing the similarities between the long-ago and faraway performances of Cibber, Charke, Sterne, Garrick, Bellamy, and Robinson and the close-at-hand performances of Michael Jackson, I don't mean to minimize the historical specificity of the eighteenth-century performers or their strategies of autobiographical performance. Rather, I aim to suggest that in their searches for new ways to publicize themselves without sacrificing their privacy, these eighteenth-century stars asked questions that have become as central to modern celebrity culture as the modern celebrity him- or herself—and that, despite changing technologies of and assumptions about the self, have never entirely disappeared. The celebrities that I examine throughout this study offered a model for those around them and for those who followed them to maintain their privacy despite a society increasingly obsessed with watching, patrolling, and controlling the selves of its citizens. They teach us how to be modern in a world that seems increasingly to offer us little choice but to see or be seen.

CHAPTER 1

The Celebrity Emerges as the Deformed King

Richard III, the King of the Dunces, and the Overexpression of Englishness

In the dead of winter, 1699, as the people of England struggled to forget the bloody images of the last half-century—a regicide, a civil war, a succession of violent rebellions—Colley Cibber shuffled across the well-worn boards of Drury Lane stage in the gleaming crown of a king.[1] It was a costume he had long tried to claim. By the late seventeenth century England's burgeoning celebrity culture had elevated actors and actresses like Cibber to a status once thought unattainable for people of such humble origins. The tragedian Thomas Betterton, born the son of an undercook to Charles I, received a lavish funeral in Westminster Abbey when he died in 1710. Anne Oldfield, once apprenticed to a seamstress, was by 1710 earning a salary greater than that of a "Gentleman" and had been offered joint ownership of Drury Lane (an offer later revoked by managers hesitant to grant such power to a woman).[2] So it was that by 1740, Cibber thought himself a notable enough person to merit an autobiography. "This Work, I say, shall . . . contain the various Impressions of my Mind," Cibber writes of his *Apology for the Life of Colley Cibber*, drawing an implicit comparison between the spectacular king and the celebrity autobiographer when he adds, "as in *Louis the Fourteenth* his Cabinet you have seen the growing Medals of his Person from Infancy to Old Age."[3]

Given the vainglory of such comparisons, Cibber's choice of his first royal role might seem a strange one. For when he stepped onto the stage in that production of 1699, he appeared not in the regal robes of an upstanding monarch but in the monstrous shape of Richard III, Shakespeare's famously hunchbacked villain.

In this chapter, I explore why Cibber should choose the character of the deformed king to make his tragic debut—and I suggest that Richard's abnormal body was part of the strategy he developed to frustrate his spectators' attempts to glean his private life from his public performances. For though he wore many crowns over the course of his long career on the stage, the three for which he is remembered are three that contorted his body into an image of deformity. One of these crowns was an enormous white wig, a prop I will discuss in detail in chapter 2 as deforming the noble body of the Restoration rake into the nonnormative body of the eighteenth-century fop. In this first chapter, I focus on two crowns separated by the forty-four years that divide their debuts and that represent the approximate span of Cibber's career. These crowns are separated also by the two trajectories of that career: Cibber as performer—decked out in the diadem of the player-king—and Cibber as poet—his humorous face framed by the laurel wreath.

Cibber achieved the first crown when he rewrote and starred in *Richard III*, taking on the first and most enduring of his several royal roles. Though critics panned Cibber's performance as Richard, no one could deny the staying power of his script: it was Cibber's adaptation (and not Shakespeare's) that was performed on English stages well into the nineteenth century. But the role served Cibber beyond merely cementing his version of *Richard III* in the English imagination. Passages in the *Apology* suggest that Cibber assumed the role of Richard because audiences—noting his short stature, his beady eyes, and his squeaky voice—could not stomach him in the romantic leading roles he coveted. Denied the role of the noble prince, he settled for that of the deformed king. The body he performed as Richard is one that, as James I. Porter writes of the disabled form in literature, "seems somehow too much a body, too real, too corporeal . . . it is a body that, so to speak, stands in its own way."[4] Assuming a body that is "too much a body," exaggerating the flaws that he could not escape, this chapter argues, helped Cibber to deflect (if not exactly to dissolve) his spectators' stares.

The second crown that Cibber wears in this chapter was thrust upon him by Alexander Pope, who named Cibber King of the Dunces in his mock-epic poem *The Dunciad in Four Books* (1743) and who mercilessly denigrates his prose—not to mention his persona—as overwrought. Pope was certainly not the only reader to express this criticism, and I examine several other writings by Cibber's detractors here. But I focus on *The Dunciad* as the work that has best stood the test of time. If Cibber's Richard exaggerates the eccentricities of his body, Pope's Dunce King might be said to exaggerate the eccentricities of his prose style. Pope portrays the newly appointed laureate as the paragon of an English culture that too often mistook heaviness for gravity and preferred Cibber's pseudoliterary loquaciousness to Pope's clipped wit.

The Cibber of Pope's *Dunciad* spouts sentences that contain many words but little meaning—many of them adapted or directly quoted from the most convoluted passages of Cibber's *Apology.* In pointing out and pointing up these eccentricities—and in parodying them in his own excessive couplets and footnotes—Pope offers an early articulation of overexpression and the challenges it presented for critics attempting to dissect or to decipher Cibber's persona.

The crowns of Dunce King and of deformed king resemble each other not only in the inflated depictions of their deformities but also in what it is they deform. Both the early modern king that Cibber's Richard corrupted and the epic hero that Pope's Dunce King mocked had once served as figureheads of their nations—a role that the celebrity, by Cibber's day, had begun to take on. Cibber's comparison of himself to Louis XIV in his *Apology* indicates that he embraced this role, but elsewhere he complains vehemently about its limitations: as symbols for a growing and diversifying nation, the celebrity, the king and the epic hero were subject to whatever meanings and representations the nation imposed upon them. To be such a person was to be watched—and perhaps worshipped—by multitudes. But it was also to surrender one's right to define oneself. Considering the celebrity's role in this way casts Cibber's Shakespearean performance—as well as his purple prose—in a new light. In this chapter, I argue that Cibber assumed the guise of the deformed king in order to maintain his position in the spotlight without imprisoning himself in his spectators' interpretations. Richard's deformed body allowed Cibber to overexpress not only his own physical eccentricities but also the English national identity that kings and epic heroes had once embodied and that mere celebrities were now forced to assume. Donning a persona that defied the increasingly rigid codifications by which the eighteenth-century body was read and classified, in other words, Cibber frustrated his spectators' attempts to interpret his performance and cleared the way to define and describe himself. We might regard the misspellings, malapropisms, and meandering sentences that Pope satirized as deformities as central to Cibber's strategy. They also provide us with a way to understand this strategy by studying its printed remains.

One final word: despite the negative implications of the word "deformity," I use it here deliberately—and not only because it is the word that Cibber employs throughout his play. I want to emphasize overexpression as a process of deformation, the deliberate dissolution of the recognizable forms of identity. Scholars of autobiography (a genre roughly coextant with celebrity) describe the autobiographical performance as an attempt to mold unruly subjectivities into established structures or conventional narratives—an attempt that leaves those subjectivities open to the appropriations and regulations of those who read them.[5] An overexpressive performer like Cibber resists this appropriation by exhibiting a deformed body that is undeniable and yet impossible for his spectator to categorize or conventionalize. In both *Richard III* and *The Dunciad*, the disabled body becomes not an obstacle to but rather an entry into the status of subject for the spectacular celebrity struggling for the right to self-definition.

THE DECLINING POWER OF THE ENGLISH MONARCH AND THE DUBIOUS POWER OF THE ENGLISH CELEBRITY

Though it may at first seem counterintuitive, Cibber's strategy of disabling inquiries into his person by transforming himself into a deformed king makes sense if we consider the celebrity culture emerging at the very moment that Cibber was coming of age. If we define the celebrity as a person as famous for what he performed in his private life as for what he performed on the public stage, we might think of Colley Cibber as one of the first. Cibber was born the son of a prominent sculptor (whose works, to Pope's delight, guarded the entrance to Bedlam Hospital for the insane). He was headed for the English army when he discovered the London stage. Cibber's unimpressive figure at first precluded him from roles as romantic hero or tragic king, and he spent his early years at Drury Lane playing bit parts and filling in for lead actors who had fallen ill or defected to the competing theater. By 1696 Cibber had become frustrated with these limited roles, and he decided to take matters into his own hands by composing a star vehicle that would highlight his unique proclivities as an actor. *Love's Last Shift* debuted to great applause, no less for its charming plot than for Cibber's outrageous performance as its fop. The role earned Cibber the fame and theatrical capital he would need to mount his adaptation of *Richard III* three years later.

At the same time that it established him as a celebrity and performer, *Love's Last Shift* also launched Cibber's career as a writer and businessman able to predict, with uncanny accuracy, the theatrical trends that would draw the fickle London audiences back to the theater again and again. By the time of his death in 1757 Cibber had composed twelve comedies, six tragedies, two ballad operas, two masques, a farce, an interlude, a "comical tragedy," and several poems.[6] Not all were successes, but despite his critics' attempts to dissuade him Cibber kept producing more. He served as English poet laureate under George II—a post he assumed in 1730—and as one of the most successful and longest-reigning managers of Drury Lane theater from 1709 to 1733. But the work for which he is best known today is his *Apology for the Life of Colley Cibber*, published in 1740. Though most often cited as a source for theater history, the *Apology* was also a literary innovation: as the first secular autobiography published in England, it declared that ordinary life might be as worth reading about as sinners' reforms or saints' conversions. "A Man who has pass'd above Forty Years of his Life upon a Theater, where he has never appear'd to be Himself," Cibber writes, "may have naturally excited the Curiosity of his Spectators to know what he really was, when in no body's Shape but his own."[7] His anticipation of his spectators' curiosity about "what he really was" was perhaps Cibber's savviest. With it, he established a literary genre that was to capitalize on an emergent celebrity culture constructed not around its heroes' public performances but around the seeming secrets of their private lives. By the middle of the eighteenth century, the son of a middle-class sculptor had come to live like a king.

Yet as often as Cibber declares his delight at the privileges that his pseudoroyal status granted him, he also registers anxiety about what this new role demands. The king's place in English society had shifted in the years following the English Civil War—the years in which Cibber's own fame was rising. In her study of the street and court performances that characterized daily life in the late Renaissance and Restoration, Paula Backscheider identifies the Stuarts as the last of the "spectacular" kings, who guaranteed their authority by performing it in elaborate displays of wealth and spectacle. By the mid-eighteenth century, such "spectacular politics" had given way to a bourgeois public sphere ruled by figures like Mr. Spectator, who guaranteed his objectivity by refusing to stand out. Cibber's career spans this shift: he first mounted the boards in 1687, two years after the death of the Stuart king Charles II; and he surrendered his official place in the Drury Lane Company in 1745, the year that the English defeat of Jacobite forces at Culloden squelched once and for all the royalists' hopes of reestablishing a spectacular Stuart on the English throne. By the time he retired, the spectacle once exclusive to the king had passed to the celebrity—and it had been stripped of the authority it once signified.

Cibber registers this shift within the pages of his *Apology*, which begins with his boyhood memories of being "carry'd by my Father to the Chapel in *Whitehall*; where I saw [King Charles] and his royal Brother the then Duke of

York, with him in the Closet, and present during the whole Divine Service."[8] But Cibber marks his entry into adulthood at the same time that he marks his entry into authorship, with the death of the spectacular king:

> King *Charles* his Death was judg'd, by our School-master, a proper Subject to lead the Form I was in, into a higher kind of Exercise; he therefore enjoin'd us, severally, to make his Funeral Oration. . . . This Oration, such as it was, I produc'd the next Morning: All the other Boys pleaded their Inability, which the Master taking rather as a mark of their Modesty than their Idleness, only seem'd to punish, by setting me at the Head of the Form: A Preferment dearly bought! Much happier had I been to have sunk my Performance in the general Modesty of declining it. A most uncomfortable Life I led among 'em, for many a Day after! I was so jeer'd, laugh'd at, and hated as a pragmatical Bastard (School-boys Language) who had betray'd the whole Form, that scarce any of 'em wou'd keep me company.[9]

Cibber's words discover in the figure of the modern celebrity the ghost of the early modern king: with the death of Charles as head of state Cibber assumes his own throne as "Head of the Form." Upon his coronation, however, Cibber finds himself in a changed world. Here, "general Modesty" holds more cultural value than spectacular display, and "Preferment" comes at a hefty price. Charles's regal performances may have made him a "Deity" capable of simultaneously representing (as effigy for) and commanding (as authority over) his English subjects. In this new world, though, Cibber finds that his own promotion merely exposes him to the jeers, the laughter, and the commands of his classmates. Less the "Head" than the figurehead of his fellows, a celebrity may wear the king's crown, but he lacks the power that such a symbol represents.

Worse, the celebrity lacks the king's power but still attracts his subjects' gaze—a gaze becoming less admiring and more critical as power shifts from royal display to public opinion. If Cibber presents his boyhood self as the ghost of the spectacular king, in other words, he portrays his classmates as precursors to Mr. Spectator. Even as late as 1740 it was Mr. Spectator to whom English readers turned to determine what made one properly English. And what seemed to make one properly English, according to Mr. Spectator, was the absence of any identifiable national characteristics that might attract an unwanted gaze. As an Englishman, he noted in 1711, "I am a *Dane*, *Swede*, or *French-Man* at different times, or rather fancy my self like the old Philosopher, who upon being asked what Country-man he was, replied, That he was a

Citizen of the World."[10] This lack of personal attributes or national characteristics, which he encouraged his readers to interpret as a lack of personal bias, made Mr. Spectator the ideal observer of his surroundings, the uninterpretable interpreter of English society.

A similar authority belongs to Cibber's jeering schoolmates, who cloak their self-interest under a "general Modesty" and who offer their commentary (dubbing Cibber a "pragmatical Bastard") in good company within the nation-in-miniature that Cibber presents. It is these school-age authorities who decide, a page later, that Cibber will compose the coronation ode that will convince the master to release them from school. It is they who determine, too, who might and who might not be elected into their society. Having produced the ode, Cibber nonetheless finds himself excluded. "They left me out of the Party I had most mind to be of, in that Day's Recreation," he laments. "But their ingratitude serv'd only to increase my Vanity; for I consider'd them as so many beaten Tits, that had just had the Mortification of seeing my Hack of a *Pegasus* come in before them. . . . I have met with much the same silly sort of Coldness, even from my Contemporaries of the Theatre, from having the superfluous Capacity of writing myself the Characters I have acted."[11] In former times, Cibber implies, his spectacular identification with and encomium to the king might have elevated him above his ordinary English classmates. Yet by the late seventeenth century such a role merely exposed him to their criticisms and robbed him of the Englishman's power of self-representation. Paradoxically, Cibber's role as his classmates' public representative excludes him from his classmates' company, just as his later role as celebrity—a symbol of Englishness—precludes him from being truly English.

Cibber's metaphorical description of his poetry as his "Hack of a *Pegasus*" is important here, because it helps to clarify what might otherwise seem a somewhat jumbled relationship between author, actor, celebrity, and king. The distinction between the schoolboy Cibber and his classmates—and the larger distinction between the spectacular celebrity and Mr. Spectator—is not a distinction between the writer and the reader. Rather, it is a distinction between the "Hack" who writes out of self-interest and the historian who disregards (or appears to disregard) his own fame in recording an objective analysis of his surroundings. Cibber invites his classmates' ire because he allows the spectacle of his overwrought prose to distract from the subject he is meant to observe, flying high on the *Pegasus* of his own poetic license and distorting history in his eagerness to "raise[e]" the king's character "to such height." In the final sentence of the passage, Cibber maps this distinction between "Hack" and historian onto the distinction between the actor, who thinks only of his own presence in the spotlight, and the playwright, who must take the larger view of the play as the reliable historian must take the larger view of history.

The problem for Cibber, of course, is that since the debut of *Love's Last Shift* his career had depended upon his playing both roles at once. As an actor he earned his spectators' praise by demanding their attention; as a playwright, by gaining their respect. As a theater manager, an autobiographer, and a "*Histor[ian] of the Stage During His Own Time*," moreover, he earned his readers' trust by eschewing spectacle and—like Mr. Spectator—performing objectivity. These roles become even more entangled when the play that Cibber is writing and performing is itself drawn from English history. History plays like *Richard III* recast the playwright as historian and invite the audience members to contrast the actors' performance as king with their shared cultural knowledge of that king's life. Setting himself the task of "writ[ing] the Characters I have acted" (Richard III among them), Cibber attempts to establish himself as both the celebrity and the authority, both the spectacle within and the spectator of his history.[12] Significantly, however, he does so by making himself so peculiar he cannot be interpreted. As I will argue in the remainder of this chapter, he finds his place not by dismounting but rather by deforming his "Hack of a *Pegasus*" into the lame and limping "Harse" of his most famous line as Richard III.

SEIZING THE HEROSTRATIC CROWN: COLLEY CIBBER AS THE DEFORMED KING

The liabilities that the role of public spectacle had assumed by the turn into the eighteenth century emerge in the very first lines of Cibber's *Richard III*. By portraying the position of spectacle as one of vulnerability, these lines set up Cibber's later development of Richard as a celebrity-king hungry for power but wary of the dehumanizing gazes such power invites. At the same time, they suggest a strong identification between the king and the celebrity portraying him, so that as the play continues, Richard's vulnerabilities become Cibber's vulnerabilities—and Richard's illegible body, Cibber's defense.

Shakespeare's *Richard III* opens, famously, with a soliloquy by the deformed king: "Now is the winter of our discontent / Made glorious summer by this son of York," Richard begins.[13] His speech evokes the imagery of the divine right of kings at the same time that it introduces his determination to undermine that right.[14] In contrast, the world that greets the audience as the curtain opens on Cibber's play seems stripped and stark. The difference speaks to how the role of spectacular king had changed in the years between the last years of the Renaissance and the dawn of the eighteenth century. In place of Shakespeare's castle Cibber presents the prison where Shakespeare's *3 Henry IV* (the final act of which Cibber has adapted as the first act of his *Richard III*) concludes. Here, Richard's predecessor languishes, awaiting news from the battlefield. And in place of Richard's extraordinary body and simile-laden soliloquy, Cibber introduces the nondescript bodies of a servant and an unnamed lieutenant, whose question opens the play:

> LIEUT. Has King *Henry* walked forth this Morning?
> SERV. No, Sir, but it is near his Hour.
> LIEUT. At any Time when you see him here,
> Let no Stranger into the Garden;
> I wou'd not have him star'd at.[15]

Reinforcing the position of spectacle as a position of humiliation, Cibber concretizes King Henry's loss of his status as subject—his demotion to the position of prisoner—by casting him as one who is "star'd at."

Cibber's attraction to this short exchange (which he lifts, unlike much of the rest of the scene, from Shakespeare's *2 Henry IV*) suggests the identification between celebrity and king that he would make explicit years later in the *Apology*, empathizing with Charles II as a man whose happiness, "like his Person," must remain "a Prisoner to its own Superiority."[16] Throughout *Richard III*, similarly, Cibber portrays the deformed king as a kind of celebrity performer whose power both depends on and is undermined by his spectators' stares. Not insignificantly, it is through a carefully orchestrated performance that Richard first seizes the crown in both Shakespeare's play and Cibber's adaptation.[17] If in Shakespeare's version such spectacles secure Richard's authority, in Cibber's play—as in his *Apology*—the king's performances suggest the "defenceless Station" accorded the object of the public gaze.[18]

Like Cibber, however, Cibber's Richard is not one to settle into such a "defenceless Station" without a fight. After dispatching his henchmen to murder the two young nephews who block his path to the throne, Richard pauses to ponder his legacy:

> Shall future Ages, when these Children's tale
> Is told, drop Tears in pity of their hapless Fate,
> And read with Detestation the Misdeeds of *Glo'ster*,

> The crook-back'd Tyrant, cruel, barbarous,
> And bloody—will they not say too,
> That to possess the Crown, nor Laws Divine
> Nor Human stopt my way?—Why let 'em say it;
> They can't but say I had the Crown;
> I was not Fool as well as Villain.[19]

With his defiant "Why let 'em say it," Cibber's Richard suggests he is no longer submitting to a narrative he cannot control but rather permitting a narrative he has helped to create. Such a suggestion seems at odds with Shakespeare's portrayal of Richard as a cursed villain whose history is both predestined and prophesied by the deformity that buckles his back. It seems at odds, too, with Richard's determination to star in the very same history he narrates. If to be "star'd at" is to be denied the ability to interpret one's own body or tell one's own story, how can Richard maintain his position as spectacular king without surrendering his position as historian? How can he play the villain-king without also playing the fool?

Cibber suggests the answers to these questions shortly after this scene, in the third act of the play, as he introduces the strategy that will become Richard's defense against his spectators' stares. This strategy is one that, as I am arguing, became integral to Cibber's own performances of self—and his own defenses against his spectators' invasive attentions. He articulates his strategy in one of the few soliloquies original to his adaptation of Shakespeare's play. Richard has spent the preceding acts killing a king, seducing and poisoning the king's daughter-in-law, arresting and executing all of the noblemen who oppose him, and plotting the murder of the remaining heirs who block his path to the throne. After a virtuosic performance of piety that earns him the crown he seeks, Richard takes a moment to ponder the stakes of his success. "A Crown!" he exclaims, donning the headpiece for the first time:

> Thou bright Reward of ever-daring Minds;
> Oh! how thy awful Glory fills my Soul!
> Nor can the Means that got thee, dim thy Luster:
> For, not Mens Love, Fear pays thee Adoration,
> And Fame not more survives from Good than Evil Deeds.
> Th'aspiring Youth, that fir'd the *Ephesian* Dome,
> Outlives, in Fame, the pious Fool that rais'd it.[20]

In this soliloquy, Cibber implicitly links his own status as celebrity to his character's status as king by portraying Richard as a spectacular (and somewhat unscrupulous) seeker of "fame." But he defines this fame as a very peculiar kind. The Ephesian youth to whom Cibber refers is Herostratus, who lends his name to the term "Herostratic fame," or fame at any cost. Eager to secure his place in the history books, Herostratus burned the domed Temple of Artemis in Ephesus in 356 BC. The Ephesian authorities tried to thwart his bid for notoriety by executing him and forbidding the pronunciation of his name. His story was later recorded, however, by the ancient historian Theopompus.[21] Herostratus thus exemplifies a figure asserting his right to self-definition, one who strikes out against a history to which he is unknown by performing himself back into that history—through whatever means necessary.

Like Cibber, Herostratus doesn't eschew spectacle in his pursuit of fame, and in the same breath that Cibber describes the "awful glory" of the deformed king's crown he evokes the blazing display of a great temple burning to the ground. Yet Herostratus's history is one known primarily for what it leaves unseeable and unsayable: the dome that Herostratus "fir'd" into nonexistence, the name legislated as unspeakable in ancient Ephesus (and left unspoken in Cibber's soliloquy). Through Herostratus, Cibber introduces the seeming paradox around which his overexpressions revolve: the paradox of a figure whose fame is undeniable yet whose history is one his countrymen are unable to retell. Through Richard, Cibber employs this paradox in his own performances of self. He replaces Herostratus's sentence of silence with Richard's determined efforts to define himself. And he discards the desperate and destructive actions through which Herostratus achieves his spectators' attentions in favor of the bent back and halting gait of the deformed king.

"WHAT BLOODY SCENE?": REFORMING THE SCRIPTS OF DISABILITY INTO PERFORMANCES OF ILLEGIBILITY

If Herostratus's status as subject depends on the destructiveness of his actions and the unspeakability of his name, Richard's status as subject (and the status of the celebrity who portrays him) depends on the illegibility of his deformed body. Like Herostratus's crimes, Richard's body earns him an undeniable and unforgettable place within his nation's history while discouraging the subjects of that nation from retelling (or rewriting) the story that now belongs exclusively to him. By portraying Richard's deformity as illegibility, in other words, Cibber's play provides an early example of the overexpressive strategy that his own performances of self would adopt. Like the overexpressive celebrity's, the maladroit monarch's eccentric features invite the attentions that secure his power while at the same time frustrating the reinterpretations that might undermine it.

With the live performances themselves lost to time, it is impossible to know how the language of Cibber's script translated to the gestures of his performance or how, exactly, Cibber suggested Richard's named deformities in his stance or costume. No images exist that can be positively identified depicting Cibber as Richard. The image that comes closest is the frontispiece to Nicholas Rowe's 1709 edition of *Richard III* (figure 1), published at a time when Cibber was still active in the role. The illustration that adorns Rowe's edition shows the climactic scene in act 5 in which Richard, sleepless on the eve of the Battle of Bosworth Field, is visited by the ghosts of all he has killed. Draperies framing the image suggest both the borders of Richard's tent and the curtains of the Drury Lane stage and seem to invite us to read the image as a representation of the play in performance. If we do, we might interpret this image as confirmation that Cibber's portrayal emphasized Richard's deformities. Richard sits bent over a table, his head in his right hand and the bulk of his hunched left shoulder suggesting an awkwardly bent back. His armor lies in disarray at his feet, the jumbled gloves and greaves echoing and emphasizing the disordered body of the man who sits beside them.[22]

There are, however, several problems with interpreting this image as a faithful representation of Cibber's performance. While a few of the frontispieces that adorn Rowe's edition *The Works of William Shakespear* may depict the plays in performance, many certainly do not. The most obvious evidence that the *Richard III* frontispiece falls into the latter category is that the play for which this image serves as frontispiece is Shakespeare's version, not the 1699 adaptation that Cibber would have been performing. The most famous recent actor to have used the Shakespearean text was Samuel Sandford, who appeared in a production led by Betterton and performed sometime before 1691–1692.[23] Cibber's version of the play had not been performed for five years before Rowe's edition appeared, and although Sandford had died eleven years before Rowe's edition saw publication, his performance was memorable enough that Cibber could discuss it at length in his *Apology* of 1740. If the illustration does depict the play in performance, in other words, it might as easily memorialize Sandford's performance as Cibber's.

A representation of Sandford is not necessarily irrelevant, since Cibber writes in the *Apology* of having borrowed heavily from Sandford's performance in his own portrayal.[24] Yet later representations of other actors in the role de-emphasize Richard's deformities as much as Rowe's illustration seems to emphasize them. William Hogarth's 1745 painting of David Garrick shows

1. Frontispiece to Nicholas Rowe's *Richard III* (1709). © Courtesy of Thomas Fisher Rare Books Library, University of Toronto.

2. William Hogarth, *David Garrick as Richard III* (ca. 1745). © Courtesy National Museums Liverpool.

the actor head on, leaning on one arm but in a posture that may suggest readiness for battle as easily as it suggests weakness or deformity (figure 2). William Hamilton's later painting of John Phillip Kemble in the role (figure 3) works in much the same way.

Despite these arguments, there is some evidence that Richard's deformities figured prominently in the audience's perception of the role, if not in Cibber's precise gestures. Rowe's own play *Jane Shore*, for instance, debuted in 1714 with Cibber taking up his old role as Richard III (a casting choice that indicates how much audiences had come to associate Cibber with the deformed king). At one moment in the play, Cibber as Richard invites his courtiers (and his audience members) to "Behold my arm, thus blasted, dry, and wither'd / Shrunk like a foul abortion, and decay'd."[25] The stage directions tell us that he animates these lines by "*pulling up his sleeves*"—a detail that suggests that Richard's deformities played some part in the spectacle of Cibber's performance.[26] Theater documents excavated by Judith Milhous indicate that Cibber wore the same costume to play the deformed king in both *Jane Shore* and his own *Richard III*.[27] Taken together, these documents suggest that there was

3. William Hamilton, *John Phillip Kemble as Richard III* (1790). © Victoria and Albert Museum, London.

some effort to make Richard's deformities visible on Cibber's costumed body in the 1699 production.

To whatever extent Richard's deformities figured into Cibber's performances, they figure heavily into his script. His portrayal of Richard's body is one of the ways that Cibber's version of the play departs most markedly from Shakespeare's—and that contributes most markedly to critics' complaints of the character's illegibility. In the earlier *Richard III*, the king endures again and again the disgust of onstage spectators who read his deformities as unambiguous markers of his villainy (and whose readings are confirmed in the play's final act). As disability scholars David T. Mitchell and Sharon L. Snyder point out, much of the dramatic tension in Shakespeare's text arises from Richard's attempts to "perform his deformity"—to defy with his own skillful language the prophecies proclaimed at his birth and made overt in his crooked back.[28] Through the poetic language that he commands throughout the play, Richard struggles for the right to self-definition against the "scripts of disability" that threaten to define him and against the spectators who offer their own interpretations of a body made all too visible by its irregularities.[29] These attempts are ultimately unsuccessful. By act 5, Richard's former eloquence has dissolved into largely monosyllabic confirmations of his body's inadequacies: "A horse! A horse! My kingdom for a horse!"[30] Shakespeare's Richard ends the play imprisoned in his own body and in his spectators' readings of that body, the victim of his spectacular performances rather than the subject who speaks his own story.

Shakespeare portrays Richard's deformities, then, as prophecies of his doom: the legible signs of his identity as a man "sealed in thy nativity / The slave of nature and the son of hell."[31] In stark contrast, Cibber's language refigures these deformities as ciphers that defy the grammar of the Enlightenment anatomy.[32] Cibber introduces the inscrutability of Richard's deformities early in the play chiefly through the observations of the deposed King Henry, who seems baffled by Richard's "Frightful" form.[33] It is not, Cibber makes clear, that Henry is a poor reader of bodies. When a lord arrives at the Tower of London fresh from the battlefield in the first act of the play, Henry intuits the tenor of his news from the expressions on his face. "[H]is Brow's the Title-Page, / That speaks the Nature of a tragic Volume," Henry predicts. "Say, Friend, how does my Queen! my Son! / Thou tremblest, and the Whiteness of thy Cheek / Is apter than thy Tongue to tell the Errand."[34] When the body before him is not the able body of the messenger but the deformed body of Richard, however, Henry seems less sure of his interpretations. "What bloody

Scene," he asks upon Richard's entrance in the following scene, "has *Roscius* now to act?"[35]

Henry's identification of Richard as the Roman actor Roscius confirms the deformed king's status as spectacle and heightens his identification with the spectacular celebrity who portrays him. It also repositions Henry from one who would be "star'd at" to a spectator casting his gaze on Richard.[36] By posing his reading of Richard as a question rather than stating it as a fact, Henry betrays some anxiety about whether Cibber's Richard will indeed stick to the "scripts of disability" that dictate how each scene, in Shakespeare's play, will end. It is worth noting that Henry's question originates with Shakespeare's *3 Henry VI*: in that play, Henry, upon Richard's entrance to his Tower cell, asks, "What scene of death hath Roscius to act?"[37] Cibber's "bloody scene," so much vaguer than Shakespeare's "scene of death," places new emphasis on the deformed body's illegibility. So, too, does the line's proximity, in Cibber's play, to Henry's description of the messenger's face as a "tragic volume." In contrast to the "tragic volume" of a narrative already completed and unalterable by the time that Henry encounters it in his messenger's face, Henry's question about Richard's body indicates a spectacle not quite contained or containable by the conventions of its form. It evokes the open-endedness of a performance that seems in danger, at any moment, of departing from its script.

Henry's inability to read Richard clears the way for Richard to define himself—and, as I will argue, mirrors the ways that the audience's inability to read Cibber's portrayal of Richard will aid Cibber's own self-creation. This move from illegibility to self-definition is prefigured in the scene in which Henry equivocates about how to characterize Richard or to predict the form his "bloody Scene" will take.[38] Henry's readings of Richard's body grow more confident as the scene progresses and he moves from questions ("wherefore dost thou come? Is't for my Life?") to conditional descriptions ("If murdering Innocents be executing, / Then thou'rt the worst of Executioners") to assertions of Richard's villainy ("thou cam'st to bite Mankind").[39] Here Henry's descriptions of Richard break off midsentence, interrupted by Richard's "I'll hear no more—die, Prophet, in thy Speech" and punctuated by Henry's murder, as Richard claims the power of self-definition as his and his alone.[40] Having silenced Henry, Richard dismisses the readings of his body that he has "heard [his] mother say" and settles, finally, on its uncategorizable peculiarity: "I am—myself alone."[41] With this line, Richard disables his spectators' attempts to read him against earlier narratives or within predetermined rules about anatomy as a key to character. He redefines himself, instead, as one who cannot be compared to—any more than he can be defined by—anyone but himself.

Cibber lifts these lines, largely unchanged, from Shakespeare's *3 Henry VI*.[42] By inserting them into the first act of his *Richard III* (in place of the famous soliloquy with which Shakespeare's Richard defines his disability as prophecy), Cibber leaves somewhat more ambiguous the significance of Richard's shape. Like Herostratus's countrymen, Richard's onlookers cannot ignore him. His deformities structure their remarks and position him, from the moment he enters the stage to the moment he exits, at the center of the gaze. Despite the spectacle that his body affords them, however, these onlookers echo Henry's trepidation when it comes to reading the character of the deformed king. As unable to interpret his deformities as they are to ignore them, the spectators must surrender to Richard the privilege to define himself, alone.

It is perhaps not just to limit Shakespeare's five acts to two hours' traffic, then, that Cibber excises so many of the speeches in which Richard or his onlookers depict his body as prophecy. Like Henry's "What bloody scene has *Roscius* to act?" these excisions reformulate Richard's deformities as questions rather than predilections of doom. As such, Cibber's script transfers the power of naming and of narrative from the unseen viewer to the deformed king, who alone can say what or how his body means. The lines that replace Shakespeare's soliloquy in Cibber's version confirm the king's power over his own history by emphasizing his continued eloquence, in stark contrast to the declining majesty of Shakespeare's babbling monarch. At the same time, as we shall see, they suggest the triumph of the spectacular celebrity who embodies the king over the cits and critics who glower at him from the pit.

Most telling are Cibber's changes to the spectacular scene in act 5 when, as Rowe's frontispiece illustrates, Richard encounters in a dream the ghosts of those he has murdered and wakes, in Shakespeare's version, having lost all sense of self. "What do I fear? Myself?" Shakespeare's Richard asks. He proceeds in the same sorts of interrogative sentences that Cibber will use to express Henry's bafflement at Richard's illegible body in his own first act. "There's none else by," declares Shakespeare's Richard: "Richard loves Richard, that is, I am I. / Is there a murderer here? No. Yes, I am. / Then fly! What, from myself? Great reason. Why?"[43] Richard's "I am I" might appear to resemble the line that marks Richard's self-definition in the first act of Cibber's play: "I am myself—alone." But in Shakespeare's final act, this apparent declaration of selfhood quickly dissolves into a meaningless tautology, as Richard replaces this statement of self with a series of questions with impossible or oxymoronic answers. ("Is there a murderer here? No. Yes, I am.") Shakespeare's Richard inhabits a body legible to his spectators but obscure to himself. His struggles at self-definition collapse, finally, in a doubly conscious internalization of his spectators' definitions of his body as villainous and in an impossible desire to "fly . . . from myself."

Cibber deletes this section. The changes that he makes recast Richard as a spectacle gaining self-awareness at the same time that Shakespeare's Richard is losing it. Departing from Shakespeare's soliloquy just before "What do I fear?," Cibber excises the nearly forty lines in which Shakespeare details, in increasingly unraveling language, Richard's unraveling powers of self-description. Replacing these lines in Cibber's play is a brief meditation on determinism ("I am but Man, and Fate, do thou dispose me"),[44] almost immediately interrupted by the entrance of Catesby, who has come to summon Richard to battle. The ghosts of the dead might rob Shakespeare's Richard of his former eloquence, but Cibber's Richard dismisses them with surprisingly little equivocation. The short, robust lines that replace Shakespeare's long soliloquy serve to reaffirm the king's powers of self-description. "No never be it said / That Fate itself could awe the soul of *Richard*," Cibber's king declares, only twenty-three lines after waking from his dream. "Hence babbling Dreams; you threaten here in vain; / Conscience avant, *Richard*'s himself again."[45]

This final phrase echoes Shakespeare's "I am I" in its reflexivity, but Cibber's revision lacks the tautological symmetry that makes Shakespeare's language turn back on itself into an expression of self-alienation. By translating the phrase into the third person, Cibber takes advantage of the idiomatic association of the reflexive pronoun with an individual's return to his proper subject position.[46] Cibber's "Richard's himself again" signifies not the splitting of the self accomplished by Shakespeare's "I am I," but rather a reunification that permits the self to speak. The grammatical eccentricity of Cibber's sentence confirms Richard's dual roles as the star as well as the author of his history. By translating Shakespeare's subject pronoun "I" into the objective case ("himself"), Cibber composes a sentence in which Richard occupies both the subject and the predicate: he serves, in other words, as both the speaking subject and the object being spoken about.

Cibber's revisions to Shakespeare's play not only emphasize the vulnerability that the spectacular king (and the spectacular celebrity) had acquired in a society that would recognize the unspectacular Mr. Spectator as its primary spokesperson. These revisions also transform Richard's deformities from the unambiguous marks of malignancy to strange hieroglyphs that make his form illegible. Undeniably visible but frustratingly uninterpretable, Cibber's Richard maintains his Herostratic fame without suffering the vulnerability of those kings who are "star'd at."[47] The same deformities that increase Richard's visibility also ensure his privacy.

That Cibber's Richard achieves his self-dissolution through increased self-reference is what transforms the scene from expression to overexpression. It is no accident that, though they lack the same self-doubt, Cibber's revisions contain the echoes of Shakespeare's "I am I." While these echoes do not rob Cibber's Richard of his coherence, as they did Shakespeare's Richard, they include an excess of self-reference. In proclaiming "Richard's himself again," Cibber's deformed king refers to himself twice (once as "Richard" and once as "himself"). This excess of self-reference, however, does not bring the spectator any closer to knowing who or what Richard is. In fact, it prevents such knowledge by replacing with "himself" any adjective that might help to elucidate the deformed king's character. A soliloquy whose excessive self-reference serves only to deflect self-description, a deformed body whose excessive visibility serves only to increase illegibility: these are the overexpressive elements that allow Cibber's Richard to reclaim the powers of self-definition from his spectators and to begin to tell his own story.

It is thus fitting that in addition to allowing Richard the power to describe his own intentions, his own dreams, his own life, Cibber should allow him the power to describe his own death as well. This decision marks a significant departure from Cibber's source. Shakespeare's play relegates Richard's death to a stage direction that prevents the king from speaking during his final scene onstage.[48] The last line we hear from him (the line that ends the scene just before this one) is "A horse! A horse! My kingdom for a horse!"—a line that, as I've already discussed, reduces the intricacies of Richard's earlier utterances to a succession of mainly monosyllables, capable only of naming his lameness.[49] Though Shakespeare allows Richard to bring the play into being through his opening soliloquy, he affords no such privilege at the play's conclusion. The end of Richard's life, like the end of the play in which he appears, is performed upon him by the stage directions—and by Richmond's announcement that "the bloody dog is dead."[50]

Not so the final moments of Richard's life in Cibber's play. The stage directions tell us that Richmond and Richard "*Fight*" and "Richard *falls*."[51] In this play, however, Richard dies with a final grand farewell that increases the overexpressive spectacle of his departure. "Perdition catch thy arm—the chance is thine," Richard exclaims to Richmond as he receives his death wound:

But oh! the vast Renown thou hast acquired!
In conquering *Richard,* does afflict him more
Than ev'n his Body's parting with its Soul.
Now let the World no longer be a Stage
To feed Contention in a lingering Act;
But let one Spirit of the first-born *Cain*
Reign in all Bosoms; that each Heart may set
On bloody Actions, the rude Scene may end,
And Darkness be the Burier of the Dead. [*Dies*[52]

Like "Richard's himself again," the first four lines of Richard's death speech guarantee his dual role as subject and object by translating his self-description into the third person. This perspective allows Richard to insert himself as the star of the story even as he seems to watch that story unfold from afar. His double functions as spectacle and spectator are even more starkly juxtaposed in the passage's idiosyncratic verb tense, as Richard describes his greatest misfortune to be the "vast renown [Richmond has] acquired" in defeating him. Speaking in the present perfect tense, Richard enjoys the perspective of an omniscient spectator able to see and to narrate not only the defeat of the king but also its consequences, the rising fame of his defeater.

Perhaps even more poignant is Richard's wish that "the spirit of the first-born *Cain*," a character whose marked body resembles Richard's, should come to "Reign in all bosoms."[53] The line betrays a desire for the inconspicuousness that guarantees the subject's power to observe others and to define himself. In a society in which Cain's deformities mark "All bosoms," Richard's own deformities will no longer seem so offensive. Significantly, Richard does not imagine achieving this inconspicuousness by contorting his own figure to fit the unmarked figures of his able-bodied fellows. Instead, he imagines forcing their figures to conform to his own. As he does so, his spectators become copies of his own body, pawns in his own plot.

It is, then, a particularly overexpressive illegibility that Richard imagines here—an illegibility that he will achieve not by minimizing but by exaggerating the spectacular proportions of his own body and the self-reference within his own sentences. It is also a typically Cibberian illegibility—or typically Cibberian according to critics' depiction of Cibber as a celebrity who doesn't conceal but proclaims his deviations and his disabilities. These disabilities were not limited, for such critics, to the body that Cibber exhibited in performance but included also the idiosyncrasies and malapropisms that littered his printed works and that his readers compared both implicitly and explicitly to the deformities of Richard's body. One pamphleteer even accused Cibber in his writings of intentionally "ty[ing] up your Wit, as a Beggar does his Limbs, to excite our Compassion and our Charity."[54]

I will turn to Cibber's critics in the final section of this chapter, where I explore how critiques by Pope, Henry Fielding, and others helped to crystallize the elements of overexpression that Cibber's own autobiographical performances suggest. First, though, I examine how the strategy of overexpression that I have defined in Cibber's performance as Richard translates to his printed works. As I will demonstrate, the purple prose and misspelled words with which Cibber "t[ied] up his wit" and deformed the printed page worked to frustrate spectators' interpretations of his printed works much as Richard's unreadable body had frustrated their critiques of his performance. Reading these works in concert with Cibber's performances as Richard contextualizes Pope's famous critique of Cibber as the deformed king of *The Dunciad* by revealing the extent to which Cibber borrowed from his onstage role to construct his offstage persona. Even more importantly, such readings suggest one model for translating the features of overexpression from the stage to the page—a model that later artists would take up, build upon, and react against.

"HOW FAIR A PAGE THOU'ST BLOTTED": DEFORMING THE PRINTED PAGE INTO THE *LINGUA CIBBERIANA*

The suggestion that Cibber's stylistic techniques might apply as easily to his printed materials as to his performances in *Richard III* might seem surprising—especially if we recall the first act of the play and the deep distinction that Henry implies between the "tragic volume" of his able-bodied messenger's face and the "bloody scene" presaged by Richard's irregular body.[55] Henry's association of a normative body with the printed page and a deformed body with performance suggests a dichotomy between print and performance—one that disability scholars reproduce in lamenting Richard's inability to perform his identity against the "scripts of disability" that circumscribe him.[56] Both formulations portray performance as ephemeral and somewhat unruly—a medium that defies form, specializing in stories (like the "bloody scene" that Richard will enact) whose plots often do not conform to recognizable patterns and whose endings cannot be predicted.

Print, on the other hand, seems in this dichotomy to belong to the depersonalized and disembodied world ruled by figures like Mr. Spectator. Like the "tragic volume" of the messenger's able body, the printed page bears none of the distinguishing marks or distracting peculiarities that might make one author's book appear different from another's, or that might distract from the reader's ability to interpret the story's meaning. This standardization was particularly apparent in Cibber's lifetime, which saw the emergence of the dictionary; the growing insistence on standards of spelling, punctuation, and grammar; and the increasingly uniform appearance not only of printed books but also of published playscripts.[57] Though dictionaries and wordbooks had begun to appear earlier in the eighteenth century, such standardization would reach its climax with the publication of Samuel Johnson's *Dictionary of the English Language* in 1755, fifteen years after the debut of Cibber's autobiography. This assumption of the printed page as rule-bound and standardized suggests one reason that the Scriblerians' complaints about Cibber's malapropisms so often coincide with their complaints about Cibber's vanity. To refuse to conform to standards of grammar and spelling was to draw unnecessary attention to oneself. Cibber's greatest crime, according to the Scriblerians, was his attempt to make a spectacle of himself not only on the spectacular stage but on the supposedly unspectacular and normative printed page as well.

Yet the foregoing discussion of overexpression suggests a way to understand Cibber's printed misspellings and malapropisms not as vanity but as its opposite: as the only means by which a celebrity of Cibber's stature could forestall his readers' tendency to interpret every word of his prose as a window into his personality. In short, Cibber's linguistic tricks constitute a strategy by which the celebrity might avoid his spectators' anatomizing gaze at the same time that he seemed to invite it. Cibber provides an illustration of this strategy in the final scene of *Richard III*, in which he reimagines Richard's story not as a "Tale . . . told" (or performed) by "future Ages" but rather as a history recorded on a printed page.[58] As he does, he suggests that this printed page is a medium as spectacular and unstable as performance.

The play doesn't end, after all, with Richard's death speech. Cibber punctuates this death with an elegy by Richard's opponent and successor, Richmond. And like Henry's "What bloody scene," Richmond's speech seems less an effort to describe or define the character of the deformed king than a confirmation of the impossibility of doing so. "Farewel, *Richard*," Richmond begins.

> and from thy dreadful End
> May future Kings from Tyranny be warn'd:
> Had thy aspiring Soul but stirr'd in Virtue,

> With half the Spirit it has dar'd in Evil,
> How might thy Fame have grac'd our *English* annals?
> But as thou art, how fair a Page thou'st blotted?[59]

Richmond's elegy mirrors the language that the Scriblerians would later use to condemn Cibber's prose by comparing it to a deformed body. Here, Richard's distinctive figure resurfaces to "blot" the pages of English history books, rendering them illegible.

Crucially, however, Richard achieves his illegibility not by leaving holes but rather by creating excesses in his self-presentations. These self-presentations play upon the excessive visibility of a body that "seems too much a body" as they do on the excessive ink that blots the deformed king's name.[60] We might perceive shadows of this blotted page in the black page of *Tristram Shandy*, a similarly excessive and similarly inscrutable memorial to a similarly disabled character, Sterne's doomed parson Yorick (a character whose fate, like Richard's, comes down to his lack of a proper horse). We might perceive its shadows as well in Cibber's description of his autobiography as "this *Chiaro Oscuro* of my Mind," a memorial somewhere in between the "oddly besmear'd" (or blotted) page of an improper memory and the "flatly white-wash'd" page of forgetting.[61] The image of a page too full of ink to be properly interpreted is one that haunts the overexpressive performances of the celebrities I examine here—and one that we shall see again.

The blotted page made illegible by its excesses certainly seems an apt symbol for the famously verbose prose that distinguished Cibber's printed works, and his Scriblerian enemies were quick to point out the resemblances between Cibber's overwrought performances as Richard and the deformed words and sentences of his prose. One of the most complete descriptions of his performance, published by an anonymous pamphleteer in 1740, is also one of the most negative. Specifically, it chastises Cibber for being too spectacular in his onstage appearance—and too peculiar in his diction. "When it came to be acted," the pamphleteer writes, "this same Mender of *Shakespear* chose the principal Part, *viz. the King*, for himself; and accordingly being invested with the purple Robe, he scream'd thro' four Acts without Dignity or Decency. . . . When in the heat of Battle at *Bosworth Field*, the King is dismounted, our Comic-Tragedian came on the Stage, really breathless, and in a seeming Panick, screaming out his line thus—'*A Harse, a Harse, my Kingdom for a Harse*.'"[62]

The pamphleteer's mocking of Cibber's lines, heavy with the drawled accent the actor assumed as fop, transforms the words that—in Shakespeare's play—mark Richard's surrender to the "scripts of disability." In Cibber's play, these same words mark language as subject to the whims and the persona of the performer. In part, Cibber's crime stems from his inability or refusal to divorce his onstage role from his offstage persona: his performance fails because he continues to play himself even when he attempts to play Richard. The critique suggests one way that the roles of Cibber as Richard and of Cibber as Cibber bled into one another, inviting audiences to read Cibber's deformed king as a commentary on his own celebrity.

Yet it is significant that the pamphleteer's critique focuses on Cibber's mispronunciation—expressed in print through a misspelling—of the play's words. Like Richard's proper name—or like Herostratus's—the misspelled "*Harse*" isn't public property. It can't be found within any of the dictionaries that emerged during Cibber's lifetime. Instead, "*Harse*" is a word that acquires its meaning not in its spelling but rather in its pronunciation—not in print but in performance. It is only recognizable to the extent that it emanates from and refers back to the body and the voice of Colley Cibber. (One of the Scriblerians' most famous members, Henry Fielding, relies on this recognition in creating a parody of Cibber for his 1730 play, *The Author's Farce*. Fielding identifies the ridiculous character Sir Farcical Comic as a mockery of Cibber by having him repeat Cibber's affected accent in foppish catchphrases—"Stap my breath!" and "Stap my vitals!"—that turn properly English *o*'s to Cibber's drawn-out *a*'s.)[63] Like Richard's blotted page and illegible body, such misspelled words belong to Cibber and only to Cibber: incorrect but unmistakable, proprietary precisely because they are improper. As such, they preserve the uniqueness of Cibber's deformed performance even within the increasingly standardized surfaces of the printed page. At the same time, they emphasize this performance's deformity and its illegibility, muddling the generic distinctions that audiences might use to categorize and interpret "our Comic-Tragedian's" performance.

Richmond's description of the blotted page of Richard's history book thus anticipates the ways in which Cibber's own histories will employ misspelled words and malformed sentences to guarantee Cibber's spectacular uniqueness at the same time that they render him illegible. Should we desire an example of the blotted pages, superfluous phrases, and overwrought words that make overexpression not only a strategy of performance but also a performance in print, we need look no further than Cibber's *Apology*. Like Richard's death speech, the *Apology* advertises itself as both autobiography and history, both an analysis of Cibber's *Life* and a *History of the Stage During His Own Time*. Cibber himself serves as the book's spectacular subject and as its objective historian. His strategy for occupying both of these roles simultaneously becomes clear when, early in the *Apology*, he defends one of his most egregious overexpressions by exaggerating it further. After explaining the grave offenses he suffered from his critics, Cibber alludes by way of example to a preface he wrote for his play *The Provoked Husband*, "where, speaking of [leading actress] Mrs. [Anne] *Oldfield*'s excellent Performance in the Part of Lady *Townly*, my Words ran thus, *viz. It is not enough to say, that here she outdid her usual Outdoing*."[64]

As Cibber acknowledges, the superfluous repetition of the already exclamatory "outdid" turned his preface to palaver, and his readers were especially vocal in their criticisms of this passage. The phrase makes a parodic appearance in *The Apology for the Life of Mr. The' Cibber*, which claims to be the autobiography of Cibber's son but was probably written by Henry Fielding.[65] It surfaces as well in *The Tryal of Colley Cibber, Comedian* (attributed on its title page to T. Johnson, but probably also written by Fielding).[66] Yet as Cibber points out, his overdone "outdoing" prevented his critics from doing little more than aping him. "I owe myself the Shame of confessing, I have no Excuse for it," Cibber admits of his overexpressive phrase. "But . . . like a Lover in the Fulness of his Content, by endeavouring to be floridly grateful, I talk'd Nonsense. Not but it makes me smile to remember how many flat Writers have made themselves brisk upon this single Expression; wherever the Verb, *Outdo*, could come in, the pleasant Accusative, *Outdoing*, was sure to follow it. . . . Nay, the very learned in the Law, have at least facetiously laid hold of it! Ten Years after it first came from me, it serv'd to enliven the Eloquence of an eminent Pleader before the House of Parliament! What Author would not envy me so frolicksome a Fault, that had such publick Honours paid to it?"[67]

Cibber's "outdid her usual outdoings" serves the intended purpose of overexpression in two ways. First, it frustrates his readers' attempts to divine the meaning of his prose, much as Richard's bent back frustrated King Henry's attempts to divine the meaning of his performance. Second, the phrase—precisely because of the nonsense it produces—coerces the most authoritative figures in England ("the very learned in the law," "an eminent Pleader before the House of Parliament," the spectators and authorities who ruled Cibber's society) into speaking Cibber's tongue. Cibber translates his eccentric phrases into the normative language by creating a syntax so spectacular that others begin to repeat it. What author, in a print world as overpopulated with critics as Cibber's was, "would not envy" that?

Cibber does not evade his critics' lambastings with his misspelled words and malformed sentences—any more than he avoids his spectators' stares with his deformed costume. Indeed, he seems to encourage these lambastings as he does those stares. Yet at the same time that they invite his critics' ire, Cibber's blatantly nonnormative sentences also render useless his critics' most powerful weapons. Unable to categorize his language as English in the strictest sense, they can hardly critique his deviations from it. Unable to understand or interpret his prose, they can only mimic it. In this they resemble the baffled Henry VI in Cibber's play, articulating what all Cibber's spectators seem to be thinking as he asks what Richard's illegible body could possibly mean.

It was not only the anonymous writer of the *Laureat*, published shortly after the release of Cibber's *Apology*, who noted the resemblances between Cibber's malapropisms in print and his bent body as Richard III. The deformity of Richard's printed pages is an image that recurs throughout the Scriblerians' writings against Cibber, so that deformity comes to stand in (much as it did for Cibber's Henry VI) for illegibility. In the final section of this chapter I turn to these writings by Cibber's critics, who often reference Cibber's role as Richard in order to justify their attacks of his written works as similarly excessive, similarly deformed. The most famous of these is Pope's *Dunciad*, and as we shall see, the crown that Cibber donned as Richard both resembles and sheds light on the laurel wreath he wears as King of the Dunces. Even more significant than the link such critiques draw between Cibber's life as performer and his life as poet is their description of the effect that Cibber's autobiographical performances had on his spectators and readers. As they repeatedly chastise Cibber's excesses for rendering his persona impenetrable, Pope and others become the first to articulate these excesses, until what was merely an idiosyncrasy of Cibber's Richard comes to seem a defining feature of Cibber's style. As they grope for ways to express what so frustrates them about the poet laureate, in other words, their critiques succeed in popularizing and in perpetuating the overexpressive methods that later artists will adopt. Through their writings, overexpression begins to come into focus as both the excess of deformity and as the inherent deformity of excess.

"TO BLOT OUT ORDER": COLLEY CIBBER AS KING OF THE DUNCES

Echoing throughout Scriblerian responses to Cibber's works is the contention that the actor's printed and performed deformities violate the standards of the English language and of Englishness itself. Paradoxically, such violations seem only to make Cibber more English. In a pamphlet published in 1740 under the pseudonym of "T. Johnson" and later produced on the pages of his periodical, *The Champion*, for instance, Henry Fielding puts Cibber on trial. The charge, as the title page declares, is "writing a Book intitled An Apology for his Life, &c. Being A thorough Examination thereof; wherein he is proved guilty of High Crimes and Misdemeanors against the English Language."[68] The trial consists of testimonies by personages proclaiming the *Apology*'s excesses as turning its syntax to senselessness. Yet the senselessness of Cibber's English language seems not to make him less English, but rather to make him more so: Fielding ends his pamphlet by acquitting Cibber of all crimes for which he stands accused. "Now I shall prove it to be *English* in the following manner," Fielding declares of the *Apology*'s excessive language. "Whatever Book is writ in no other Language is writ in *English*. This Book is writ in no other Language; *Ergo*, It is writ in *English*: Of which Language the Author hath shewn himself a most absolute Master; for surely he must be absolute Master of that whose Laws he can trample under Feet, and which he can use as he pleases."[69]

Fielding's mock-logical conclusion that a book "writ in no other Language" must be "writ in *English*" makes more sense if we recall Mr. Spectator's description of the ideal Englishman as a "Citizen of the World."[70] The Englishman is an unmarked man who avoids the peculiarities of other nations and seeks only to remain unremarkable and unremarked upon as he mixes with the crowd. Cibber, according to Fielding, seeks a similar illegibility. While Mr. Spectator achieves his Englishness by blending in, however, Cibber does so by standing out—highlighting the excesses, the deformities, and the improprieties that make the *Apology* such an uncategorizable book.

Reviews and discussions of Cibber's printed works by his contemporaries reiterate Fielding's suggestion that the very excesses of Cibber's language make his works impossible to dissect and that the oddities of his Englishness render him somehow more English. The writer of the *Laureat* faces just such a difficulty in describing Cibber's 1712 tragedy *Ximena*, an adaptation of the French neoclassical play *Le Cid*. "Our Laureat, some Years ago," the pamphlet explains, "presented the Public with a Thing he called a Play, something in Imitation of the *Cid* of *Corneille*, I cannot call it a Translation into *English*, for it is not *English*, 'tis a Sort of *Lingua Cibberiana*, which, as they say the *Lingua Franca* is a commercial, is a Sort of Theatrical Language, peculiar to himself and the Stage."[71] As the pamphleteer describes it, Cibber's language hovers between originality and anonymity, between being monstrous and being unmarked. Such language is not quite the standardized "*English*" of the bourgeois public sphere, he declares, but a "*Lingua Cibberiana.*" The words of this language are nonstandard, "peculiar to" Cibber and to "the Stage," where the pronunciations of individual performers take precedence over the iterative words churned out by the printing press. At the same time that he marks such language as the exclusive property of Colley Cibber, however, the pamphleteer implies that such language is unmarked. It is a *Lingua Cibberiana* that, like the "commercial" *Lingua Franca*, does not belong to a particular nation and does not mark its speakers as of a particular character. As he did in Fielding's *Tryal*, Cibber earns his national identity by relinquishing all national markers. Speaking a language both "peculiar to" himself and unidentifiable as anything else, Cibber guarantees his Englishness by overexpressing it.

The nonnormative body at the center of Cibber's performances and the improper words that punctuate their prose guarantee the Scriblerians' representation of the celebrity not only as "Beggar" or as actor but also, of course, as king.[72] In his *Tryal*, Fielding descries Cibber's tendency to regard history as his own property rather than a commonality he shares with his "Countrymen"—and to treat language as his own "absolute power."[73] Here again Cibber assumes the crown of the deformed king, reclaiming his language as an "absolute power" that, unlike the standardized pages legible to anyone, could not be reinterpreted by Cibber's readers. Fielding's fellow Scriblerian, Alexander Pope, would make a similar accusation just two years later when, composing a new fourth book to his 1728 mock-epic *The Dunciad*, he removed the crown of the Dunce King from the head of Lewis Theobald and placed it squarely on the skull of his new nemesis, Colley Cibber.

The Dunciad did not begin as a poem about Cibber—or even as a poem about celebrity. In 1728, angered by the publication of *Shakespeare Restored; or a Specimen of the many Errors as well Committed as Unamended by Mr. Pope in his late edition of this poet* by his rival Shakespearean editor Lewis Theobald, Pope published an anonymous three-book mock-epic. This first *Dunciad* satirized Theobald as a proud and pedantic sovereign who represented all that was wrong with Grub Street printers and English letters. A second version, *The Dunciad Variorum* (largely unchanged but with a long prolegomenon) appeared in 1729.

As the years passed, however, Pope's enemies changed—or merely multiplied. Pope had met Cibber through their mutual friend Joseph Addison in 1713, and the two became civil if cautious acquaintances. This civility collapsed when Cibber, in a performance of Buckingham's *The Rehearsal*, ad-libbed a speech designed to give injury to Pope and his fellow Scriblerians. The speech sparked a pamphlet war that eventually waned only to wax again in 1730, after Cibber assumed the post of poet laureate. Complaining vehemently (and perhaps accurately) that the appointment had less to do with poetry than with politics, Pope took advantage of Cibber's well-known malapropisms and accused him of mangling the English language. Cibber only added fuel to the fire with his publication of the *Apology* in 1740, prompting Pope to compose a fourth book for his *Dunciad*. It appeared in 1742 and bestowed upon Cibber the dubious prize of the Dunce King's crown. Less than a year later, Pope had published a new, complete version of the poem—*The Dunciad in Four Books*—now focused not on Lewis Theobald but on Cibber himself.

Though composed forty-three years after Cibber debuted his *Richard III*, *The Dunciad* seems haunted by the play that was still in repertoire when Pope was writing. As Laura Rosenthal, G. S. Rousseau, and others have pointed out, the poem alludes frequently to theatrical images and devices.[74] The invocation that launched the fourth book describes Pope's nightmare vision of a world without culture. Setting the scene for the poem's final, climactic moments, Pope writes:

> Now flam'd the Dog-star's unpropitious ray,
> Smote ev'ry Brain, and wither'd ev'ry Bay;
> Sick was the Sun, the Owl forsook his bow'r,
> The moon-struck Prophet felt the madding hour:
> Then rose the Seed of Chaos, and of Night,
> To blot out Order, and extinguish Light.[75]

Pope's use of the word "blot" here recalls Richmond's lamentation, in the final scene of Cibber's *Richard III*, for the "fair page" of the "*English* annals" that Richard's deformity has "blotted." Evoking Cibber's reimagining of Richard's deformed body as a blotted page, this image plays into one of Pope's central objections to Cibber as a man who has earned his laurels through performance rather than print, spectacle rather than sense. At the same time, his critique registers the growing separation between celebrity and author—or between spectacular, flash-in-the-pan fame and literary renown—that had begun to structure the London arts scene. The English culture that Pope fears throughout the *Dunciad* is precisely the English culture that Cibber creates in his overexpressive performances and prose: an English history "fir'd" into nonexistence by the "annals" that obscure rather than remember their subjects, an English literature so superfluous that it becomes nonsensical, and an English monarchy headed by a deformed and illegible king.

Pope's anxieties about the uncategorizability of Cibber's haunting performances and illegible print surface even before the final, four-book poem begins, in a short introduction that heads the 1743 version and articulates many of the qualities that later artists would adopt as the cornerstones of overexpression. In the voice of "Ricardus Aristarchus" (a mocking pseudonym for another Shakespearean editor, Richard Bentley), Pope compares his poem to the "*greater Epic[s]*" of authors such as "Homer and Virgil."[76] The mock-epic he presents differs from these "*greater Epics*" in part because it descends from a play rather than a poem: it is a genre, Pope writes, "come down to us amongst the Tragedies of Euripides."[77] In addition to tracing the origins of the mock-epic genre to the stage, then, Pope locates it more specifically in the "Tragedies" of an author known for violating Aristotle's admonitions against spectacle. (It is likely the most notorious scene of Euripides's tragedy *Medea* that Pope is evoking when he imagines Cibber "mounting the wind" on "grinning dragons" in Book III.)[78] Cibber has earned Pope's ridicule, this allusion implies, because he has confused the spectacular display of the actor with the authoritative objectivity of the historian. "It is from their *actions* only that Princes have their character, and Poets from their *works*," Pope writes in a footnote to Book IV.[79] To combine these two roles—to attempt to earn literary fame through spectacular "actions"—is to violate Pope's rules of order, and to plunge all of England into Dulness.

Yet this is precisely what Cibber does in his determination to "write the Characters I have acted."[80] And Pope's inability to dissect Cibber's character or critique his nonsensical prose seems to rescue Cibber's private self—if not his public persona—from the most vicious of Pope's attacks. Significantly, Pope traces Cibber's success at avoiding such barbs to two excesses characteristic of all the actor's self-presentations: the excessive "*actions*" that deform his English body, and the excessive words that deform his English language. Pope's identification of Cibber's excesses as both performed and printed suggests a resemblance between the qualities that, for him, define Cibber's works and the qualities that I have attributed to overexpression—a resemblance that the continuation of the introduction (as well as the poem it introduces) will confirm.

Pope defines the first of these excesses in the same preface in which he describes the origins of the mock-epic form. Though he refers to the mock-epic as the "lesser Epic," he distinguishes the form from its classical predecessors by noting its exaggerations—and, in particular, the exaggerated persona of the man who serves as both the hero of the poem and the representative of his nation.[81] "In the *greater Epic*," Pope explains (by way of contrast), "the prime intention of the Muse is to exalt Heroic Virtue, in order to propagate the love of it among the children of men."[82] Pope's definition of the classical epic as a poem meant to declare and define a national hero who might serve as a model for "the children of men" is one that more recent critics have also attributed to the epic form. Like the early modern king, as scholars such as Richard Terry, Ulrich Broich, Gregory C. Colomb, and Claude Rawson note, the traditional epic hero serves as an embodiment of an entire nation. He is a symbolic personage rather than a person, whose every virtue and whose every vice suggest the collective virtues and vices of his countrymen. Like the celebrity, the epic hero represents his nation but loses his relevance at the moment that his values no longer accord with those of his countrymen.

In the early eighteenth century, the same shifts that had depleted the power of the English monarchy seem also to have depleted the power of the English epic. By Pope's lifetime, writes Rawson, "The epic had become impossible to write. A loosening sense of universal coherence, however emphatically asserted, a progressive fragmentation of faiths, vast accretions of knowledge in the particulars of the universe, could not be expected to sustain confident or consensual articulations of a universal vision, in much the same way as the evolution of bourgeois society and the growth of anti-war sentiment made it harder for good poets to write epics."[83] If epic heroes, like early modern kings, serve as symbols of "their lands and times," the mock-epic hero of Pope's poem, like the celebrity-king of Cibber's play, seems a deformation of these predecessors.[84] He seems a hero who has become uncategorizable through the very excesses of his person and personality.

Pope suggests these excesses—and the ways that they destroyed the mock-epic hero's suitability as representation of his nation—in Aristarchus's lengthy introduction. "But then it is not every Knave, nor (let me add) Fool, that is a fit subject for a Dunciad," he writes. "There must still exist some Analogy, if not resemblance of Qualities, between the Heroes of the two Poems [the greater epic and the lesser]; and this in order to admit what Neoteric critics call the *Parody*, one of the liveliest graces of the little Epic. Thus it being agreed that the constituent qualities of the greater Epic Hero, are *Wisdom, Bravery*, and *Love*, from whence springeth *heroic Virtue*, it followeth that those of the lesser Epic Hero, should be *Vanity, Impudence*, and *Debauchery*, from which happy assemblage resulteth *heroic Dulness*, the never-dying subject of this our Poem."[85]

As he delves into the "particulars" of each quality comprising the identity of the lesser Epic Hero, Pope suggests that "*Vanity, Impudence, Debauchery*" and "*heroic Dulness*" are the qualities of the epic hero deformed: they are

"*Wisdom, Bravery, Love*" and "*heroic Virtue*" in excess.[86] "It is the character of true *Wisdom*," Pope explains, "to seek its chief support and confidence within itself; and to place that support in the resources which proceed from a conscious rectitude of Will—And are the advantages of *Vanity,* when arising to the heroic standard, at all short of this self-complacence? Nay, are they not, in the opinion of the enamoured owner, far beyond it?"[87] "Far beyond" the "true *Wisdom*" possessed by the English hero, Cibber's "Vanity" as the mock-epic hero exaggerates the qualities recognizable as English. They become, like Cibber's nonsensical words and deformed performances, unrecognizable as anything in particular. The pattern holds for the remainder of the mock-epic hero's qualities. These include not simply *Bravery* but "courage in so high and heroic a degree, that it insults not only Men, but Gods" and begins to resemble blasphemy; not only "*Love*" but love that, "when it is let alone to work upon the *Lees*, . . . acquireth strength by *Old age*; and becometh" debauchery; and, not merely "*Magnanimity*" but "*Buffoonery*, the source of *Ridicule*, that 'laughing ornament' . . . of the little Epic."[88] Pope illustrates each of these heroic qualities with a direct quote from Cibber—either from his *Apology* or from his indignant and widely circulated 1742 pamphlet, *A Letter from Mr. C—— to Mr. P——*.

Despite a name that deems him "lesser" than his epic predecessors, then, Cibber's ridiculousness stems from an abundance rather than a dearth of wisdom, bravery, love, and heroic virtue. If the epic hero of England exemplifies these qualities, Cibber exceeds them. And if the epic hero stands as an embodiment of his nation, Cibber's excessive identity deforms that same embodiment: he becomes less an emblem than an overexpression of Englishness. The epic hero's virtues might "manifest [themselves] in every limb," Pope suggests, but Cibber's qualities as the mock-epic hero are less revealing of his or his countrymen's characters. Promising a glimpse into the Englishman's true character but offering up only the superficial and spectacular Cibber, Pope portrays these same qualities in the mock-epic hero as those "all collected into the *Face*."[89]

This face is, of course, a deformed one—and its deformities make it at once unmistakable and unreadable. "Nor can we be mistaken in this happy quality a species of *Courage*," Aristarchus continues of Cibber's "high courage of blasphemy," "when we consider those illustrious marks of it, which made his *Face* 'more known (as he justly boasteth) than most in the kingdom,' and his *Language* to consist of what we must allow to be the most *daring* Figure of Speech, that which is taken from the *Name of God*."[90] In place of poetry Cibber pronounces blasphemy, according to Pope; he speaks in curses and irregular utterances because he cannot speak sense. Samuel Garth, Pope's contemporary and the supposed inventor of the mock-epic form, described the new genre as characterized by its "barren Superfluity of Words."[91] His description reappears, not insignificantly, as the epigraph to the *Laureat*'s diatribe against the verbosity of Cibber's *Apology*.[92] That Pope employs a form at once "barren" and "superfluous" to describe the indescribable aspects of his arch nemesis suggests Cibber's simultaneous omnipresence and indescribability. The "marks" that make Cibber's face so well known might be "illustrious," but they are hardly illustrative. While they make him famous, they do not make him knowable.

Pope's introduction thus characterizes Cibber's self-representation in terms of its spectacular exaggerations. The epic hero exemplifies substance, but Cibber performs empty spectacle. The epic hero exemplifies the qualities by which his countrymen are categorized and known, but Cibber, in exaggerating these qualities into deformities, cannot be categorized and cannot be known. As Aristarchus's notes on Cibber's blasphemous "*Language*" make evident, Cibber achieves this spectacular unknowability not merely through the exaggerated Englishness of his character but also through the excessive words and phrases of his written works. These works, like the body they evoke again and again, are distinguished by their deformities. "All my Prose and Verse were much the same," declares the King of the Dunces in Book I:

> This, prose on stilts; that, poetry fall'n lame.
> Did on the stage my Fops appear confin'd?
> My Life gave ampler lessons to mankind.
> Did the dead Letter unsuccessful prove?
> The brisk Example never fail'd to move.
> Yet sure had Heav'n decreed to save the State,
> Heav'n had decreed these works a longer date.[93]

The final two lines link the roles of celebrity, of epic hero, and of king, poking fun at Cibber's self-characterization as a representative of his nation whose "works" might "save the State." Yet the first two lines suggest that Cibber will attempt to save his nation through a deformed and irregular language, a prose marked by the prosthesis of stilts or a poetry "fall'n lame."

Pope goes beyond mentioning the "lame[ness]" of Cibber's poetry: instead, he demonstrates it. The mock-epic style that Pope at once theorizes and exemplifies to mock-honor the deformed King of the Dunces twists even the lines celebrated for his regularity into the deformed excesses of Dulness. Pope's parody of Cibber's excessive style is evident in the excessive footnotes that litter—and in many places overwhelm—the text of his poem. These appear as well in the three-book *Dunciad*, poking fun at editors like Bentley and Theobald—who (Pope claims) attempt to redirect the reader's attention from the text itself to their copious emendations of it. Retaining many of these footnotes in his later *Dunciad in Four Books*, Pope draws an implicit comparison between overzealous editors and spotlight-seeking historians. Such, of course, was Cibber, a man whose bids for stardom had overshadowed his observations about the theater and who had polluted his *Historical View of the Stage During His Own Time* with an *Apology for [His] Life*.

Similar deformities haunt Pope's characterizations of Cibber and of his poetic kingdom throughout *The Dunciad* and suggest the syntactical and formal qualities of overexpression as a strategy printed as well as performed. Much has been made, for instance, of Pope's heroic couplets, a form he is credited with perfecting in earlier works such as *The Essay on Man*. Updating W. K. Wimsatt's famous description of these couplets as embodying the dialectic pattern of Enlightenment thought, J. Paul Hunter characterizes them as "a careful pairing of oppositions or balances but no formal resolution. . . . Rather than privileging one half or the other of the conflict or negotiating a successful compromise, the closed couplet tends to privilege the balancing itself—the preservation and acceptance of difference rather than a working out of modification or compromise."[94]

Yet if Pope's perfectly rendered couplets suggest balance and rational thought, as Hunter implies, what might we make of the excessive couplet that launches *The Dunciad*? Following the form of the epic, Pope's mock-epic begins with an invocation to the muse of the Grub Street hacks: "The Mighty Mother, and her Son who brings / The Smithfield Muses to the ear of Kings, / I sing."[95] The first two lines of the poem firmly establish the verse form for which Pope is so well known, imposing the characteristic balance that Hunter describes through the perfect rhyme of "brings" with "Kings." But the third line upsets this precarious balance by inserting an extra rhyme: "sing." This additional rhyme acts as a sort of poetic third wheel (or a deformed poetic foot) to Pope's couplet. Top-heavy beneath this excessive rhyme, Pope's couplet topples into chaos, his perfect poetic form suddenly taking on Cibber's poetic deformities.[96]

As the poem continues, Pope develops such excesses and deformities as the particular provenance of Cibber and his minions—and as the very qualities that make his works uninterpretable. After his description in Book I of the stilted prose and "lame" poetry that exemplify Cibber's print productions, Pope pauses momentarily to allow the Queen of Dulness to take stock of her collected verses and her celebrity verse-maker. "All these, and more, the cloud-compelling Queen," he writes, "Beholds thro' fogs, that magnify the scene."[97] Pope's epic epithet here identifies the "cloud-compelling Queen" as one who gathers obfuscation about her rather than dispersing it, who encourages darkness rather than enlightening her surroundings. Significantly, the "fogs" she gathers do not merely obscure but rather "magnify the scene." Recalling Cibber's blotted page, in other words, they achieve their indecipherability through the excess rather than through the dearth of meaning. Under the pen of such a dunce and under the reign of such a queen, sentences and verses exceed their communicative power and endeavor instead, as Pope writes in Book IV, to "explain a thing till all men doubt it."[98]

In its mocking praise and parodic imitations of Cibber's language, *The Dunciad* articulates several of the strategies that Cibber employs to invite his spectators' stares while frustrating their interpretations—strategies that I have joined under the rubric of overexpression and that will resurface in the writings of Cibber's successors. Cibber achieved the illegibility that would prevent his spectators from dissecting his private life, first, by adopting a persona (what Pope would call the "*lesser Epic hero*") characterized by an unreadable excess of the qualities that might make him readable, in this case, as an Englishman.[99] Second, he exaggerated the originality of his written works through the use of misspelled words, superfluous clauses, and phrases—like "outdid her own outdoings"—so exclamatory they ceased to make sense. By articulating these qualities in his *Dunciad*, Pope—as well as his fellow Scriblerians—helped to publicize Cibber's excesses and to identify the helplessness they caused in Cibber's spectators and thus, as further chapters will suggest, to popularize overexpression as a strategy for frustrating critics that future stars would take up. Pope didn't decipher overexpression as a particular strategy of Cibber's, in other words. But by railing against the illegibility of Cibber's autobiographical performances and by naming precisely what qualities of Cibber's works produced this illegibility, he began to articulate both the qualities and the effects of Cibber's style on Cibber's critics. Ironically, it was the critics declaring their own impotence in interpreting or articulating Cibber's style that provided the first coherent descriptions of overexpression and that allowed later artists to imagine Cibber's idiosyncrasies as a single, effective strategy for disabling the critics' barbs.

CONCLUSION: THE UNCREATING WORD

In attempting to deny Cibber the privilege of writing his own history, then, Pope, Fielding, and others seem only to confirm this privilege. *The Dunciad* claims to fulfill the prophecies that Cibber's *Apology* predicted but that Cibber's Richard struggled so determinedly against, promising in Ricardus Aristarchus's introduction not to "hinder [Cibber's] own Prophecy of himself."[100] In a footnote to Book IV of the poem, Pope points out that he has kept this promise. He expresses his hope that his poem "hath not injured [Cibber], but rather verified his Prophecy (p. 243 of his own Life, 8vo. ch. ix) where he says '*the Reader will be as much pleased to find me a* Dunce *in my* Old age, *as he was to prove me a brisk* blockhead *in my* Youth.' Wherever there was any room for Briskness, of Alacrity of any sort, *even in sinking*, he hath allowed him; but here, where there is nothing for him to do but to take his natural rest, he must permit his Historian to be silent."[101] By declaring himself to be Cibber's "Historian," Pope reverses the actor's claim—both in the autobiography and, implicitly, in *Richard III*—to be both historical subject and historian of his own life. But if the prophecies are those that Cibber himself pronounced, does Pope's poem merely further Cibber's designs in writing himself into history?

The question of who writes history and who is written by it is one haunting even the final couplets of Pope's nearly final poem. Pope's own dark prophecies for the destruction of English culture seem to have been fulfilled in these couplets, and the last vision he leaves us is that of a world descended into chaos: "Lo! thy dread Empire, CHAOS! is restor'd; / Light dies before thy uncreating word: / Thy hand, great Anarch! lets the curtain fall; / And Universal Darkness buries All."[102] Here again, Pope joins print and performance, the "uncreating word" with the "curtain" that sweeps the stage. Most critics read in the reign of Universal Darkness Pope's lament for a literature he cannot rescue from the destruction of modern letters and for the culture he cannot salvage from the decay of modern times. But it is possible, I think, to see in the hand letting fall the curtain to bury the world in "Universal Darkness" an image of overexpression through which Cibber guarantees his spectacular authorship.

Dustin Griffin reads this curtain as the curtain of a theater and interprets the final lines as a further declaration of Pope's supremacy, his power over the poetic spectacle with which he has just entranced us. "Can we perhaps say that the final couplet is designed as one last reminder that Pope has always been present in and behind the poem that he has presented to us, the readers," Griffin asks, "a bizarre, monstrous spectacle, a staged triumph of Dulness and de-creation of the world? What may we do, as spectators in the well-lit Augustan playhouse but applaud Pope's magnificent artifice?"[103] In Griffin's formulation, Pope's "de-creation" of the world only confirms his authorship, his mastery of his text and our imaginations. But of course, it is Cibber and the Queen of Dulness that Pope is addressing as "great Anarch" here, and it is Cibber who controls the openings and closings of this curtain as he controls—to Pope's great frustration—the openings and closings of the curtain on the Drury Lane stage. Cibber becomes, here, king of spectacle; and he becomes spectacular king. But he is also (quite literally) a stagehand, the invisible authority manipulating the spectacle from the shadows behind the curtain.

If we recall Peggy Phelan's argument that performance "becomes itself through disappearance," Pope's evocation of performance in these final lines seems fitting.[104] Chaos, too, becomes itself through disappearance—living up to its name only when it has become something we can no longer interpret or describe. So, too, does the modern author in the eighteenth-century public sphere declare his authority, paradoxically, by disappearing—retreating, like Mr. Spectator, behind the spectacle of the objects he is observing and recording. Like his description of the mock-epic, Pope's description of the Chaos that inspires it suggests the overexpressions of Englishness that made Cibber's deformed body and performing prose at once spectacular and impossible to interpret. We might imagine the pages of Cibber's *Apology* or the lines of his *Richard III* as littered with "uncreating words" that destroy as they accumulate, so that the more Cibber says the less we know about him. As Pope struggled to articulate what made these words so destructive and what made Cibber's person so deformed, he provided later celebrities with a strategy to strive for. And only twelve years after the publication of Pope's four-book *Dunciad*, Cibber's daughter, Charlotte Charke, would produce an autobiography—obviously modeled after her father's—that would do precisely that.

CHAPTER 2

The Growth of Celebrity Culture

Colley Cibber, Charlotte Charke, and the Overexpression of Gender

Like the early modern kings whose images he evoked (and deformed), Colley Cibber passed on to his heirs not only his elaborate headdresses and his celebrity status, but also his strategy of overexpression. His youngest daughter, Charlotte Charke, describes her inherited celebrity as a curse when, in a curious scene from her own autobiography of 1755 (a narrative heavily indebted to her father's), her recognizable figure prevents her escape from some angry creditors. Charke's proclivity for male attire doesn't seem to help matters, and her pursuer easily picks her out of a crowd, she writes, "by Dint of a very handsome lac'd Hat I had on, being then, for some substantial Reasons, EN CAVALIER [i.e. dressed as a man]; which was so well described, the Bailiff had no great Trouble in finding me."[1]

The pitfalls of fame were not foreign to the irascible Charke, who spends much of her narrative in deep debt and in male dress, pursuing the promise of a steady income and dodging the creditors who pursue her through her many failed careers as strolling player, puppeteer, merchant, sausage seller, baker, and gentleman's gentleman, among others. Her adoption of the celebrity autobiography to tell her story—and her adaptation of overexpression to scramble it—provide insights into how eighteenth-century women might use such strategies differently from their male counterparts. Charke's *Narrative of the Life of Charlotte Charke* has attracted some notice in recent years from scholars of eighteenth-century genders and sexualities, who have attributed Charke's transvestitism to everything from a feminist desire to challenge the status quo of eighteenth-century gender categories to a homosexual desire for her female companions to an unfulfilled desire to be welcomed as the long-lost son of the father who disowned her.[2] None of these possible motives, however, explain the actions that follow her arrest in her "handsome laced hat."

Betrayed by a costume too easily visible and marked out in a cap "so well described," Charke is dragged off to jail. She is soon released, but worries that without a disguise she will be spotted by still more creditors. So she improvises: "The Officer [of the prison] advised me to change Hats with him, that being the very Mark by which I was unfortunately distinguished, and made known to him," Charke writes. "My Hat was ornamented with a beautiful Silver Lace, little the worse for wear, and of the Size which is now the present Taste; the Officer's a large one, cocked up in the Coachman's Stile, and weightened with a horrible Quantity of Crape to secure him from the Winter's Cold. . . . [W]e each of us made very droll Figures; he with his little laced Hat, which appeared on his Head of the Size of those made for the *Spanish* Ladies, and my unfortunate Face smothered under his, that I was almost as much incommoded as when I marched in the Ditch, under the insupportable Weight of my Father's."[3] Charke describes in miniature the cultural shifts (and the sartorial shifts) that, as chapter 1 addressed, were transforming the ways that selves were expressed and regarded in the eighteenth century. As an increasingly secular nation was replacing the spectacular king with the unmarked bourgeois man as the locus of English authority, Charke replaces the spectacular laced hat linked to the cavalier courts of the early modern era with the less dressy and markedly more middle-class cap of the "Coachman's Stile."

Yet if Charke means her change of clothes to make her less conspicuous within the increasingly bourgeois and increasingly gendered public sphere, it seems odd that she should trade her old hat for one that is even larger, even more spectacular, and—"cocked up" and "weightened with a horrible Quantity of Crape"—even more obviously transvestite. Odder still is the trick's effectiveness. While it renders her figure more "droll," Charke's dress here seems to enable her disappearance: she strolls out of the prison unafraid of further assault, for, she assures us, "this smoaky Conveniency (for it stunk insufferably of Tobacco) was a Security and absolute Prevention from other threatening Dangers."[4]

Charke's conspicuous disguise makes sense only if we consider it not as her attempt to transform herself into a man, but rather as her attempt to exaggerate into illegibility the signifiers—and the accessories—that mark a body as male or female. These signifiers include the headpiece that, when Charke wore it, seemed an obvious index of masculinity but that, on the officer's head, resembles a hat "made for the *Spanish* Ladies." They include the "cocked-up" cap that shifts from a symbol of normativity to a symbol of spectacular masculinity atop Charke's "unfortunate face." And they include also the overweight wig of Charke's father, to which she alludes in the final line of the passage and which exemplifies the oddly gendered performances I examine throughout this chapter. All of these accessories suggest not mere disguise but overexpression, the only strategy available to a woman "so well-known [she] needs no description." Unable to make herself nondescript, Charke destabilizes the signifiers of eighteenth-century gender to make herself indescribable—and she slips through the London streets "droll" but undetected.

I begin with this anecdote because it introduces two features of overexpression that this chapter will develop and to which future chapters will return. First, Charke's trading of her "cavalier" costume for a cocked-up cap demonstrates how her overexpressions deviated from her father's—and suggests one way an eighteenth-century woman's overexpressions must necessarily deviate from those of an eighteenth-century man. As *Mr.* Spectator's title indicates, the eighteenth-century man need not disguise or obscure his gender (whatever he might conceal about his "Name, [his] Age, and [his] Lodgings") in order to pass freely through London's public spaces.[5] But a woman lacked this liberty, and thus all of the women that I examine throughout this book—including Charke—had to portray themselves in a role that made their publicity permissible before they could overexpress that role in ways that made their privacy imaginable. For Charke, this role was sometimes the role of the bourgeois man—dressed "en cavalier." And it was sometimes, more specifically and more poignantly, the role of her bourgeois father, whose words (and whose wigs) haunt her own autobiography.

Like her father's, Charke's autobiographical performances in male dress seem at some points to be the effects of a clever disguise and at other times to be the expressions of her inner desires (for the liberty of a man, for the love of a woman, for the recognition of her father). The difficulty Charke's audiences had in distinguishing between these two meanings suggests the cleverness of the overexpressive project. Yet while Cibber's audiences merely threw up their hands in frustration, Charke's audiences, as we shall see, worked even harder to impose their meanings on her words and her costumes. In this sense, Charke's overexpressions—and, indeed, the overexpressions of all the women I examine throughout this book—failed to deflect her spectators' examinations. In the second half of this chapter I ask why. What is it about the extra disguises that women like Charke, Bellamy, and Robinson must take on to appear in public that make their overexpressions, ultimately, ineffective?

Charke's curious allusion to her father's wig in this passage suggests a second point that will become crucial to the theory of overexpression that this book explores: that is, the way that this strategy destabilizes seemingly static signifiers (a costume piece, a stage property, a printed word) and attaches their meanings to the body that wields them. We might think here of Cibber's wig, as well as of the "cavalier" cap that signifies masculinity on Charke's body but becomes feminine as soon as it is placed on the officer's head. The hat's transformation is surprising, since we often consider the sartorial signifiers of gender to be stable even if the bodies they signify are not: a skirt, for instance, will always convey femininity within a certain culture, as a "cocked-up" cap will always be read as masculine. If an accessory changes meaning every time it changes bodies, however, what hope might the spectator have of interpreting it? Similarly, if a word's meaning depends on and always refers back to the famous body that writes it, what hope do we have of interpreting a book unless we know something of its author?

Overexpression works in part by inviting its spectators to ask such questions, challenging again and again the languages through which identity, in the mid-eighteenth century, was read. But Charke's suggestion that an accessory's meaning shifts depending on the body that wears it does something else, too. By attaching the object's meaning to the body that performs with it, Charke implies that the object's meaning holds only so long as the performer lives—only so long as the show goes on. In this way, the object takes on the ephemerality of performance. And, like the gesture or attitude of a performance, it changes slightly every time a new body takes it up—ensuring, as it does, that the power of meaning-making lies with the performer rather than the spectator and depends on his or her (fleeting, elusive) presence.

In the pages that follow, I explore this phenomenon by focusing on the great white wig that Cibber wore in his most popular role, the fop Sir Novelty Fashion (later crowned Lord Foppington), and that, by 1740, had become an emblem of his identity. The eighteenth-century wig was a symbol of upright masculinity that transformed, on Cibber's body, into a symbol of suspect sexuality—and that transformed again as soon as Charke slipped it onto her head. The wig's shifting meanings frustrate any attempt to interpret it—or the celebrity that wields it—as masculine or feminine, as normative or not. The words of Cibber's *Apology* and Charke's *Narrative* work in much the same way, replacing their dictionary definitions with personal inflections and thus locating the meaning of a printed page, like the precise shape of a performed gesture, in the body that tries it on. This argument will lay the groundwork for my discussion of Laurence Sterne's odd language in *Tristram Shandy*, taken up in chapter 3. More broadly, it will begin the exploration of women's overexpressions—and why they so often fail to protect their performers—that I will continue in chapters 4 and 5. By tracing the tendrils of Lord Foppington's great wig as they wind through Cibber's most celebrated stage roles, through some of the most memorable scenes in his *Apology*, and through the pages of *The Narrative of the Life of Charlotte Charke*, this chapter explores overexpression as a strategy that not only endures past Cibber's 1699 performance of Richard III but that takes up and takes part in many of the debates central to the formation and the imagination of the eighteenth-century self.

THE TROUBLE WITH EIGHTEENTH-CENTURY GENDERS

Part of what made Cibber's and Charke's manipulations of gender signifiers so frustrating to their spectators—and so clever as overexpressive strategies—was the importance that gender and sexuality began to assume in mid-eighteenth-century discourses about identity. It was during this time, as Dror Wahrman and others have argued, that "prevailing gender norms were redefined as essential and natural, thus pulling the cultural rug from under behavior or images that seemed to offer alternatives to these dominant norms."[6] Even as deformities like Richard III's were becoming less prescriptive and more performative, in other words, genders and sexualities were increasingly regarded as traits permanently grafted onto the body that bore them. All one need do to police these traits would be to probe that body, to strip it of its disguises and gaze upon it.

If these new gender ideologies demanded a body stripped of its disguises, we might expect the theater, with its dependence on disguise, to be one of the last places that such ideologies might take hold. In part this is true, and Kristina Straub includes both Cibber and Charke in her book *Sexual Suspects*, which describes the complications that eighteenth-century actors and actresses introduced to emergent gender norms. Yet as Straub points out, the theater also offers a kind of magnifying lens through which we might view these emergent ideologies in high resolution. Many of the developments in theatrical practices during Cibber's and Charke's lifetimes might be understood to reflect developments in ideologies of gender and sexuality that portrayed the naked body as natural, bounded, and clearly gendered. Whereas the theater of the Renaissance and Restoration seemed to delight in disguise and deception, the sentimental plays of the early eighteenth century betrayed some anxiety about any character who lied about his or her "true" desires or covered his or her "natural" body, and it rewarded characters unafraid to reveal themselves. Thus the English stage went from being the site of the character's dressing up (in, for instance, the dressing-room scenes so essential to the portrayal of the Restoration rake) to the site of the character's dressing down, revealing to the audience the naked sincerity of his or her "true" feelings, his or her "authentic" self.

This transformation is evident in the changing attitudes toward cross-dressing and gender play in the English theater with which Cibber and Charke were familiar. In the all-male companies of the Renaissance and early Restoration stage, men cross-dressed as women, and audiences accepted the femininity of their costumes as synecdoche for the femininity of the characters they portrayed. With the introduction of women into the acting companies in the late seventeenth century, however, cross-dressing roles became the purview of female players—like Charlotte Charke—who used masculine costumes not to conceal their gendered bodies but to reveal them. Their form-fitting breeches were designed to show off their feminine figures and to remind their spectators (coyly or not so coyly) of the "true" identities peeking from behind their assumed roles. These developments allowed the English stage to participate in the gender significations that had begun to designate bodies as either male or female and accessories, attitudes, and object choices as either normative or not.

What this meant for celebrities like Cibber and Charke was that the theater and its disguises no longer offered concealment from a nosy public determined to trace a star's "true" self. For what Felicity Nussbaum calls the "Interiority Effect"—the suggestion of an interior self beyond that or aligned with that of the character the actor played onstage—works both ways. The moment that the spectator perceives the illusion of interiority in one actress's performance, he or she begins to expect it in all performances. As the Interiority Effect took hold on the eighteenth-century stage, praise for a player's performance began increasingly to take the form of praise for his or her personal character. Hence the vocabularies of literary and theatrical criticism, of celebrity gossip, and of gender critique often, in this period, overlap and intertwine. So much is clear from an anonymous pamphlet entitled *The Laureat*, published in 1740. Attacking Cibber as an "Author who is obscure, unconnected, and wrapt up and conceal'd in the clinquant Tinsel of Metaphor, and unnecessary figures," the pamphlet promises "to explain the Meaning, or to expose the no Meaning, to take off the Vernish of the rhetorical Flowers, and to undress a certain Book lately publish'd, intituled, An APOLOGY FOR THE LIFE OF MR. COLLEY CIBBER."[7]

The pamphleteer's attack confirms the early eighteenth century's privileging of the naked and naturalized body over the disguised body, the new preference for a self that was revealed rather than constructed. Moreover, it links this body explicitly—through metaphors of dressing and undressing—to the text that describes it. Cibber's book, like his body, is unsatisfactory because it remains "wrapt up and conceal'd in the clinquant Tinsel of Metaphor, and unnecessary figures." In order to be understood it must be "undress'd." Of course, the same undressing that reveals the meaning of Cibber's prose—and, metaphorically, the gendered contours and sexual desires of his body—also leaves him vulnerable to the pamphleteer's critique. The language of *The Laureat* emphasizes the position of the early eighteenth-century celebrity as a catch-22: to "wrap up and conceal" oneself in disguise and metaphor was to invite one's critics to undress one—and to dress one down. But to present oneself as sincere and undisguised was to leave oneself—in Cibber's words—"helpless, and expos'd" to an increasingly normative gaze.[8]

The pamphleteer's language thus helps to explain the particular form that Cibber's and Charke's overexpressions of gender would take. The celebrity who wishes to stave off such critiques—to prevent such "exposure"—cannot simply disguise him- or herself, for critics and spectators will simply strip him or her of all disguises. Instead, he or she must seem to reveal a naked body—an "authentic self"—while at the same time dismantling the binary between the naked body and its disguises, between "authentic" desires and dissembling. This means both imbuing the naked body with the same dissembling power as the body in costume, and it means destabilizing the way that the costume itself signifies or constructs character. In other words, it means mixing up the body natural and the body performed, blurring the boundaries between corpus and costume. And this, as I will argue in the next part of this chapter, is precisely what Colley Cibber does.

BIG WIGS: THE FOP'S HAIR AS EXCESSIVE MASCULINITY IN CIBBER'S SENTIMENTAL COMEDIES

Cibber's performances of nakedness begin with his performances as the fop, a Restoration character known for self-conscious outfits and fawning speeches but who, in Cibber's eighteenth-century version, became a character so elaborately dressed as to be naked and so overt as to be unreadable. I will explain these apparent oxymorons by examining Cibber's most famous costume piece, a large white wig that he wore in his role as Sir Novelty /

Lord Foppington but that soon became part of his everyday dress—and that we might interpret either as a disguise over or as a metonymy for the male anatomy. Similarly, I will argue, we might associate the fop's gender as easily with superfluous as with insufficient masculinity. Understanding the complex significations of the mid-eighteenth-century fop—as well as the complex significations of his most obvious costume piece, the wig—helps us to understand why Cibber should adopt such a persona for his ramblings on stage, on street, and on page—and how Charke would revive and revamp these significations in her own performances of self.

Even more than the deformed king, the fawning fop marked Cibber's celebrity persona and made his career. In 1696, frustrated by his inability to rise in the Drury Lane company, Cibber created a star vehicle for himself in his comedy *Love's Last Shift*. The play introduced the world to Sir Novelty Fashion, who would reappear (as Lord Foppington) in two later plays: *The Relapse* (1696), Sir John Vanbrugh's sequel to *Love's Last Shift*; and Cibber's *The Careless Husband* (1704). The fop soon became a recurring role in Cibber's career—and, later, a role ghosted with his memory. David Garrick named his own fop "Fribble" (in his 1747 comedy *Miss in Her Teens*), echoing Henry Fielding's parodic tribute to Cibber in *The Author's Farce* (1730). As his fame in the part grew, Cibber began to incorporate the fop's elaborate dress and flowery language into his everyday performances of self.

It was an odd persona to settle on. Like the gender ideologies that shaped them, the significations of the fop were changing rapidly by the time Cibber introduced Lord Foppington. In one of the earliest articles on Cibber's foppishness, Lois Potter argues that the character acted less as a threat to than as a model of masculinity, a (somewhat less successful) version of the Restoration rakes and princely heroes that Cibber had once longed to play. Susan Staves, similarly, has described the Restoration fop as a precursor to the properly domesticated man of the sentimental stage. Such arguments suggest that the fop presents not an alternative to masculinity, but an excess of it.

In more recent criticism, however, scholars have more often characterized the fop as an outmoded throwback to the spectacular politics of the previous era. Both Kristina Straub and Thomas A. King oppose the fop to the normative identity of the unmarked eighteenth-century man: the fop's obsession with self-display, they argue, associates him with a diminished or even with a castrated masculinity. For King, the castration of Cibber's private manhood results from his imitative production of a public manhood. In describing a portrait of Cibber in which an elongated quill pen points to a "negative space in his breeches," King writes that Cibber's quill/phallus "requires the displacement of his penis . . . and therefore of his own personal embodiment into a chain of imitations. At the same time the quill points to the place of mimetic transformation, signaling that Cibber's writings and his foppish display do not originate or inhere 'in' his body but in the structure of publicness."[9] Cibber is unfit for the new order of the bourgeois public sphere and the unmarked signifiers of eighteenth-century manhood, according to King, because he requires an exterior prop to indicate a masculinity that should be inherent.

But in what is otherwise an insightful reading of Cibber's portrayal of the fop, King neglects to mention the most famous stage property with which Cibber's fops performed their masculinity: Lord Foppington's great wig. Wigs were not uncommon atop the heads of eighteenth-century men, and they were often read as signifiers of masculinity. But Cibber's wig was uncommonly over the top: puffed and plumed, curled and furbelowed—and, when it appeared in *The Relapse*, large enough to require a servant with a sedan chair to haul it across the stage. An engraving by John Simon from the first part of the century shows Cibber's hair standing in twin bouffants on top of his head and cascading down his back (figure 4). In such magnificent proportions, Cibber's wig blurs King's neat division between a masculinity "originat[ing] or inher[ing] 'in' [Cibber's] body" and the "structure of publicness" that constitutes, for King, Cibber's failed privacy. Such proportions blur even the division between the territories of interiority and exteriority—between corpus and costume—upon which King's argument depends. As a marker of gender identity, in other words, the wig was problematic, and in eighteenth-century representations it might indicate either masculinity or femininity, either total discretion or egregious insincerity, depending on how (and when) it was worn. In choosing as his emblem the eighteenth-century wig, Cibber is picking up and playing up the ambiguous significations of the wig as both a signifier of masculinity and metonymy for the male body it conceals. On Cibber's body and within his texts, however, the wig becomes a costume piece whose very overtness makes it suspect and whose excessive masculinity makes it illegible.

The ambiguous representations of the eighteenth-century wig are the subject of a recent article by Lynn Festa, who traces the accessory's transformation over the course of the century from "a sign of the autonomy" of the middle-class male subject to "a humbling intimation that we may be possessed as much by things as things are possessed by us."[10] The wig's importance as a constitutive part of the male body has been noted elsewhere by Marcia Pointon, who writes that the wig "might be seen as a register of socialized masculinity from the seventeenth to the beginning of the nineteenth

4. John Simon (after Giuseppe Grisoni), *Colley Cibber as Lord Foppington in* The Relapse *by John Vanbrugh* (ca. 1700–1745). © National Portrait Gallery, London.

century."[11] In several representations from the long eighteenth century the wig served as a metonymy to the male body: its loss or disorder indicated a depletion of masculine virility or a disruption of a decidedly masculine decorum. Illustrative of the wig's inseparability from the body and its sexual significations was the popularity throughout the eighteenth century of the merkin, a wig especially designed for the pubic region of both male and female bodies. Wigs on the head—as well as those less in sight—served as both the expression of a healthy sexuality (since hair loss was one of the most recognizable symptoms of syphilis) and as a practical defense against lice. For this reason, they became synonymous with virile masculinity.

Yet even as it symbolized, the wig also disrupted the eighteenth-century notion of the proper masculine subject. Festa notes in particular the problems that the periwig presented for the notion of "possessive individualism" that, as C. B. MacPherson argues, formed the basis for English subjecthood in the eighteenth century. Most peruke makers, Festa explains, fashioned their wigs from human hair that they had collected from the heads of lower-class country girls, a fact that literalized anxieties about the body's permeable boundaries and the potential for men's subjection to and dependence on inferior women. "The paradox of the wig in the context of 'possessive individualism,'" according to Festa, "lies in the fact that the object meant to proclaim its wearer to be a freestanding individual is harvested from the bodies of other people: to wear a wig is to make another's parts an integral part of one's own appearance."[12] For this reason a wig too unwieldy—a masculinity too overwrought—might signify nonnormativity and chaos just as easily as the modest wig advertised masculinity and decorum.

Against King's description of Cibber as a "residual pederast" who mistakes the nonnormative identity of the eighteenth-century fop with the more acceptable masculinity of the Restoration fop, I want to suggest that Cibber assumed his foppish accouterments and donned his enormous wig precisely in order to call up the confusion of identity that King interprets as nonnormative. Cibber's wig is not merely a signifier of femininity, in other words. It is, more complexly, a signifier of bourgeois masculinity so overt that it becomes ambiguous. In short, it is an overexpression of Cibber's gender that allows him to remain in the spotlight without ever being "expos'd."

The unstable significations of the gentleman's periwig surface again and again in Cibber's most two most successful comedies, *Love's Last Shift* and *The Careless Husband*. Both plays feature Sir Novelty / Lord Foppington as the hero of their comic subplots, and both suggest Sir Novelty's wig as a signifier of masculinity that in its very obviousness becomes impossible to interpret.

In order to understand the associations of the wig and the meaning of masculinity in Sir Novelty's subplots, however, it's important that we look first at the plays' main plots. Both *Love's Last Shift* and *The Careless Husband* are typical of the sentimental comedies that were so popular in Cibber's day in that both pivot around a promiscuous libertine's transformation into a proper gentleman and a model of upright masculinity. And in both plays, the libertines in question negotiate their newfound masculinity through the putting on or the taking off of a periwig.

In *Love's Last Shift*, the rake Loveless is transformed into a sentimental man and a loving husband after his long-suffering wife, Amanda, lures him into her bed by disguising herself as a high-class courtesan. Significantly, it is a wig that greets Loveless and his servant, Snap, when they enter Amanda's house in pursuit of the promised liaison. The stage directions inform us: "*The SCENE changes to an Anti-chamber, a Table, a Light, a Night-Gown, and a Periwig lying by.*"[13] Amanda, it seems, has placed the periwig in anticipation of her husband's arrival, and Loveless takes the hint: "Ha! this Night-Gown and Peruke don't lie here for nothing," he tells Snap. "I'll make my self agreeable.—I have baulk'd many a Woman in my Time for want of a clean Shirt.—*[Puts 'em on.*"[14] Here the periwig seems an integral part of Loveless's masculinity, a costume he must put on in order to enjoy intimate and heteronormative relations with a woman he later learns is his wife. Laura Brown pinpoints Loveless's conversion in the final act of the play as an important moment in the transformation of the comedy of manners—a genre that rewarded wit and social affect—into the sentimental comedy—a genre that celebrated naked sincerity.[15] Loveless's wig crowns his own transformation from Restoration wit to eighteenth-century man of feeling and serves as a metonymy for the naked and undisguised body he will offer up to his wife.

The wig reappears with a similarly metonymic purpose in *The Careless Husband*, though its contours have grown even larger and its significations of masculinity even more complex. In this play the rake to be redeemed is Sir Charles Easy, who spends much of the first four acts pursuing indiscreet affairs with everyone except his wife. The climax of the sentimental plot occurs when Lady Easy comes upon her husband and her lady's maid sleeping near each other in a parlor, their clothes in disarray. Most disturbing to Lady Easy is not that her husband has betrayed her (she has known about his affairs since act 1) but that now he sleeps before her with his head indecorously uncovered, his wig having become unfastened during the strenuous activity of the preceding hour.

"Ha! Bare-headed, and in so sound a Sleep!" she says to herself as she stands before his prostrate body. "Who knows, while thus expos'd to th' unwholesome Air, / But Heav'n offended may o'ertake his Crime, / And, in some languishing Distemper, leave him / A severe Example of its violated Laws."[16] As in *Love's Last Shift*, so in *The Careless Husband* the gentleman's periwig stands not as an emblem of but rather as a shield against the now transgressive libertinism of the previous era. Without it, Sir Charles "expos[es]" himself to disease—both physical and moral—and provides a "severe Example of [Heaven's] violated Laws." The solution here is moderation: if an improper man is one who exposes too much of himself to those outside his domestic sphere or too little of himself to those within it, the proper man is one who reveals his sincere self willingly, but only to those in his family and only at the appropriate time.

This is the lesson that Sir Charles has learned by the end of the play, as he returns to his wife openly shedding tears of shame and of sentiment. But complicating the gendered symbolism of this scene is the method by which Lady Easy teaches her husband this lesson, corrects his "expos[ure]," and elicits his emotions. Rather than replacing the wig or waking Sir Charles to reproach him for his unfaithfulness, she discreetly "*Takes a Steinkirk* [handkerchief] *off her Neck, and lays it gently on his Head.*"[17] A late eighteenth-century painting of the scene by Francis Wheatley emphasizes the discretion of Lady Easy's action, the delicacy with which she places the handkerchief on her husband's head without disturbing his rest (figure 5). Charles, waking to find his head covered with his wife's handkerchief and his wig still lying nearby, suddenly feels the pangs of conscience. He returns the wig to his head and, reformed, rushes off to beg Lady Easy's forgiveness.

The wig signifies masculinity, then, but it also suggests an uneasy alliance between proper masculinity and proper femininity. Sir Charles's masculinity is redeemed from the charges of a deviant and indiscreet libertinism only after his head has been covered in the clothes of a woman. Discretion—the prized quality of the unmarked eighteenth-century man—seems here to depend on at least a modicum of sexual ambiguity and of empathy, the ability to put oneself into the shoes (or under the headpiece) of a member of the opposite sex. In suggesting a masculinity allied with or empathetic to femininity, Sir Charles Easy's modest wig seems less distinguished from than aligned with Sir Novelty Fashion's more ostentatious updo. This alignment suggests that the masculinity of Cibber's fop characters differed from that of their sentimental acquaintances in degree, not in kind: if Charles Easy's wig was a symbol of a new sort of masculinity, Foppington's wig was merely its overexpression. And by inviting us to read Foppington's wig through the canopy of

5. Francis Wheatley, *Lady Easy's Steinkirk: A Scene from "The Careless Husband" by Colley Cibber (Act V, Sc. 5)* (late eighteenth century). © Victoria and Albert Museum, London.

its more masculine companions, Cibber prevents us from reading it as a clear or stable signifier, whether of femininity or of a nonnormative sexuality.

In order to tease out the ambiguous significations of Lord Foppington's great wig, let's turn briefly to the *Apology*, which itself makes frequent reference to its actor-author's signature prop. In a much-discussed (and much-maligned) passage toward the middle of the autobiography, Cibber describes the wig's role in establishing his friendship with Colonel Henry Brett, a nobly born but financially strapped rake (and later a comanager of Drury Lane theater) who has come to London in pursuit of a wealthy wife. Cibber links

Brett's performances as libertine to his own performances as fop through the exchange of the famous wig, which Brett admires while watching Cibber's performance in *Love's Last Shift*.[18] In a complexity prefigured in Cibber's most famous comedies, the wig serves at once as an expression of Brett's nonnormative libertinism and as the vehicle of his reform into a happily (and heteronormatively) married man. But these categories of rake and fop and of normative and not become increasingly difficult to distinguish in the heaped-up clauses of Cibber's prose.

Cibber describes his meeting with Brett in the sexually ambiguous language typical of the *Apology*'s most overexpressive moments:

> And though, possibly, the Charms of our Theatrical Nymphs might have had their Share, in drawing him [backstage]; yet in my Observation, the most visible Cause of his first coming, was a more sincere Passion he had conceiv'd for a fair full-bottom'd Perriwig which I then wore in my first Play. . . . Now whatever Contempt Philosophers may have, for a fine Perriwig; my friend . . . knew very well, that so material an Article of Dress, on the Head of a Man of Sense, if it became him, could never fail of drawing him to a more partial Regard. . . . This perhaps may soften the grave Censure, which so youthful a Purchase might otherwise, have laid upon him: In a word, he made his Attack upon this Perriwig, as your young Fellows generally do upon a Lady of Pleasure; first, by a few, familiar Praises of her Person, and then, a civil Enquiry, into the Price of it.[19]

Cibber is intent on assuring his readers that Brett's "sincere passion" for the periwig is part and parcel of Brett's sincere passion for women: his comparison of the wig to the Lady of Pleasure implies, in one sense, an identification of the wig as a commodity circulated among heterosexual men, one that confirms both their heterosexuality and their masculinity within a homosocial network.

On the other hand, the wig seems at times indistinguishable from (or metonymy for) the body of the man who wears it—an observation that might further explain Cibber's nervous anticipation of "whatever Contempt Philosophers may have" for Brett's object choice. If the wig is a mere accessory that can be taken off and given away like an ill-fitting coat, it serves here as a tool abetting Brett's pursuit of a worthy woman—and thus a signifier of both men's normative heterosexuality. Cibber's surrender of it to Brett indicates, in that case, his possession of a "true" identity not dependent on his possessions and not subject to the changes in his attire.

But if the wig is a metonymy for Cibber's body, as Loveless's wig is a metonymy for his body, it signifies Brett's pursuit of Cibber himself. The sartorial clues that might allow Cibber's spectators to distinguish a feminine identity from a masculine one—or well-ordered discretion from outlandish display—thus become entangled within the fop's great mop of hair. By adopting and adapting the eighteenth-century man's wig as the emblem of his identity offstage as well as onstage, Cibber creates a gender identity so blatant it is ambiguous and presents to his audience a body so unabashedly visible that it can be neither denied nor described. In this way, he preempts his critics' threats to "undress" him by seeming to strip without actually "exposing" anything of himself.

Perhaps the most brilliant articulation of Cibber's overexpressions of gender occurs in *The Relapse*, composed by Cibber's friend and eventual business partner, Sir John Vanbrugh. It is Vanbrugh who promotes Sir Novelty to Lord Foppington—and who promotes the wig to its most monstrous proportions. He also introduces Foppington's wigmaker. "My lord, I have done what I defy any prince in Europe t'outdo," the wigmaker tells Lord Foppington as he unveils his newest creation. "I have made you a periwig so long, and so full of hair, it will serve you for hat and cloak in all weathers."[20] So much more than your average accessory, Foppington's wig serves a number of different purposes for a number of different personae: it is both hat and cloak in both summer and winter; it is (much like Cibber himself) both frustratingly impenetrable and unabashedly obvious; and it is both a signifier of upright masculinity and a signifier of excessive femininity. But even when it constitutes full dress in and of itself, the wig is not full enough for Lord Foppington. He demands that the peruke maker enhance his hair even further, for, he says, "A periwig to a man, should be like a mask to a woman nothing should be seen but his eyes."[21]

Lord Foppington's declaration drips with the uneasy significations of the eighteenth-century hairpiece: his words establish the wig as the marker of masculinity (the opposite of the mask as the marker of femininity) even as they suggest a destabilizing affinity between wig and mask, between what has come to signify "man" and what has come to signify "woman." In *Nobody's Story*, her book about the self-fashioning strategies of women in the eighteenth-century literary marketplace, Catherine Gallagher discusses the woman's mask—a common costume piece of the eighteenth-century prostitute—as an accessory that "signals the availability of the body but also implies the impenetrability of the controlling mind."[22] She presents the mask as a metaphorical tool for the female writer who must sell her work as self-representation while withholding "her true self" as the unseen and unseeable "sold self's seller."[23] The mask, in other words, changes the gendered dynamic between subjectivity and objectification, allowing the women to be the object of the gaze without surrendering herself entirely to the gaze's penetration. Cibber's wig achieves a similar effect, but it does so by enhancing rather than by concealing his distinguishing features. By scrambling precisely what these distinguishing features distinguish, by vacillating uneasily between masculine and feminine identities, the wig makes Cibber illegible and impenetrable. In doing so, it reduces his body from something that is seen to something that does nothing but see. Peering from behind his unwieldy wig, Colley Cibber as Lord Foppington becomes an overexpressive version of Mr. Spectator, "nothing seen but his eyes."

"THE PUBLICK EYE" AND THE PUBLIC "I": LOOKING AT CIBBER'S LANGUAGE

I have described the foppish wig that Cibber adopted in his performances of self as a stage property that capitalizes on eighteenth-century anxieties about men's dependence on women and on things. In emphasizing the wig's ambiguous significations, Cibber creates a persona that is as illegible as it is seemingly revealing and a nakedness that is impossible to read. As he does, he reminds his spectators that sartorial signifiers are not as stable or as legible indicators of gender as we might like to believe. It is a reminder that Charlotte Charke will take up and expand as she incorporates Cibber's famous wig into her own performances and adapts its gender significations to her own purposes.

Before I turn to Charke's *Narrative*, however, I want to linger for a moment on Cibber's autobiography in order to explore how his written language takes on the same sexual and gender ambiguities as his sartorial choices. In his promise to "undress" Cibber's prose, the writer of *The Laureat* implies that sentences, like clothes, encode and dissemble, and all one need do to interpret the persona they describe is to strip them down to their simplest elements—much as the new sexual ideologies taking shape during Cibber's lifetime promise that we can identify a person's "true" gender by stripping him or her down to a naked, naturalized body.

Yet as Cibber's cascading wig destabilizes the distinctions between naturalized body and theatricalized costume and between masculinity and femininity, so his convoluted prose resists attempts to interpret it. In particular, Cibber destabilizes the grammatical distinctions between subject and object—that is, between who is speaking and who is being spoken about, who is looking and who is being looked at. As Straub and others have argued, these distinctions were, in the late seventeenth and early eighteenth centuries, increasingly gendered. By confusing the hierarchical relationship between the subject and the object of his sentences—much as his wig confuses the hierarchical relationship between the subject and the object of the gaze—Cibber destabilizes not only the gendered significations of the fop's fawning language but also the power dynamics that these significations imply. His prose becomes as illegible as his body—and as immune to attempts by his critics (like the anonymous writer of *The Laureat*) to "undress" it.

The Laureat focuses on a particular passage early on in Cibber's autobiography, chastising it as full of the superfluous clauses and ambiguous sexuality that, he argues, was so typical of Cibber's prose. Significantly, the passage is one in which Cibber, addressing his unnamed patron, attempts to mediate between the (often feminized) visibility required of his profession and the invisibility demanded for admission into the (masculine) bourgeois public sphere. "When I see you lay aside the Advantages of Superiority, and by your own Cheerfulness of Spirits, call out all that Nature has given me to meet them," Cibber begins, "then 'tis I taste you! then Life runs high! I desire! I possess you! Yet, Sir, in this distinguish'd Happiness, I give not up my farther Share of that Pleasure, or of that Right I have to look upon you, with the publick Eye, and to join in the general Regard so unanimously pay'd to that uncommon Virtue, your *Integrity!* . . . This it is, that discourages, and keeps silent the Insinuations of Prejudice, and Suspicion; and almost renders your Eloquence an unnecessary Aid, to your Assertions: Even your Opponents, conscious of your *Integrity*, hear you rather as a Witness, than an Orator—— But this, Sir, is drawing you too near the Light."[24]

King reads this passage as further evidence of Cibber's residual pederasty, arguing that Cibber's unbridled obsequies to his patron exemplify the kind of deference appropriate of a lower-class man addressing his social superior in the seventeenth century but marked as nonnormative and emasculating by the beginning of the eighteenth.[25] Yet Cibber is savvier than King gives him credit for. His refusal to reveal his patron's name indicates some awareness that spectacle no longer guarantees power, and that revealing his patron's identity might in fact diminish the patron's authority by "drawing him too near the Light."[26] Wedged somewhere between spectacular politics and Mr. Spectator, Cibber attempts to recognize his benefactor without undermining his benefactor's authority in a public sphere that awards anonymity over self-display.

Cibber's deference to his benefactor's desire for invisibility indicates that he is aware of the new politics of spectatorship emerging as he is writing. He is aware, too, that his own position as actor, as autobiographer, and as public icon—at the same time that it elevates his fortune and his social status—bars him from seizing such power for himself. "As there is no Hazard, or visible Terror, in an Attack, upon my defenceless Station" in the public eye, he writes, "my Censurers have generally been persons of an intrepid Sincerity."[27] When his career choice makes it impossible for him to escape public display, Cibber flaunts it: to his patron's anonymity Cibber contrasts his own "Nakedness of Temper" and claims, "I am content, to be gaz'd at, as I am, without lessening my Respect, for those, whose Passions may be more soberly cover'd."[28]

Again, we might read such declarations as pleas for attention by a man unaware that such attention will no longer guarantee him the authority he seeks. Certainly this has been the assumption of several of Cibber's critics, both modern and contemporary. The anonymous author of *The Laureat* detects in Cibber's declaration of public "Nakedness" and in the breathless encomiums of the earlier passage the evidence of a sexuality that, deemed non-normative, must be critiqued: "*I taste you, I desire, I possess you*," the pamphlet mocks. "Fye, *Colly*, Fye; have some small Regard to Decency; you cou'd go no higher than this if your *Patron* were of the *Feminine Gender*."[29] The same ambiguities that drew his contemporary's "Fyes" have also caught the eyes of Cibber's more recent readers. Straub interprets the *Laureat*'s critique as evidence for the growing cultural anxiety about spectacle and disguise, as well as for an increasingly common tendency to label as deviant the man who puts himself on display. Such readings take Cibber's declaration of his own "Nakedness" at face value, interpreting it as Cibber's sincere wish to lay himself bare for the perusal (and at the mercy) of his audience members.

Yet what strikes me as odd about the *Laureat*'s critique of Cibber is the way that it chastises the author for revealing himself blatantly—with no "small Regard to Decency" or decorum—at the same time that it scolds him for "conceal[ing]" himself beneath the "clinquant Tinsel of Metaphor" and the obscurities of overly elaborate prose. What might we make of the contradictions in such a critique? And what might we surmise from the fact that, when Cibber does finally embark on the "honest Examination of [his] Heart" that seems to offer up his persona in all of its "Nakedness," the only fault he admits is a "natural Vanity"—a quality that might make us suspect that its very naturalness is contrived?[30] I want to suggest that what King and Straub describe as Cibber's "queerness" here—the overly spectacular and ambiguous language that so bothers the author of *The Laureat*—is part of the overexpressive strategy through which Cibber guarantees his privacy. As we shall see, the language he employs in the dedication of the *Apology*, like the wig he wore both on and off the stage, actually works to dissolve the distinction that his critics draw between the spectator and the spectacle, between the speaking subject and the object of the gaze.

Nowhere is this dissolution more apparent than in the very passage that invites *The Laureat*'s ire: "When I see you lay aside the Advantages of Superiority, and by your own Cheerfulness of Spirits, call out all that Nature has given me to meet them," Cibber writes, "then 'tis I taste you! then Life runs high! I desire! I possess you!"[31] The most obviously overexpressive moments in this sentence lie in the exaggerated enthusiasm of those final exclamations—exclamations that, as Straub notes, muddy the distinction between homosocial politics and homoerotic desire and that complicate our attempts to read Cibber's gender identity as either masculine or feminine or to read his relationship with the patron as either normative or not.[32] I want to focus, however, on the confusion between subject and object that results from the sentence's great heap of clauses and its proliferation of sensory verbs.

The primary agent of the first part of the sentence seems to be Cibber's patron, who "lays aside" his noble birth in order to "call out" his description of Cibber. Here the patron acts as the subject of the sentence and as the spectator charged with the task of seeing and defining Cibber, the object of his gaze. But the additional clause that launches Cibber's overexpressive sentence complicates this structure. Introducing the main action of the sentence with "when I see you lay aside" transforms "you" (the patron) into an object, and "I" (Cibber himself) into the primary agent and definer. With the addition of this seemingly superfluous clause, in other words, Cibber metamorphoses from spectacle to spectator, from "Orator" to "Witness," from defined to definer.

The confusion between subject and object grows as the paragraph continues and Cibber—formerly "content to be gaz'd at, as I am"—sidles slyly out of the spotlight and declares "that Right I have to look upon you, with the publick Eye."[33] Here again, Cibber tempers his earlier admissions of "Nakedness" by casting himself as a gazer gazing upon his patron—only to find that his patron, seen "rather as a Witness, than an Orator," is casting his gaze back on Cibber. Cibber hovers around (or yo-yos rapidly between) his role as "publick Eye" and his role as public "I" until the distinction between spectator and spectacle becomes impossible to discern. Accordingly, the gendered hierarchies that Straub and King (not to mention the author of *The Laureat*) assign to this relationship begin to dissolve. Cibber here, as elsewhere, is both on display and indescribable, both object and subject—"Naked" but nonetheless not "expos'd."

It is telling that even the author of *The Laureat*, despite his determination to "undress a certain Book lately publish'd, intituled, AN APOLOGY FOR THE LIFE OF MR. COLLEY CIBBER" should, finally, give up his attempts to interpret Cibber's prose.[34] "Upon reading and endeavouring to understand this difficult Author," he writes, "I found, that to go thro' and examine him particularly wou'd be more than an *Herculian* Labour, and that the cleansing this *Augean* Stable, was a Work unequal both to my Inclination and Strength. And therefore I determined only to give the Publick just so much of him as might convince them, that this long and labour'd Performance of our most celebrated Laureat, is something over-rated."[35] Instead of interpreting Cibber or attempting to "examine him particularly," the pamphleteer can do nothing but repeat the most egregious excerpts of Cibber's "long and labour'd Performance." Unable to "explain the Meaning" of Cibber's complex sentences, he must be content merely to "expose the no Meaning" to which Cibber freely admits.[36] Like the author of *The Laureat*, many critics of Cibber's work lodged their complaints in the form of parody or in a hybrid of parody and critique. It was as if, incapable of distilling Cibber's rampant exaggerations and superfluities into their own words, they could do nothing but exaggerate and repeat them further.

After abandoning his attempt to interpret Cibber's *Apology*, the author of *The Laureat* admits that all those labyrinthine sentences and crowded pages that make it up actually reveal startlingly little of the private life they promise to explicate: "Colley Cibber is not the Character he pretends to be in this Book," the author declares, "but a mere *Charletan*, a *Persona Dramatis*, a *Mountebank*, a Counterfeit *Colley*. . . . In my Opinion, his very Nakedness is a Disguise."[37] It isn't, the critic makes clear, that Cibber refuses to reveal himself to us. It's that the very substance of his self-revelations—the big wig with which he makes himself up and the uncreating words through which he marks himself out—make him impossible to decipher, to dissect, or to "expose." If we can't rely on the stability of sartorial signifiers or of subject-object relations, we can no more define the limits of Cibber's body than we can translate the meanings of his prose. In the great wig that scrambles even as it seems to proclaim his masculinity and with the convoluted sentences that dissolve even as they seem to promise his self-revelations, Cibber even in his nakedness seems somewhat overdressed.

Yet even Cibber himself could be outdone. In the second half of this chapter, I turn to the performances and printed works of Charlotte Charke,

Cibber's youngest daughter, who published her own *Narrative of the Life of Charlotte Charke* in 1755, fifteen years after Cibber's *Apology* set the tone for celebrity autobiography. Charke's *Narrative* recalls the *Apology* in more than its genre. As we shall see, the role of heir to the great Colley Cibber was one of many roles that Charke adopted—and altered—in her own interpretations of overexpression. These interpretations—like the autobiography itself—begin when, as a four-year-old child, she places the great white wig of Lord Foppington on her own small head. As she does, she complicates even further the significations that the wig contains. If we interpret the wig as a signifier of proper masculinity when donned by Loveless or Sir Charles Easy and as an identifiable but illegible trademark of Colley Cibber as fop when worn by the man himself, how should we read it when it reappears on the body of Charlotte Charke—a woman, but a woman known for dressing as a man? This question leads me to two others that the remainder of this chapter will take up. First, how does Charke's gender affect her performances of overexpression? How, in other words, do societal anxieties about women in public roles necessarily change how female celebrities adopted and adapted Cibber's strategy? (And how do they account for Charke's ultimate failure?) Second, how does overexpression change when it is incorporated into a new performance, enacted by a different body? How is overexpression passed down?

OVEREXPRESSION ON OTHER BODIES: CHARLOTTE CHARKE'S "UNACCOUNTABLE LIFE"

At the beginning of her 1755 *Narrative*, Colley Cibber's youngest daughter sets herself a seemingly impossible (and undoubtedly overexpressive) task: "to give some Account of my UNACCOUNTABLE LIFE."[38] Her *Narrative* keeps its promise, introducing a narrator nearly as descriptive as she is impossible to describe.[39] If Cibber's story can be traced through the boldly printed appearances of his given name in periodicals and gossip columns, playbills and puffs, Charke's story must be told in a series of pseudonyms. In her youth she was Charlotte Cibber, the favorite daughter of a famous father until her marriage to Richard Charke changed her name and estranged her family. Before the passage of the 1737 Licensing Act made employment on the stage harder to come by, she was Miss Charlotte Charke, famed for her roles in breeches and as impudent servants—as well as for parts that parodied her father staged by his nemesis (and Charke's sometime employer) Henry Fielding. To readers of novels she was Miss Charlotte Evelyn or Jane Elstone or even Henry Dumont, the long-suffering protagonists of fiction often read as autobiographical. And throughout much of her adult life she was Mr. Brown, a male guise that allowed her to pursue several careers denied to women and that facilitated her living with (and sleeping with?) a mysterious female companion whom she called, simply, "Mrs. Brown."

Like her father before her, Charke vacillates throughout her autobiography between craving visibility and legibility as a means of acquiring property for herself and avoiding visibility and legibility as a trap by which she might become the property of someone else. Yet as this series of pseudonyms and costumes hints, Charke's status as a woman makes her status as a celebrity somewhat more complex. Like Cibber, Charke must negotiate between her own desire to be a private individual—that is, one relatively protected from the jibes, jests, and critiques of the public—and her audience's demand that she be a celebrity—that is, one who willingly surrenders herself to her public as if she has nothing to hide. Charke's audience had another demand that further complicated the first: that Charke be a woman—a role that denied her entry into many public spaces (like the coffeehouses that Mr. Spectator was said to have inhabited) and that charged her with impropriety should she venture from the private sphere. In appearing onstage or in public, in other words, Charke was fulfilling the demands for celebrity at the same time that she was violating the rules for womanhood. Not only did her public life open her up to her spectators' dissections of her private thoughts and activities; it opened her up to her spectators' critique of her gender as well. A detailed examination of Charke's description of her first appearance onstage reveals several similarities and a few key differences between her brand of overexpression and her father's—and begins to suggest some reasons why her overexpressions, ultimately, failed to blunt her spectators' critiques.

Charke's means of acquiring property depended on her willingness, as a player, to show herself off, as well as her willingness, as a celebrity, to make herself legible. She enjoyed her first taste of financial independence as an actress of bit parts on the Drury Lane stage—an experience she introduces by describing her eagerness to see her name written legibly and recognizably in the playbills. "I must beg Leave to give the Reader an Idea of that Extacy of Heart I felt, on seeing the Character I was to appear in the Bills," Charke writes about snagging her first role, as Mademoiselle in Vanbrugh's *The Provok'd Wife*; "though my Joy was somewhat dash'd, when I came to see it inserted, *By a young Gentlewoman, who had never appear'd on any Stage before.*"[40]

For the young actress, the passage implies, her legitimacy as a professional and as a wage-earner depends on her legibility as a name on the Drury Lane playbills.

Craving the recognition of her name rather than a general reference to her station, Charke is delighted when, upon her second appearance, she is upgraded from a "*young Gentlewoman*" to a proper noun. "My name was in Capitals [in the playbills] on this second Attempt," she continues; "and I dare aver, that the Perusal of it, from one End of the Town to the other, for the first Week, was my most immediate and constant Business: Nor do I believe it cost me less, in Shoes and Coaches, then two or three Guineas, to gratify the extravagant Delight I had, not only in reading the Bills, but sometimes hearing myself spoken of, which luckily was to my Advantage."[41] Thus Charke celebrates her legibility and visibility, enjoying the repetition and distribution of her name "from one end of town to the other" and taking great pride in "sometimes hearing [herself] spoken of." Like her father, the young actress is quick to recognize that increased visibility produces increased privilege and increased profits.

Such visibility also, however, produces increased liability. Only a page later Charke has found much to regret in her newly minted fame. She echoes her father's discomfort with the scrutiny exacted upon the eighteenth-century actor when she reveals her apprehensions that her first attempts should suffer by comparison to the performances of the great actresses of her day. "Now I leave to any reasonable Person, what I went through, in undertaking two such Characters, after two of the greatest Actresses in the Theatre, *viz.* Mrs. *Oldfield* and Mrs. *Porter*," Charke writes of her early performances as an understudy. "I solemnly declare, that I expected to make an odd Figure in the Bills of Mortality——DIED ONE, OF CAPITAL CHARACTERS."[42] By "CAPITAL CHARACTERS" Charke suggests not only the choice theatrical characters that she will play in lieu of her more famous peers but also the "name in capitals" that clearly identifies her on the playbills. While they are necessary to Charke's acquisition of property, both sets of characters also betray Charke by forcing her "odd Figure" into a set of conventionalized definitions—the standardized language of the playbill, the standardized letters of the printed page, and the stock characters of the eighteenth-century stage. Like the identity supposedly expressed by her "handsome lac'd Hat," the obvious significations of such "capital characters" imprison Charke in an identity that can be "so well described."[43] The same visibility that facilitates her possession of property also marks Charke as the property of the spectators who gaze upon her and rename her according to the nouns they think she deserves.

Charke's problem here resembles her father's, if it increases the stakes: for both father and daughter, fame demands servitude to increasingly normative ideals of gender—and to others' definitions of self. But for Charke, unlike for Cibber, obscurity is not only unthinkable (her fame, after all, was thrust upon her at birth); it also bars her from one of the few (and certainly the most profitable) careers available to eighteenth-century women. With her social status more precarious, Charke must discover a strategy more radical than her father's. She does so, I will suggest, by adapting Cibber's overexpressive strategies to perform her gendered body as a blank. While Cibber's overexpressions portray his gender as both-at-once—the wig so masculine it is feminine—Charke's restage her gender as neither-at-all. And while Cibber strips down to a "Nakedness" layered with both masculine and feminine signifiers, Charke presents a nakedness to which no gender can be assigned and through which no gender can be interpreted.

Charke hints at this strategy when she imagines her appearance in the "Bills of Mortality" not as a male or a female (as the bills often divided the dead) but rather as the ungendered pronoun "one." She develops this strategy further throughout her *Narrative*, in which her layers and layers of disguises serve only to emphasize the illegibility of the body they seem both to express and to conceal.

Charke's promising career as an actress on London's licensed stages was short-lived, for soon after her debut she was banned from Drury Lane by decree of the theater manager Charles Fleetwood (the primary target of Charke's biting satire *The Art of Management*) and banned from all other city stages by the decree of the 1737 Licensing Act. Banned, too, from her father's household, Charke struck out on her own, wandering London and the countryside beyond in the employ of several companies of strolling players—and in the guise of a man. The stories she relates of her adventures suggest the ways that she used gendered costumes, gendered props, and gendered language to overexpress a body marked as feminine until it became blank of any recognizable gender at all.

One of Charke's most successful ventures after 1737 was as a puppet master, a disguise that allowed her to earn money without disobeying the Licensing Act's ban on "plays" in the strictest sense. Extant playbills and puffs advertising Charke's popular performances list as their headliner a spectacular Punch "in petticoats."[44] A stock character of eighteenth- and nineteenth-century English puppet theater, Punch was a doll marked by a bulbous nose and overly enlarged facial features that suggested a rampant and overly legible masculinity. Punch wears his masculinity on his sleeve in much the same way that Cibber wore his masculinity on his head—or, rather, in his flowing, phallic wig. Cibber's wig invites us to read his exterior as an indication of what lay beneath. By dressing Punch "in petticoats," however, Charke seems to suggest a disconnect between Punch's body and his costume—a disconnect that renders his gender as nonnormative as that of the woman who operated his body (and who was known, on occasion, to don a "cocked-up" cap).[45]

Yet even as we draw comparisons between Charke's transvestitism and that of her petticoated Punch, it's important to keep in mind that Punch is but a puppet. Charke's reference to a puppet's gendered anatomy necessarily calls to mind not only Charke's own anatomy but also the most famous scene of Ben Jonson's *Bartholomew Fair*—a play frequently in repertory over the course of Charke's career. The climax of the scene occurs when a puppet lifts his costume to reveal his lack of genitalia, thus exposing not only his blank gender but also the hypocrisy of his antitheatrical interlocutor, who has been fooled into thinking him a man. Playing with the gender of a performer that by definition has no gender, Charke suggests that the bulbous nose and unmistakable face that expose Punch's "natural" masculinity are as performative as the petticoats that supposedly conceal this "nature." Beneath his nose—as beneath his clothes—Punch's gender is a blank. Similarly, Charke implies, any spectator who looks for her gender or sexuality beneath the clothes she wears necessarily exposes himself as a fool who looks for an interior self where there is, she suggests, no interior at all. Here again, Charke's gendered performances trump her father's: his exaggerated costumes suggest a body so masculine it is feminine, but her exaggerated puppets challenge the very existence of—or at least the relevance of—a gendered body beyond its exterior performance.

When Charke incorporates the details of her puppet show into the pages of her *Narrative*, the confusion that her performance suggests between masculine bodies and feminine bodies and between costume and corpus reappears as a grammatical confusion between subject and object. "For some Time I resided at the *Tennis-Court* with my Puppet-Show, which was allowed to be the most elegant that was ever exhibited," Charke boasts. "I was so very curious, that I bought Mezzotinto's of several eminent Persons, and had the Faces carved from them. Then, in regard to my Cloaths, I spared for no Cost to make them splendidly magnificent, and the Scenes were agreeable to the rest. This Affair stood me in some Hundreds, and would have paid all Costs and Charges, if I had not, through excessive Fatigue in accomplishing it, acquired a violent Fever, which had like to have carried me off, and consequently gave a Damp to the Run I should otherwise have had, as I was one of the principal Exhibiters for those Gentry."[46]

Unclear throughout the passage is who, in Charke's puppet show, fulfills the role of the critic and who is criticized. Who, in other words, is being exposed here? In his book *Puppets and Popular Culture*, Scott Cutler Shershow points out that the exaggerated facial features of Charke's puppets transform into a low-brow, "popular" form the faces of the "several eminent persons" who likely made up at least a portion of Charke's audiences. Charke reinforces the class dynamics of this transformation when she mentions that her caricature-like puppets have been carved from "Mezzotint[s]." Because of its relative expense, mezzotint was a form of printmaking consumed mainly by the upper classes. Charke has taken expensive portraits of her upper-class neighbors and reproduced them as caricatures. By projecting her patrons' faces back to them in these deformed, distended versions, Shershow argues, she makes her spectators into the spectacles, as she conceals herself behind the stage on which her marionettes perform.

The syntax of Charke's sentences accomplishes a similar reversal. When she describes herself as "one of the principal Exhibiters for those Gentry" who attended her shows, her wording leaves ambiguous whether she exhibits her puppets for the pleasure of the upper classes or whether she exhibits the upper classes themselves. The convoluted clauses of the sentence following this one only compound the ambiguity of the spectator-spectacle/subject-object relationship: "I was one of the principal Exhibiters for those Gentry; whose Mouths were, like many others we have seen MOVE without any Reality of Utterance, or at least so unintelligible in the Attempt, they might as well have closed their Lips, without raising an Expectation they were unlucky enough to disappoint, whether ORATORS or PLAYERS, is not material."[47] The antecedent to which Charke's "whose" here refers is, like the subject of the earlier sentence, significantly ambiguous. Is Charke describing as "unintelligible" the utterances of her patrons, who speak in a tongue so class-consciously verbose that it is nonsensical? Does this description apply instead to Charke's puppets, whose mouths move as she lends them a voice as "unintelligible" as the sentence that describes it? Or is the description instead a commentary on those tragic players who fail as orators by strutting and fretting their hour upon the stage—actors, perhaps, like Charke's father, who was parodied as a nonsensical puppet in *The Author's Farce* and whom Charke ventriloquizes throughout her own *Narrative*?

I return to Cibber here because Charke's refusal to distinguish between subject and object in this passage from her *Narrative* recalls Cibber's similar refusal to distinguish between "Witness" and "Orator" in the Dedication to his *Apology*. Like Cibber's, Charke's convoluted sentences dissolve the standard (and often gendered) hierarchy of subject over object, observer over observed. Yet like her performances, Charke's language, too, goes above and beyond her father's. Referring to but revising her father's gendered language, Charke presents a gender identity that cannot be described as either masculine or feminine—and that cannot even quite be described as Cibberian. Instead, as a further example will confirm, it becomes unrecognizable, indescribable—as the gender of the body that writes it becomes a blank.

Both the self-consciousness and the gendered significance of Charke's borrowings from her father come into focus late in the *Narrative*, when Charke recalls (but does not quite reproduce) one of her father's most egregious misspellings. The scene begins when Charke, her puppet show dissolved and her London theater career unsuccessful, takes her show on the road. After the grandeur of the London stages, the resources of the traveling players seem impoverished. "One Scene and a Curtain, with some of the worst of their Wardrobe, made up the *Paraphanalia* [*sic*] of the Stage, of which I was Prime Minister," she writes; "and, though under as many Disadvantages as a Set of miserable Mortals could patiently endure, from the before-mentioned Reasons, and an inexhaustible Fund of Poverty, through the General Bank of the whole Company, . . . we all went into a joint Resolution to be industrious."[48] As in her earlier replacement of the laced hat of the "CAVALIER" for the crepe-covered hat of the "Coachman," Charke rejects the royal spectacle for which her father was known. If Cibber portrayed himself as the deformed king of the theater, Charke strips herself down to the accouterments of its more modest (and more unmarked) "Prime Minister."

Charke's misspelling of the word *paraphernalia*, however, implies a performance that is less normative—and more Cibberian—than an initial reading might suggest. As Fidelis Morgan notes in her edition of the *Narrative*, Cibber himself had famously misspelled this word (as "para*phon*alia") in his preface to *The Provok'd Husband*.[49] (This was the same preface, interestingly, where he committed his most egregious overexpression in describing an actress who "*outdid* her usual *Outdoings*.") The mistake delighted Cibber's critics, most notably Henry Fielding, who immortalized it in *The Author's Farce*, a play with which Charke was intimately familiar. I will return to Charke in a moment, but I want first to examine Cibber's use of the word—and its gender implications—in order better to understand the significance of Charke's repetition of it.

Cibber's preface to *The Provok'd Husband* consists mainly of praise for the play's leading lady, Anne Oldfield, who appeared as the reformed female rake Lady Townly. Cibber writes, "The Qualities [Oldfield] had *acquired,* were the *Genteel* and the *Elegant*. The one in her Air, and the other in her Dress, never had her Equal on the Stage; and the Ornaments she herself provided, (particularly in this Play) seem'd in all Respects, the *Paraphonalia* of a Woman of Quality."[50] In Cibber's usage, the word refers to the stage properties and "Ornaments" that make Anne Oldfield into a "Woman of Quality"—or, more accurately, to the stage properties that she supplies to express her true identity as a "Woman of Quality." Like the wig that enables the transformation of Cibber's male rakes into men of feeling, *paraphonalia* suggests the accessories that refer to Oldfield's naked sincerity, which enable her properly (and legibly) gendered performance as the reformed Lady Townly.[51]

Cibber's misspelling of the word works against the apparent propriety and legibility of this gendered performance, problematizing the relationship between Oldfield's performance and increasingly codified categories of gender as it problematizes the relationship between Cibber's word and increasingly standardized methods of spelling it. It was perhaps for this reason that Fielding—an author already known for scolding Cibber's deformations of language as well as for depicting and descrying nonnormative genders in works like *The Female Husband*—chose the misspelled *paraphonalia* to anchor a ballad he inserted into *The Author's Farce* (1730). In his lullaby for the Queen of Nonsense in the play within Fielding's play, Sir Farcical Comic (a foppish writer of comedies who bears a marked resemblance to Cibber) croons:

Can my Goddess then forget
    Paraphonalia,
    Paraphonalia?
Can she the crown to another head set,
    Than of her Paraphonalia?
    If that had not done too,
    Remember my bone too,
My bone, my bone, my bone.
Sure my goddess never can
    Forget my marrow bone.[52]

Morgan points out that Fielding's repetition of the word "bone" pokes fun at a particularly unpopular double entendre later in *The Provok'd Husband*, when the innkeeper Mrs. Motherly asks her guest Sir Francis Wronghead,

"Will you give me leave to get you a broiled Bone, or so, till the Ladies come home, Sir?"[53] In Cibber's play, "bone" suggests the male genitalia. Fielding plays with this suggestion in his parody, which converts *paraphonalia*, too, from a word that signifies Oldfield's accouterments to a word that signifies Cibber's male body as he offers it up to his Queen. Fielding's association of this *paraphonalia* with the Queen of Nonsense, moreover, attaches the word to the former age of spectacle rather than his own age of the unmarked bourgeois. But Fielding echoes Cibber's own overexpressive language and suggests the illegibility of Cibber's gender as he repeats ("my bone, my bone, my bone") and deforms (the perpetual misspelling of *paraphonalia*) these words.[54] As Jill Campbell has noted, Fielding often expresses some ambivalence about whether gender constitutes an essential or a performative aspect of identity.[55] His language here suggests that Cibber's gender, at least, is performed, but performed poorly, made illegible by its overexpressive accouterments.

When Charke takes up these accouterments in her own performance, she renders them even more illegible, miring them even deeper in contradictory meanings. In Charke's *Narrative*, as in Cibber's preface, "*Paraphanalia*" suggests the accessories of a gender identity; it signifies the props and costumes that Charke employs in her performances in breeches roles. Rather than the props and ornaments of a "Woman of Quality," however, Charke's "*Paraphanalia*" consists of the trappings of a man. The same word that for Cibber suggests a recognizably female body and for Fielding a deformed (or a too obviously performed) male body suggests for Charke a body that is unrecognizable according to the definition of either. By misspelling *paraphernalia*, Charke evokes her father's overexpressed, illegible signification of gender. But by misspelling it differently than her father has misspelled it, she goes beyond the efforts of his parodists—who simply reproduce his overexpressions—and instead dissolves their meanings even further. Not recognizably feminine, not recognizably masculine, and not even recognizably Cibberian, Charke's language here makes both undeniable and unreadable the "CAPITAL CHARACTERS" through which an identity might be "so well described" and through which a well-accoutered body might be arrested and contained.[56]

Such passages shed new light on the first and most famous passage from her *Narrative*, in which the four-year-old Charke rises early, creeps to where her father's "enormous bushy Tie-wig" hangs on its hook, and places its billowing bulk on her diminutive head. The episode has become the centerpiece not only of Charke's 1755 autobiography but of recent critics' readings of that autobiography as well: a way of including Charke among the queer writers hunting for ways to express their nonnormative genders in normative language. I want to suggest, however, that Charke's first adventure in transvestitism marks her indoctrination not into queerness—a failed masculinity that we must read as her attempt to express nonnormative gender—but rather into overexpression—an exaggerated masculinity that we should read as her attempt to avoid expressing any gender at all.

Charke's many adventures in male dress begin, as she narrates them, just shy of her fifth birthday, when she enters the servants' hall of her father's summer home in Twickenham before the rest of the family has awakened. "By the Help of a long Broom, I took down a Waistcoat of my Brother's, and an enormous bushy Tie-wig of my Father's," she writes, "which entirely enclos'd my Head and Body, with the Knots of the Ties thumping my little Heels as I march'd along, with slow and solemn Pace. The Covert of Hair in which I was conceal'd, with the Weight of a monstrous Belt and large Silver-hilted Sword, that I could scarce drag along, was a vast Impediment in my Procession: And, what still added to the other Inconveniences I labor'd under, was whelming myself under one of my Father's large Beaver-hats, laden with Lace, as thick and broad as a Brickbat."[57] Modern readers of Charke's *Narrative* have described its most famous passage as Charke's trying on a masculinity that proves insufficient. "Charke's textual cross-dressing," writes Kristina Straub, "acts out with a vengeance a threat posed by the cross-dressed actress as a reflection of 'failed,' ideologically inadequate masculinities" such as the castrated male, a role that Straub identifies with Cibber's fops.[58]

As we have seen, however, Cibber's wig signified not a "failed" but rather an overly abundant masculinity—one that, in its overtness, troubled the boundaries between the body natural and the body performed. So, too, Charke's description of her father's costume emphasizes not its inadequacies bur rather its excesses. What is most striking about this passage is the sheer enormity of Charke's masculine attire. On Cibber the wig was hardly discreet, but on Charke's body it appears voluminous—even more so as an accompaniment to the "monstrous belt and large [and phallic] silver-hilted sword," the beaver lined with lace that, far from suggesting delicacy, is "as thick and broad as a brickbat." Like the cocked-up cap of Charke's generous bailiff, the costume she assumes here suggests a masculinity that exceeds its bounds.

Where queer readings of Charke's transvestitism fall short, then, is in their failure to account for the obviousness of the signifiers she employs. Despite their disagreements, such readings share the assumption that her performances on stage, street, and page attempt to express an identity that doesn't fit into normative categories of gender and sexuality. Instead, Charke's ambiguously gendered performances work to dissolve and unmark her identity by suggesting that the very signifiers that mark those categories don't mean what they are assumed to mean. Charke's performances are not expressions of an interior self struggling to make itself known through inadequate languages. Rather, they are attempts to expose the signifiers of gender as not so clear after all—and as such to enjoy the privilege of being looked at without suffering the limitations of being defined.

The overexpressive implications of Charke's gendered performances compound as the passage continues. After her playful description of taking the wig from its hook and marching through the back halls of her father's house, she decides to proceed into town. "Being thus accoutred," she writes, "I began to consider that 'twould be impossible for me to pass for Mr. *Cibber* in Girl's Shoes, therefore took an Opportunity to slip out of Doors after the Gardener, who went to his Work, and roll'd myself into a dry Ditch, which was as deep as I was high; and, in this Grotesque Pigmy-State, walk'd up and down the Ditch bowing to all who came by me."[59] The print composed for early editions of the autobiography (figure 6) makes some sense of the staging that Charke describes in the first sentence quoted here. Wearing a large man's coat and small girl's shoes, the four-year-old child stands in a ditch as high as her shoulders, so that her head, burdened with its big wig and beaver hat, is just seen over the top of the ditch by the passers-by who stand outside of it.

Her tumble into the ditch, Charke notes, has covered her in dirt, leaving her in a "Grotesque Pigmy-State" that indicates both exaggeration and indescribability. As a grotesque, Charke appears a clown: a figure, much like her Punch in petticoats, marked by exaggerated and distorted body parts, an all-too-visible corporeality. Yet at the same time that this corporeality is overt it is also unreadable. Describing herself as a "Pigmy," Charke compares her dirt-encrusted face to the dark skin of an unreadable racial Other.[60] The effectiveness of black paint at transforming an actor's famous face into illegibility was well known by Charke's contemporaries: fourteen years before the publication of Charke's *Narrative*, David Garrick made his professional debut as Aboan in Thomas Southerne's adaption of *Oroonoko*—"a part in which his features could not easily be discerned," notes Thomas Davies. "Under the disguise of black countenance, he hoped to escape being known, should it be his misfortune [in his first attempt on the stage] not to please."[61]

Here, the mud on her face seems not only to obscure Charke's features but also to remove her from categories of non-normative genders and sexualities altogether. The racial identity she takes on seems to exempt her from all considerations of the gender or sexual identity she embodies. Charke proposes

6. Francis Garden, *An Exact Representation of Mrs. Charke Walking in the Ditch at Four Years of Age* (1755). © Trustees of the British Museum.

her "Grotesque Pigmy-State" as an alternative to the implied ridiculousness of trying to "pass for Mr. *Cibber* in Girl's Shoes." Unable to reconcile her male dress with her "Girl's Shoes," she implies, she instead takes on an identity that makes such reconciliation unnecessary—an identity that, like that she creates with her misspelled *Paraphanalia*, is so Other that it presents her gender as a blank.

Combining the illegibility of the unknown "Pigmy" and the supreme visibility of the "grotesque," then, Charke's performance in her father's wig erases her identity even as it makes her the center of attention. And yet like so many of her borrowings from her father, this one takes Charke above and beyond even Cibber's most outrageous overexpressions. If the wig is large on him, it is even larger on her. If on him it suggests an identity so masculine it is feminine, on her it points to the ridiculousness of making such distinctions and the foolishness of any spectator who analyzes a celebrity's costume—or even dissects his or her anatomy—for signifiers of his or her "self."

CHARLOTTE CHARKE AND THE FAILURE OF OVEREXPRESSION

Charke's overexpressions in performance and print, in big wigs and misspelled words, differ from her father's overexpressions in one other significant way, however, and that is in their failure. Like the anonymous author of *The Laureat*, declaring himself incapable of the "*Herculian*" task of translating Cibber's prose or of determining Cibber's sexuality, Cibber's critics ultimately surrender their efforts to interpret him.[62] Not so the readers of Charlotte Charke. Before I conclude this chapter, I want to turn briefly to Charke's reception by both contemporary and modern readers to ask why, in her case, overexpression failed to make her illegible.

As I have discussed, several critics attempted to mimic or parody Cibber's *Apology*, and faux autobiographies of Cibber and his descendants proliferated in the years following the book's 1740 publication. Charke's imitators, however, went a step further. In October 1755, only a few months after *The Narrative of the Life of Mrs. Charlotte Charke* appeared in bookshops, the *Gentleman's Magazine* offered its own story of Charke's life. The short article was not a parody or a tribute. It reproduced excerpts from Charke's *Narrative* nearly verbatim, but with one crucial difference: the (unauthorized) biography translated Charke's first-person narrative into a third-person narrative, replacing all of the subjective pronouns "I" with the distancing and obviously gendered "she." Further contributing to the normative language of the *Gentleman's Magazine* excerpts were several interjections by the editor pointing out the unacceptability of Charke's behavior toward her father and of her gender play.[63]

The *Magazine*'s appropriations of Charke's text represent a failure of overexpression in three ways. First, the magazine's plagiarism of Charke's text weakens her attempts to make money by her visibility by siphoning off her royalties from readers who might decide to purchase the *Magazine* rather than her *Narrative*. Second, its commentary on Charke's actions impose on her prose precisely the normative viewpoint that overexpression attempts to elude or avoid. Third—and perhaps most interestingly—the *Magazine*'s rewriting of Charke's pronouns circumscribes the precise relationship between subject and object (changing "I" to "she," the person speaking to one who is spoken about) and between masculinity and femininity (replacing the ambiguous "I" with a clearly gendered "she") that Charke's *Narrative* itself seems bent on keeping ambiguous. The revisions suggest a discomfort with the blank gender that Charke presents, an effort to replace Charke's evacuation of a gendered body and a gendered identity with a clear affirmation of her as a woman, as a nonnormative sexuality, and as the object of the gaze.

As egregious as these attempts by the *Gentleman's Magazine* to determine and cement Charke's gender and sexuality may be, we can see hints of that same desire in the more recent, "queer" readings that have dominated criticism of Charke's *Narrative* for the past three decades. By excerpting Charke's *Narrative* in her 2003 collection *The Literature of Lesbianism*, for instance, Terry Castle emphasizes the very passages that the *Gentleman's Magazine* condemned; and her attempts to mark Charke's pointedly ambiguous prose as definitively sexual recall the *Magazine*'s similar attempts to mark her pronouns as definitely gendered. By labeling her transvestitism as either an inner proclivity toward a masculine identity or a deep desire for her father's love, moreover, scholars like Erin Mackie, Cheryl Wanko, and Felicity Nussbaum imply that we must read Charke's ambiguous *Narrative* for its true confessions.

Overexpression, however, gives us a new way of thinking about autobiography: it is no longer only an attempt—necessarily imperfect—to express the self through normative language. It may also be an attempt to avoid expressing the self—or, more accurately, to make a self impossible to read. So why do we seem to be so much more hesitant to give up on interpreting Charke's meaning than we were to interpret her father's? Why do we continue to ask, more than 250 years after Charke published her ambiguous and gender-bending *Narrative*, who she *really* was or what inner desires she was *really* trying to express?

I want to hazard a speculation that later chapters will flesh out more fully, and that is that our understanding of Charke as a female writer makes us more willing to read her autobiography as a confession—or her performances as expressions—of her true self. If we understand a man's costume as covering or distracting from his true self, in other words, we understand a woman's costume as expressing that self; and if we understand Cibber's eccentricities or omissions as clever manipulations of his persona, we are always tempted to understand Charke's eccentricities or omissions as attempts, never entirely successful, to confess her true self in a language that seems inadequate to her femininity, or to her lesbianism, or even to her relationship with her father. Such readings are conditioned, too, by the impact that studies of the novel—to the exclusion of performance—have had over theories of the eighteenth-century self. Works like Ian Watt's *The Rise of the Novel* and Nancy Armstrong's *Desire and Domestic Fiction*, as well as more recent studies such as Wahrman's and McKeon's, have taught us to understand the emergence of a stable and legible self in eighteenth-century England as both inevitable and essential to the makings of modernity. Charke's struggles to exempt her body and its performances from the categories of selfhood emerging to contain them, however, suggest the powerful advantages that illegibility might offer the modern individual and the crucial role that performance studies—in its attention to disappearing selves, illegible selves, and unstable selves—might play in our understanding of eighteenth-century culture.

In excavating what I have described as the overexpressive elements of Charke's prose and performances, then, I have tried to resist this temptation to read all of Charke's public pronouncements as private confessions. What happens, I have asked, if we allow Charke (as we have allowed Cibber) a public persona separate from any private inclinations? How might our readings of women's autobiographies in the eighteenth century change if we understand their eccentricities not as failed attempts to express an inexpressible identity but rather as clever attempts to overexpress personae that their audiences demanded they make public?

In my examinations of the autobiographies of George Anne Bellamy and Mary Robinson in chapters 4 and 5 I attempt to do precisely that, and, in doing so, to understand how and why overexpression works differently for the women than for the men that I examine. For now, I want only to suggest that the differences have to do not with the way women write or perform their autobiographies but rather with the ways that we read those writings, those performances. Faced with the absent or ambiguous gender that Charke's autobiographical performances produced, we must resist the temptation voiced by the *Gentleman's Magazine* to fill in the blank. If we do, we might understand Charke's *Narrative* not as a confession but rather as an overexpression, designed to resist rather than to construct a gender identity.

CONCLUSION: IF THE CAP FITS, SPARE IT

Charke's debt to her father does not end with her 1755 *Narrative* but haunts her three novels and her extant plays as well. She begins her 1735 satire *The Art of Management* with an epigram that introduces her father's 1704 comedy *The Careless Husband* and that reverberates, as well, throughout the *Narrative*: "*Qui capit ille facit*"—or, "If the cap fits, wear it."[64] In Charke's *Narrative* the cap in question is a masculine one: the big beaver hat and whitened wig of Charke's father, or the cocked-up and creped-over hat of Charke's generous bailiff—both of them humongous appendages that dwarf her feminine body. In *The Careless Husband*, the cap isn't a cap at all, but a woman's handkerchief, a feminine accessory that tops the rakish head of Sir Charles Easy and turns him into a proper man. In neither work does the cap exactly fit. But in their ill-fitting clothes and their misfit identities, in the copiously capital characters of their autobiographies and performances, Cibber and Charke achieve a sort of imbalanced equilibrium between celebrity and spectatorship, between publicity and privacy, and between the spectacular politics of the early modern period and the politics of the gaze that had come to dominate the gender ideologies of the early eighteenth century.

And as the ill-fitting cap slides from body to body—from the foppish head of Lord Foppington to the all-too-masculine head of Colley Cibber, from the body of an actor to the body of a bailiff, and from the masculine frame of an English celebrity to the tiny form of his four-year-old daughter—as the cap slides from body to body and from gender to gender, it suggests the ways that methods of self-concealment like overexpression, too, might be passed down. The words and costumes that Charke employs don't exactly reproduce those for which her father was known, but by referring to and expanding on her father's performances Charke implies that the tools he used to render his persona illegible comprised not an isolated strategy but a grammar of sorts: a tradition that could be adopted and adapted to individual need. Of course, Charke herself—cast out of the theater at a young age and dying penniless in a hovel—lacked the influence to take this grammar into the mainstream. Such a task would require a man who was eccentric enough to see the value of concealing his private foibles, savvy enough to theorize it, and famous enough to spread it far and wide. As luck would have it, in the very years in which Charke was reaping the meager rewards from her autobiography's publication, a poor parson in the town of York was madly scribbling away at a book that would make him just such a man.

CHAPTER 3

The Canon of Print

Laurence Sterne and the Overexpression of Character

"I wrote not [to] be *fed*, but to be *famous*."[1] With these words, Laurence Sterne announced to a critic his ambitions for *The Life and Opinions of Tristram Shandy, Gentleman*, shortly after its first two volumes appeared in print in 1759. Formerly a subparson in the relative backwater of York, Sterne became an overnight sensation when his bawdy, blustery, and partially bowdlerized book arrived in London, soon to be followed by its attention-seeking author. As the book's fame grew, Sterne crafted a public identity around his fictional personae: he signed his letters as Tristram, published his sermons as Yorick, and cavorted through London as the crack-brained fool, "Shandy[ing] it away" in what Thomas Keymer calls "a highly visible form of performance art, through which Sterne's social existence could become an extension of his fictional text."[2] If Sterne composed his fiction as a bid for fame, he got his wish.

And it is tempting to regard Sterne's clever quip as a true confession. He seems, after all, to welcome fame (and the invasions of privacy it entails) when he encourages his readers to interpret his fictional characters as versions of himself. As he notes in *Tristram Shandy*, the celebrity he sought depended on spectators who "find themselves ill at ease, unless they are let into the whole secret from first to last, of every thing which concerns" their celebrated authors.[3]

But we must be cautious about expecting too many self-revelations from a writer known for his slipperiness. Upon closer examination, Sterne's remark seems less a revelation of his inner self than a sly allusion to his exterior features—specifically those features often caricatured in the press. Anyone who had read about Sterne in the mid-eighteenth century would have been able to pick him out of a crowd by virtue of his emaciated frame—by virtue of a body, that is, that seemed for far too long to have sought "fame" at the expense of "good feeding."[4] A caricature of the author painted in 1765 shows him bowing congenially to a skeleton representing Death, his black-clad profile only marginally meatier than his interlocutor's (figure 7); and everyone could appreciate the humor when, in a popular mock-lecture analyzing the oddities of London's celebrities in 1765, the performer George Alexander Stevens joked that Sterne had "died, at length, of mere hunger."[5] By embedding in his supposed self-description such references to the exterior features that his public deemed his trademarks, Sterne feigns self-revelation while revealing only that which his public already knows. The reader who looks to Sterne's language to discover the interior self it promises finds himself staring at the superficial celebrity of his own creation—a celebrity who may or may not *be* hungry for fame but who is famous for *appearing* hungry. It is possible to see in Sterne's supposed revelation, in other words, an especially clever evasion—and it is telling that when he repeats the phrase (twice) in *Tristram Shandy*, he does so in the very moments he is clarifying his relationship with his critics: once in Volume V, as Tristram launches his explanation of the *Tristrapoedia*; and once in the "Author's Preface" as he addresses "my dear Anti-Shandeans, and thrice able critics."[6]

Yet the most damning piece of evidence against the sincerity of Sterne's confession is its source: his words recall and reverse a pronouncement made in a popular pamphlet from 1742, "I wrote more to be Fed, than be Famous." The pamphlet was published in the form of an angry epistle to Alexander Pope, and its author was none other than Pope's infuriatingly overexpressive nemesis, Colley Cibber.[7]

I begin this chapter with Sterne's allusion to Cibber in order to introduce a body of work that might otherwise seem anomalous within the pages of this book. Sterne was not a stage actor, and *Tristram Shandy* is not an autobiography—not explicitly or exclusively, anyway. Part of what I want to suggest in this chapter, however, is that studying *Tristram Shandy* in the context of the celebrity autobiography helps to explain some of the book's most perplexing idiosyncrasies, from its off-kilter methods of characterization to its typographical oddities and digressive prose. I examine these idiosyncrasies as some of the most articulate answers that eighteenth-century culture offered to the question of how a celebrity might protect his or her privacy from the public eye. *Tristram Shandy* is central, then, to popularizing and cementing the features of overexpression as a literary and performative tradition recognizable enough that other artists could either adapt or react against it: its popularity ensured that the idiosyncratic strategy that originated with Cibber (to whom Sterne frequently alludes) could be passed down

7. Thomas Patch, *Sterne and Death* (ca. 1768). © Trustees of the British Museum.

to later celebrities like Garrick, Bellamy, and Robinson (several of whom cite Sterne directly). I explore Sterne's debt to celebrity autobiography (and to Cibber's autobiography in particular) in the first section of this chapter.

Yet Sterne did more than simply to repeat and perpetuate the strategies that Cibber and Charke had developed; and in later volumes of *Tristram Shandy* we see evidence that Sterne revised many of the strategies that his predecessors had introduced (and to which his book frequently makes reference). The second section of this chapter examines Sterne's experiments with the form of the book as attempts to achieve the illegibility of Cibber's and Charke's eccentric performances and misspelled words using the mass-produced, standardized, and disembodied medium of the printed page. Such experiments resist promises, like those made by Samuel Johnson's *Dictionary of the English Language* four years before *Tristram Shandy* debuted, that the printed word was somehow more stable or more legible than the spoken word—or similar promises made more recently by eighteenth-century scholars that printed books develop more stable selves than performance. By insisting on the relevance of his performances outside and around his books to the characters printed within his books, I argue, Sterne suggests an affinity between performing selves and printed selves that dismantles the assumptions by which critics claim to "know" their characters or because of which celebrities suffer being known. He suggests, too, the myriad ways in which our interpretation of the words printed within a text depends on our interpretation of the performances, personalities, and publications dancing outside that text—a suggestion that Sterne's claim to write "not to be fed, but to be famous" implies and that the famous marbled page of Volume III, as I read it, makes clear.

The external factors that influence our interpretation of a book include not only the byline on the book's cover or the gossip surrounding the book's publication but also the critics interpreting the book's meaning. In the third section of this chapter, I consider how later volumes of *Tristram Shandy* respond to and even collaborate with such critics. By inserting spurious versions of his work into the heart of his story and by littering his pages with blanks (asterisks, ambiguities, euphemisms) that the reader must fill in, Sterne invites his fans and detractors to help create his work only to chastise them later for the choices they have made. Transforming the reader from critic to collaborator and from spectator to spectacle, he also dismantles the tools that such a reader might use to critique his published work or to declaim upon his private character. This technique seemingly bears little resemblance to Cibber's brand of overexpression but, I argue, emerges from the same tradition and shares similar goals. And as we shall see, it reappears in the autobiographical performances of Mary Robinson.

In this chapter I examine Sterne's musings on fame and his defense against his critics by examining the two characters whose personae he most often adopted: the parson Yorick and the autobiographer Tristram, both of whom reveal in different ways and to varying degrees what I am calling the overexpression of character. By choosing this phrase as the subtitle of this chapter I am drawing on several meanings of the word *character*. It refers, first of all, to the personages like Tristram and Yorick who populate *Tristram Shandy* and who burst from its pages to join seamlessly into Sterne's own performances of self. It evokes the hobbyhorsical methods of characterization that modern scholars have linked to both the novel and the satire but that I read as Sterne's commentary on the celebrity autobiography. And it suggests, too, the printed characters that comprise Sterne's words—words that appear no different from those neatly organized and defined in Johnson's *Dictionary* but that seem to carry meanings that Johnson could not have predicted. Of course, this subtitle might refer just as well to most of the chapters in this study, which deal in different ways with celebrities who exaggerate into illegibility the marks by which their spectators might recognize them. That such a generally applicable phrase heads this chapter is meant to signify *Tristram Shandy*'s importance in canonizing strategies familiar to us from Cibber's and Charke's performances, in translating them to print, and in introducing them to later generations of Londoners.

In selecting the printed book as the theatrical prop around which this chapter revolves, I mean to emphasize the overlaps between printed characters and performed selves that works like Johnson's *Dictionary* deny but that *Tristram Shandy* demands. Like his performances, Sterne's books are eccentric, uncategorizable, and inseparable from the body and the reputation of their author. And unlike the books that Johnson idealizes as insignificant (and standardized) containers for important ideas, Sterne's books insist on their idiosyncrasies as physical objects in and of themselves—most emphatically in the black, marbled, and white pages around which I have organized the three sections of this chapter. Tellingly, Sterne introduces the first of these pages as he introduces Yorick, one of the two characters whose persona he habitually adopted in his own public performances. It is in Yorick's portrait that Sterne unveils the methods of characterization that have so perplexed scholars of *Tristram Shandy* but that reveal most pointedly the influence of overexpression. Thus it is to Yorick's portrait that I'd like, now, to turn.

THE BLACK PAGE, THE PARSON YORICK, AND THE PRICE OF FAME

The well-meaning but tactless cleric who shares a vocation with *Tristram Shandy*'s living author and a name with Hamlet's dead jester seems at first an unlikely candidate to introduce the strategy that will allow Sterne to market his public persona while shielding his private life. In Shakespeare's play, the name *Yorick* is synonymous with fame that is fleeting and futile. In Sterne's narrative, the name seems no more auspicious. Yorick dies in the first volume of *Tristram Shandy*, after his tendency "of scattering . . . his gibes and his jests about him" invites the ire of his parishioners, and he is buried beneath the seeming obscurity of the black page.[8] But he returns to rescue Phutatorius from a poorly placed chestnut in the fourth volume of *Tristram Shandy*, to lend his name to *The Sermons of Parson Yorick* (actually the sermons of Laurence Sterne) and to narrate his travels in *A Sentimental Journey*—a work set (according to the arithmetic of *Tristram Shandy*) fourteen years after his death.

Yorick thus exemplifies a fictional character that floats outside the boundaries of the fictional text, attaching his person and his name (a name that originates, significantly, not in a novel but in a drama) to extratextual bodies. The most prominent of these extratextual bodies is the body of Laurence Sterne. In the spring of 1760, shortly after the first two volumes of *Tristram Shandy* appeared, Sterne arrived in London to market his book by parading about town in the guise of its most prominent characters. One pamphleteer complained of the lengths Sterne went merely "*to be pestered with the compliments of the silly and the idle; . . . to run gossiping from tea-table to tea-table, and cry, 'Here am I the wonderful author—there are no works like mine,' [to] hawk his face about . . . to all the portrait-painters in town, vainly begging to have his mazard multiplied.*"[9] The description captures not only the apparent suddenness with which celebrity had descended on the man who claims to have spent the first forty-six years of his life in "quiet Obscurity," but also the eagerness with which he pursued it.[10] Before his arrival in London Sterne persuaded his paramour, the performer Catherine Fourmantel, to sign her name to a letter singing the book's praises and to drop it at the door of David Garrick, the greatest celebrity of the age. The gimmick worked: when Sterne arrived in London a few months later, Garrick greeted him with friendship, a box seat at Drury Lane, and letters of introduction to the nation's most influential citizens.[11]

For the next ten years Sterne was one of the most famous men in England. Critics panned his later volumes (III–VI in 1761, VII and VIII in 1765, and the final volume just before Sterne's death, in 1767); but even then the author continued to present himself, in public, in the persons of his most popular characters. "I have converted many into Shandeism," Sterne wrote to Garrick during a trip to France in 1762; "for be it known I Shandy it away fifty times more than I was ever wont, talk more nonsense than ever you heard me talk in your days—and to all sorts of people."[12] I discuss the links that Sterne draws between his printed characters and his performing body in more detail in the next section, but I bring them up here in order to emphasize the ways in which a book that seems to have taken the form of a novel nonetheless relies on characters developed partially in performance. In this overlap between novelistic and theatrical devices of characterization Sterne's narrative resembles another genre coming to prominence in the mid-eighteenth century: the celebrity autobiography. And to note the resemblance between *Tristram Shandy* and the celebrity autobiography is to see in Yorick's rise and demise a thinly veiled version of the vulnerabilities and strategies first articulated by the inventor of that genre, Colley Cibber.

The allusions to Cibber that pepper Sterne's works are not the only indications of his familiarity with and admiration of the laureate's writings. In a letter to his bookseller in 1762, Sterne lists "The Dramatic Works of Cibber—& Cibber's life" among six English books to be sent to his friend Denis Diderot in Paris. (Others included Pope's poetry and Sterne's own "6 Vols. Of Shandy.")[13] Later that year, Sterne wrote to a friend about his having organized and performed an amateur adaptation of Cibber and Vanbrugh's *The Provoked Husband* to entertain visitors at Christmas.[14] And Cibber's 1742 *Letter from Mr. Cibber to Mr. Pope* was one of two books that scholars can confirm Sterne owned.[15] Sterne's early readers noticed similarities between Cibber's foppish persona and Sterne's crack-brain'd fool: several eighteenth-century actors' biographies allude explicitly to Sterne as continuing the tradition of the celebrity tell-all that Cibber had established.[16] And a parody of *Tristram Shandy* published in 1760 adds to Tristram's known deformities—his flattened nose, his injured penis—an "envious mountain on my back" that a few well-placed allusions link to Cibber's *Richard III*.[17]

Sterne's early interest in Cibber may have stemmed not from the celebrity that greeted him in London upon the publication of his book's first two volumes but rather from the recognizability—less widespread but no less potent—that he experienced as a popular preacher in York. His sermons earned him some status among the town's inhabitants, and in a later letter to Garrick Sterne would make the connection between preacher and celebrity explicit by comparing a French clergyman—"one Pere Clement"—to the French actress "Madam Clairon, who you must know, is the Garrick of the stage here."[18] Yet his public position also became a liability when his publication of a political pamphlet in early 1759 embroiled him in controversy and most likely curtailed his ecclesiastical ambitions.

Shortly after his pamphlet appeared, Sterne began Volume I of *Tristram Shandy*, including in it a seeming allusion to his recent notoriety. For like Cibber and like Sterne himself, Yorick is a victim of his own quest for fame, and it is in the tale of his death—which paradoxically begins the tale of his life—that we discover the most self-conscious imitations of Cibber's *Apology* and the strategies of self-protection that it introduced. As Sterne notes, the public gaze follows Yorick wherever he rides his hobbling, broke-backed excuse for a horse. "To speak the truth," Sterne writes, "he could never enter a village, but he caught the attention of both old and young."[19] Alas, poor Yorick quickly discovers that such attention leads not only to fame but also to vulnerability, and like his author he soon finds himself at the center of a local scandal.

The parson suffers, it seems, from an impulse to speak too plainly. "He was a man," Sterne explains, "unhackneyed and unpractised in the world, and was altogether as indiscreet and foolish on every other subject of discourse where policy is wont to impress restraint. *Yorick* had no impression but one, and that was what arose from the nature of the deed spoken of; which impression he would usually translate into plain *English* without any periphrasis . . .—he had but too many temptations in life, of scattering his wit and his humour,—his gibes and his jests about him.——They were not lost for want of gathering."[20] Unlike his savvier parishioners and critics, who wield "gravity" as a "cloak for ignorance, or for folly," Yorick exposes his inner character promiscuously and without regard to how his words and actions might be misinterpreted by his public.[21] Such misinterpretations inevitably arise, as when Yorick's parishioners mistake his eagerness to hire a midwife for the town as a self-serving effort to avoid lending his own horses to villagers fetching a doctor. "No sooner did he bestir himself in behalf of the midwife," Sterne explains, "and pay the expenses of the ordinary's licence to set her up,—but the whole secret came out; every horse he had lost, and two more than ever he had lost, with all the circumstances of their destruction, were known and distinctly remembered.—The story ran like wild-fire."[22]

Yorick's tendency to occupy the center of such stories—and the center of attention—is reminiscent of Cibber's willingness to play the fool in his *Apolo-*

gy and anticipates Sterne's tendency, in the words of his critic, "*to run gossiping from tea-table to tea-table, and cry, 'Here am I the wonderful author—-there are no works like mine.*'"[23] Unfortunately, this tendency also leads directly to his death at the hands of his "grave" neighbors (neighbors who themselves bear a striking resemblance to the "graver gentry" of critics whose uncharitable attacks on his book and his person Sterne will deplore in his "Author's Preface" of Volume III).[24] In the end, Yorick falls victim to these retaliations against his indiscretions, as Sterne reminds us in the moral he offers to Yorick's tale: "To wind up the last scene of thy tragedy, CRUELTY and COWARDICE, twin ruffians, hired and set on by MALICE in the dark, shall strike together at all thy infirmities and mistakes:—the best of us, my dear lad, lye open there."[25] To be famous as Yorick is famous and to speak one's mind in "plain *English* without any periphrasis," Sterne implies, is to "lye open" and vulnerable as one's gravely cloaked companions analyze and anatomize both body and text in an effort to define the author's character.

Sterne's declaration that "the best of us . . . lye open" to the public's curiosity evokes the image of body lying openly—and opened—before an operating theater of wide-eyed and discreetly costumed dissectors. We might think here of the autopsy report that Benjamin Victor includes in his biography of Barton Booth, or of David Garrick's comparison of a critic to the dissector of an actor's performance. But Sterne's phrase also contains an oxymoron that, in its startling ambiguity, reverses Yorick's tragic vulnerability and inches toward the *Chiaro Oscuro* strategy of concealment that he borrowed from Cibber and Charke. "Lye" is, after all, a word that might describe not only a physical but also a verbal activity; to lie is not only to make prostrate one's body but also to perjure one's words. And saying that one perjures "open[ly]" begins to sound like a description of overexpression: a method of characterization that arrives at concealment through the illusion of openness and hides the self under an excess of self-revelations. Out of the very sentence that threatens to anatomize him, Sterne constructs his solution to the vulnerabilities that Yorick suffers. And the best solution for those given—like Cibber, like Charke, like Yorick, and like Sterne himself—to "speak *English* without any periphrasis" is not to stop speaking. It is instead to load one's speech with as much periphrasis—as many digressions and elaborations and misdirections—as one can manage.[26] The solution is, in other words, to block the reader's entry into the interiority of the character not through the inclusion of too few details and descriptions and extratextual bodies, but rather through the inclusion of too many.

If we turn the page on Yorick's ignominious death, we find precisely such a solution—too late for Yorick but just in time for Sterne. As an epitaph that promises to record Yorick's life, the black page is overwrought, and its excess of ink works to cover up the very self that it promises to describe. Beneath its inky periphrases, its words printed over and over until they become illegible, we might discover a printed page that has taken on the qualities of performance, displaying a self so obsessively documented that it seems to disappear.

When we understand such connections between *Tristram Shandy* and the celebrity autobiographies that surrounded its publication, its overexpressive features seem almost too obvious to warrant explication. We might cite, for instance, an aging Tristram's frustration that his literary labor only drags him further and further from his task's completion: "The more I write, the more I shall have to write—and consequently, the more your worships read, the more your worships will have to read."[27] We might consider Sterne's lament that the accumulation of knowledge leads only to its own destruction:

> Thus it is, by slow steps of casual increase, that our knowledge physical, metaphysical, physiological, polemical, nautical, mathematical, aenigmatical, technical, biographical, romantical, chemical, and obstetrical, with fifty other branches of it, (most of 'em ending, as these do, in *ical*) have, for these two last centuries and more, gradually been creeping towards that Ἀκμὴ [apex] of their perfections. . . .
>
> When that happens, it is to be hoped, it will put an end to all kind of writings whatsoever;—the want of all kind of writing will put an end to all kind of reading;—-and that in time, *As war begets poverty, poverty peace,*——must, in course, put an end to all kind of knowledge.[28]

Or we might think, instead, of the resemblance between Cibber's enormous (and somewhat phallic) wig and Slawkenbergius's enormous (and unquestionably phallic) nose—an appendage that, like Cibber's, inspires some debate about whether "'Tis a true nose" or whether "'Tis made of a fir-tree."[29]

Deidre Lynch has described this tale as Sterne's parody of "overloaded characters" and the recognition scenes that, through obviously physical markings, had become increasingly unfashionable in the aesthetic theory of the mid-eighteenth century.[30] A few scholars have gone so far as to describe this "overloadedness" as a kind of tribute to—or parody of—Cibber's *Apology*, noting how both authors, in the words of Melvyn New, adopt "a voice of self-exposure rather than self-examination."[31] Beyond some brief mentions by New and Kristina Straub, however, the connections between Sterne's work and the celebrity autobiography have been largely unexplored in recent scholarship. This is particularly surprising given the discussions of genre and of characterization that have dominated Sterne scholarship for the past fifty years and to which the celebrity autobiography might offer an illuminating response. For the celebrity autobiography, as I will explain, presents a middle ground between the methods of characterization associated with the satire and those attributed to the novel, the two genres dominant in scholars' discussions of *Tristram Shandy*'s origins.

Key to these discussions are the idiosyncrasies that make Sterne's characters seem both overexposed and impenetrable. In one camp are those scholars who agree with Viktor Schlovsky's famous description of the narrative as "the most typical novel of all world literature," based on its tendency to "lay bare" the inner workings of both its literary devices and its characters' minds.[32] Scholars in this camp interpret Tristram's digressions and elaborations as evidence that Sterne has taken to extremes the novel's promise to "ma[k]e [its] subject the exploration of the personality as it is defined in the interpenetration of its past and present self-awareness."[33] Opposing these scholars are those, led by New, who link *Tristram Shandy* to an older tradition of satire, a genre that presents its characters not as psychologically realistic individuals but as representative types whose vices are often made visible by certain prominent physical features.[34]

Yet Sterne seems to reject both the psychological and the physical methods of characterization—which modern scholars have labeled as the novelistic and the satirical—in an explanation of his techniques that directly follows the black page. Many authors of character-driven narratives like his, Sterne begins, long for the aid of "*Momus*'s glass," a literal window to the soul named for the Greek god of mockery, who tried to persuade Hephaestus to install a porthole in men's breasts when he created them. "Had the glass been there set up," Sterne hypothesizes, "nothing more would have been wanting, in order to have taken a man's character, but to have taken a chair and gone softly, as you would do to a dioptrical bee-hive, and look'd in,—viewed the soul stark naked . . .——then taken your pen and ink and set down nothing but what you had seen, and could have sworn to."[35] A view of the "stark-naked" soul is precisely the promise made by the novelists who promised their spectators a peek at their subject's secret histories or of the biographers who, like Benjamin Victor, offered up a glimpse of a celebrity's innards. Such a promise is, however, impossible to keep. "But this is an advantage not to be had by the biographer in this planet," Sterne writes, where "our minds shine not through body, but are wrapt up here in a dark covering of uncrystallized flesh and blood; so that if we would come to the specifick characters of them, we must go some other way to work."[36]

If the interiorized characters of the novel won't serve Sterne's purposes, neither will the exaggerated characters of the satire, as he makes clear in enumerating a few other methods of characterization employed by his colleagues:

> One of these you will see drawing a full-length character *against the light*;—that's illiberal,——dishonest,——and hard upon the character of the man who sits.
>
> Others, to mend the matter, will make a drawing of you in the *Camera*;—- that is most unfair of all,—-because, *there* you are sure to be represented in some of your most ridiculous attitudes.[37]

Portraits that paint the character in shadowy silhouette ("*against the light*") or in blinding illumination ("in the *Camera*") are perhaps less invasive than those that rely on "*Momus*'s glass," for they represent merely the physical features of the subject in black and white. Yet they are no more desirable: like satire, they show the subject in "some of your most ridiculous attitudes" and can be as "dishonest" as they are "hard upon the man who sits." Sterne refuses the satirical means of "taking a man's character" as readily as he has refused the novelistic.

In his pairing of a portrait drawn "in the *Camera*" with that arranged "*against the light*," however, Sterne recalls another celebrity who refused to submit his life either to the "flatly white-washed" panegyric or to the darkly "besmear'd" condemnation under which so many of his colleagues' memories suffered.[38] The resemblance with Cibber here is telling. For in the very next sentence Sterne introduces the method of characterization he will employ—one that, he promises, will avoid both the satirical and the novelistic and that will present his personae spectacularly but without revealing too much. "To avoid all and every one of these errors, in giving you my uncle *Toby*'s character," he writes, "I am determin'd to draw it by no mechanical help whatever; . . . in a word, I will draw my uncle *Toby*'s character from his HOBBY-HORSE."[39]

Just as Cibber defends himself by means of the *Chiaro Oscuro* that obscures by seeming to clarify his character, so Sterne "lye[s] open[ly]"[40] through the figure of the "HOBBY-HORSE"—his word for a particular preoccupation that manifests itself as a myopic obsession in the conversations of Sterne's most memorable characters. Tristram's uncle Toby, a war veteran who interprets every word pronounced in his presence as a reference to military strategy, is only one example: Tristram's hobbyhorse might be his nose or his name, and Yorick's the (literal) horse he rides until its death from exhaustion. The hobbyhorse is, in other words, an obsession so excessive that it colors all the other traits or preoccupations that make up a character, reducing a complexly psychologized individual to a single feature. In doing so, the hobbyhorse turns a novelistic character into a satirical one and a complex individual into a flattened-out portrait reducible to a single thought or activity.

Crucially, however, the author who draws his characters from their hobbyhorses achieves this flattened-out portrait not (as the author of a satire might, according to scholarly taxonomies of those genres) through the exaggeration of an exterior trait. Rather, he produces this portrait through the exaggeration of his character's interior thought process, a Lockean association of ideas that originates in the inner recesses of the character's mind. The hobbyhorsical portrait arrives at the external by way of the apparently internal; it juxtaposes interiority and exteriority as Cibber's *Chiaro Oscuro* juxtaposes black and white. "My Lord, if you examine it over again, it is far from being a gross piece of daubing," Sterne writes, defending himself against charges that his characterizations are overly simplistic, in the dedication that directly precedes Yorick's tale; "the dark strokes in the HOBBY-HORSE, (which is a secondary figure, and a kind of back-ground to the whole) give great force to the principal lights in your own figure, and make it come off wonderfully."[41] Arriving at the external by way of the internal, exaggerating a psychologized self into a superficial one: these are, of course, the tools of Cibber's own strategy of overexpression, which Sterne's comparison between "dark strokes" and "principal lights" seems to call up.

To ask whether Sterne's characters owe more to satire or to the novel, then, is to pose the wrong question. In revealing so much about their inner lives that they reveal nothing at all, Sterne's hobbyhorsical characters betray a debt to the celebrity autobiographies that translated the larger-than-life stars of England's stages into the form of a novel and that used counterintuitive strategies to protect those stars from the penetrating gaze that the novel's form invited. It is thus telling that, just as Cibber's *Apology* drew complaints both for revealing too much and for revealing too little, *Tristram Shandy*'s critics remark nearly as often on its incompleteness as on its excesses. Jonathan Lamb describes Sterne's allusiveness, for instance, as "a tactical and tough-minded experiment with privation, breach, shortage and emptiness"; and Wayne Booth begins his influential essay by posing the question, "Did Sterne complete *Tristram Shandy*?"[42]

It was this incompleteness—and not Sterne's "voice of self-exposure"—

that constituted the most obvious link between *Tristram Shandy* and the celebrity autobiography for Sterne's contemporaries. Eighteenth-century readers were quick to note the features the narrative shared with works like Cibber's *Apology*, and they poked fun at these features in works like a 1765 parody of an actress's memoir, titillatingly entitled *Miss C——Y's Cabinet of Curiosities; or, the Green-Room Broke Open* and purportedly written "By Tristram Shandy." The story grinds to a halt when a reader suddenly breaks into the narrative to protest its dearth of promised revelations. "The *Genuine and Authentic Memoirs* of Miss C——Y were . . . Husks and Nutshells, of no Value or Consequence," the reader exclaims. "On looking it over very attentively, the Devil a Word did I see the Amours of any eminent Personage whatsoever—no theatrical Anecdotes—and no secret Histories."[43]

Rereading the early volumes of *Tristram Shandy* as Sterne's imitation and innovation of Cibber's overexpressive strategies allows us to reconcile New's description of Sterne's voice as "a voice of self-exposure" with these other views of it as mere "Husks and Nutshells." These seemingly paradoxical readings are the result, in other words, of strategies that Sterne adapts from Cibber and that allow Sterne to market himself while protecting himself from the barbs that his many critics let fly.

In later volumes of *Tristram Shandy* the overexpressive features that Sterne introduced in his explanation of the hobbyhorse continue to proliferate. At the same time, Sterne's own experience of fame (and of notoriety) as pronounced as Cibber's called for a more sophisticated—and a more individual—method of concealing while appearing to reveal his private life to his ever more vociferous critics. Instead of merely reproducing Cibber's strategies on the printed page, Sterne began to experiment with the intersections between the materiality of the printed page and the assumed immateriality of the words printed on its surface, as well as with the ways that his caperings around and outside of his text might affect the ways his readers interpreted the characters within it. Sterne exhibits these experiments most clearly in Yorick's triumphant return in Volume IV of *Tristram Shandy*, which I explore in the next section.

"IF THE TYPE IS A VERY SMALL ONE": PRINT, PERFORMANCE, AND THE MARBLED PAGE

Volumes I and II of *Tristram Shandy* hit the booksellers' shelves late in 1759, and by the time Sterne arrived in London his quirky character was quickly becoming a household name. Like the local fame he had earned from his preaching and pamphlets in York, however, the attention Sterne garnered from his bawdy books wasn't all fawning. The disapproval of common Londoners and scribbling critics seemed not to bother him ("I wish they would write a hundred such," he admitted to Stephen Croft in 1760, after discovering "a shilling pamphlet wrote against Tristram").[44] He seemed somewhat more chagrined at the offense his book had caused among London's literary elite. After the *Royal Female Magazine* reported that Sterne would parody the powerful bishop and literary patron William Warburton by casting him as Tristram's pedantic tutor in forthcoming volumes, Sterne wrote a series of solicitous letters to the bishop, complaining bitterly of such apparent misrepresentations. "These strokes in the Dark, with the many Kicks, Cuffs, and Bastinados I openly get on all sides of me, are beginning to make me sick of this foolish humour of mine of sallying forth into this wide & wicked world," he lamented in the spring of 1760.[45]

Sterne's complaints reveal that not even he, despite a savviness about celebrity culture that his allusions to Cibber demonstrate, was immune to the barbs and "Bastinados" of even savvier critics—and that his hobbyhorsical methods of characterization, despite their effectiveness against the common hacks, weren't exactly foolproof. Fortunately, he had a few other tricks up his sleeve. When he published the third and fourth volumes of Tristram's *Life and Opinions* a year later, Sterne abandoned his apparent plans to mock Warburton and inserted a seeming repudiation of the strategies of autobiographical excess that he had, at one time, endorsed. Cleverly couched in this repudiation is an even more elaborate example of the overexpressive strategy that protects the author's identity by seeming to bare all. Yet as his characters and his narrative developed, so too did Sterne's manipulations of such strategies. And in later volumes of *Tristram Shandy*, Sterne experiments more and more with how the strategies that Cibber introduced in performance might work within the confines of the printed page.

As chapters 1 and 2 suggested, overexpression had never been entirely limited to performance, and part of what made Cibber's strategy so successful was his ability to translate the superfluous clothes of his fops into the misspelled words and malapropisms of his *Apology* and other writings. He did so, as previous chapters have noted, by breaking the rules of spelling and of grammar and thus lending his pages the same eccentricity and illegibility of his uncategorizable performances. Sterne's innovation was to achieve the same eccentricity and the same illegibility using words that might be found in any dictionary and constructions that would pass the most stringent grammarian's muster. In doing so, he gave the lie to his contemporaries' assurances—reproduced in current narratives of the rise of the printed novel and its stable subjects—that the self described in printed words was somehow more stable and more legible than the persona exhibited in performance.

Leading these assurances that Sterne would work against was Samuel Johnson, whose comprehensive *Dictionary of the English Language* (1755) appeared only four years before Volumes I and II of *Tristram Shandy*. In his preface to the *Dictionary*, Johnson expressed his desire to reign in a language "too long neglected: suffered to spread, under the direction of chance, into wild exuberance, resigned to the tyranny of time and fashion, and exposed to the corruptions of ignorance, and caprices of innovation."[46] The *Dictionary* promises this stability in language by dictating the proper spelling and usage of words and cementing these words on the printed page. Johnson assures his readers that the standardization promoted by the *Dictionary* will protect the English language from decay in two senses. First, by promoting the publication of books that look more or less the same, standard spellings will encourage the reader to look past the materiality of the book to read between its lines and understand its ideas. "Language is but the instrument of science, and words are but the signs of ideas," Johnson argues; "I wish . . . that the instrument might be less apt to decay, and that signs might be permanent, like the things which they denote."[47] To regard words as things rather than as signs, according to Johnson, is to give in to the "decay" and impermanence that should infect only the embodied arts (like performance). Second, by providing an authoritative source against which the whims of individual speakers and authors might be measured and contained, the standardization promoted by the *Dictionary* will encourage the reader to forget the materiality of the body that created the book. The detachment of the printed book from the body of its author and of the printed word from the bodies and voices (as well as the dialects and idiosyncrasies) of its users guarantees its stability and its universality across time and space.

Of course, the *Dictionary* fails in both of its tasks of stabilizing and of universalizing language. Before his preface has concluded, Johnson admits the impossibility of "embalming" a living language; and before his own body was cold Johnson's friend James Boswell had written a biography of the lexicographer that elucidated the individual behind the *Dictionary*'s composition and aimed at "*Johnsonizing* the land" by encouraging all Britons to speak and write like him.[48] Nonetheless, the promise of a language immune to the eccentricities of its individual speakers lived on—except, that is, in the printed pages of *Tristram Shandy*. As his defenses against his critics mounted, Sterne adapted the principles of overexpression to fit the requirements of an increasingly standardized and apparently disembodied printed page. In emphasizing the inseparability of this page from the bodies (including his own body) that performed around and because of it, Sterne emphasizes also the precariousness of the printed page's legibility. Tellingly, he introduces this precariousness as he sheds new light on the persecutions that led to Yorick's death in Volume I—persecutions precipitated, Sterne now reveals, by a powerful ecclesiastical authority with an uncanny resemblance to William Warburton.

Yorick is conspicuously absent from Volume II of *Tristram Shandy* (when the other characters deliver his sermon in his stead) and largely absent, too, from Volume III. He reappears in Volume IV to accompany Walter Shandy and uncle Toby to the visitation dinner, where they will appeal to the ecclesiastical authorities to nullify Tristram's botched christening. The scene opens (somewhat abruptly, for Tristram has deleted the chapter preceding it) on Yorick's complaints about the "unspeakable torments" he has suffered "in bringing forth" an unidentified sermon.[49] These complaints echo Sterne's description of the "Kicks, Cuffs, and Bastinados" to which his fame has subjected him and once again suggest Yorick as a stand-in for Sterne—and his attempts to evade his critics as a metaphor for his author's.[50] "I was delivered of it at the wrong end of me," Yorick says of the sermon he has brought forth. Lest we misconstrue which "wrong end" he means, he quickly clarifies: "It came from my head instead of my heart . . .—To preach, to shew the extent of our reading, or the subtleties of our wit . . .—is a dishonest use of the poor single half hour in a week which is put into our hands—'Tis not preaching the gospel—but ourselves—For my own part, continued *Yorick*, I had rather direct five words point blank to the heart."[51] As in Volume I, here too the similarities between Yorick and his author are unmistakable, for reverberating throughout this description of Yorick's sermon are the same objections that Sterne's early critics had lodged against the first two volumes of *Tristram Shandy* as a book whose "subtleties of wit" often got in the way of its judgment or decency: "It were to be wished," wrote a reviewer for the *Royal Female Magazine* (in the same 1760 article that exposed Sterne's intentions toward Warburton), "that the wantonness of the author's wit had been tempered with a little more regard to delicacy, throughout the greatest part of the work."[52]

Such echoes—and Sterne's refusal to identify the sermon to which Yorick refers—might tempt us to interpret Yorick's diatribe against "preach[ing] . . . ourselves" as Sterne's own mea culpa for the indiscretions of his first two volumes.[53] From now on, Sterne implies, he and his characters will adhere faithfully to their intended genre: Yorick to "preaching the gospel" and Sterne to a novel unhindered by the extratextual echoes of his physical body or of a biography now well plumbed by his critics and admirers.

The very fact that Sterne evokes his own critics in a description of his character should tip us off to the disingenuousness of such promises—as should the reappearance, only a few pages later, of a vaccine against self-exposure that looks much like the autobiographical performances we've seen before. For Yorick's promises to preach the gospel are curtailed by the blood-curdling curses of Phutatorius, one of the assembled authorities. It turns out that Phutatorius's ill-timed exclamation expresses less frustration at Yorick's line of argument than alarm at the red-hot chestnut that has just tumbled from the table to fall, unfortunately, into Phutatorius's breeches.[54] He is quick to blame his accident on Yorick's malfeasance (a mistake that motivates his persecution of Yorick in Volume I). Sterne reveals, however, that the true cause lies with Phutatorius's own failure to fasten his fly.[55]

Or, perhaps, the true cause lies not in Phutatorius's exposure of himself through the undoing of his pants, but rather in the exposure of himself through the licentiousness of his prose. Some might argue, Sterne explains, "that the chestnut's taking that particular course, and in a manner of its own accord—and then falling with all its heat into that one particular place, and no other—was a real judgment upon *Phutatorius*, for that filthy and obscene treatise *de Concubinis retinendis*, which *Phutatorius* had published about twenty years ago—and was that identical week going to give the world a second edition of."[56] Like Yorick and like Sterne himself, it seems, Phutatorius, too, suffers from an impulse "of scattering his wit and his humour,—his gibes and his jests about him"—and of offending his graver and more guarded colleagues in the process. The alliance between Yorick and Phutatorius might seem odd, given Phutatorius's future role as Yorick's most vociferous critic. However, it echoes a similar effort, in the letters Sterne wrote to and about Warburton, to appeal to the bishop's empathy as a fellow celebrity rather than addressing him as an opponent.[57]

Phutatorius's self-exposure differs from Yorick's in one crucial aspect, however: while Sterne does not specify whether Yorick's offending "gibes and jests" are performed or printed, he is explicit in defining Phutatorius's offenses as emanating both from his body and from the apparently disembodied page. In making ambiguous whether it is the exposure of the bishop's person or the bawdiness of his book that has spawned Phutatorius's controversy, Sterne repeats a joke that recurs throughout *Tristram Shandy* and that links pen and penis, refiguring the published text as the author's ill-advised attempt to expose his private parts with his private life to his public. The links between Phutatorius's exposed body and his published works also hint at the limitations of Johnson's description of print as disembodied and universal. Not surprisingly, then, the cure to Phutatorius's exposures very much resembles the solution to Yorick's persecutions—except that, like the exposures it addresses, this cure works through (and emphasizes the links between) the material body and the printed page. This cure conceals Phutatorius's vulnerabilities by seeming to expose them further; and, though it seems to plumb the depths of his interiority, it is most effective when applied topically.

Appropriately, it is Yorick and his friend Eugenius (whom we have already encountered as Yorick's ally against the critics in Volume I) who recommend to Phutatorius a solution that, like Cibber's, works through the proliferation rather than the elimination of words. Eugenius begins: "If you will send to the next printer, and trust your cure to such a simple thing as a soft sheet of paper just come off the press—you need do nothing more than twist it round—The damp paper, quoth *Yorick* (who sat next to his friend *Eugenius*) though I know it has a refreshing coolness in it—yet I presume is no more than the vehicle—and that the oil and lamp-black with which the paper is so strongly impregnated, does the business."[58] As Yorick and Eugenius see it, the best antidote for the author whose immodesty has exposed him to his society's censure (or to the odd hot chestnut) is more immodesty; the best protection against unwanted intrusions into one's private life or one's private parts is to send more pages to the printing press.

Yet in Sterne's description of Phutatorius's cure we discover a challenge not only to the critics who attempt to dissect a public figure by dissecting his printed pages, but also to any reader who, like Johnson, looks to the disembodiment of the printed page as guaranteeing the stability or the legibility of its meanings. Crucially, the "sanative particles" that soothe Phutatorius lie not in the ideas that the words on the page convey but in the ink that dots its surface and "impregnates" its paper. In drawing attention to the printed page as ink and paper, Sterne rejects Johnson's description of words as signs and as the printed page as immaterial so that the printed page seems as material—and thus as subject to decay, impermanence, and misinterpretation—as an ephemeral performance. And as he does, he hints at the difficulties of interpreting any word on a printed page as if its meaning is stable and universal—and any character elucidated by such printed words as knowable or known.

Such a character is Phutatorius, whose autobiography Sterne never reproduces and thus whose life story we know merely as a series of "sanative particles" pressed against his penis rather than as a narrative that explains his self. Such a character, too, is Yorick himself, a man whose name has been printed the same for generations but whose name's meaning seems nonetheless subject to decay, as Sterne has already indicated in Volume I. "Yorick was this parson's name," he explains,

> and, what is very remarkable in it, (as appears from a most antient account of the family, wrote upon strong vellum, and now in perfect preservation) it had been exactly so spelt, . . . without the least variation or transposition of a single letter, for I do not know how long; which is more than I would venture to say of one half of the best surnames in the kingdom; which, in a course of years, have generally undergone as many chops and changes as their owners. . . . But a villainous affair it is, and will one day so blend and confound us all together, that no one shall be able to stand up and swear, "That his own great grand father was the man who did either this or that."[59]

By declaring his own character's name "so exactly spelt, . . . without the least variation or transposition of a single letter," Sterne seems to distinguish himself from the misspellings and misinterpretations that Cibber and Charke embraced and that Johnson's *Dictionary* worked hard to prevent. The meanings of Cibber's misspelled words might deform his printed pages with the resonances of his particular performances of self. But by copying the word *Yorick* directly from Shakespeare's text to his own, Sterne seems to imply, the meanings of both his alphabetic characters and his fictional characters are available and interpretable to anyone in possession of Johnson's *Dictionary* (or at least of Shakespeare's printed plays).

There are, however, several problems with interpreting the stable spelling of Yorick's name, passed down "without the least variation or transposition of a single letter," as affirming the stable meaning of the printed word. For one thing, Sterne refuses Johnson's suggestion that the printed word is necessarily less embodied or less material than the performing body when he mentions Yorick's name as preserved "upon strong vellum"—a kind of paper made from calf's skin and thus, Sterne implies, a material body in and of itself.

And as a material object made from bodies, the written word that names poor Yorick is as impossible to "embalm" or arrest as a live performance. Despite his apparent relation to his Shakespearean namesake, Yorick, "by what I can remember of him, and by all the accounts I could ever get of him," Sterne writes, "seem'd not to have had one single drop of *Danish* blood in his whole crasis; in nine hundred years, it might possibly have all run out:——I will not philosophize one moment with you about it; for happen how it would, the fact was this:—That instead of that cold phlegm and exact regularity of sense and humours, you would have look'd for, in one so extracted;—-he was, on the contrary, as mercurial and sublimated a composition,——as heteroclite a creature in all his declensions;——-with as much life and whim, and *gaité de coeur* about him, as the kindliest climate could have engendered and put together."[60] Yorick's name may have survived "exactly spelt" and "in perfect preservation" for nine hundred years between Shakespeare's character and Sterne's, but its meaning has changed, as has the kind of character it elucidates. Against Johnson's ideal of a printed language that remains disembodied and "embalmed"—and against critics who claim to be able to "read" a person by translating the language used to name him—Sterne presents a Yorick as unreadable, untraceable, and uninterpretable as the black page that memorializes him.

If Yorick's character is unreadable despite the standardized spelling of his name, even more unreadable is the book that contains him (not to mention the celebrity author known to wear that name as his own). *Tristram Shandy* abounds, after all, with printed words that can be found "without the least variation or transposition of a single letter" within the pages of Johnson's *Dictionary* but that have taken on meanings that Johnson could never have foretold (and might never have permitted). Scholars have long remarked upon the bawdy connotations and nonstandard definitions that Sterne's new contexts and superfluous explanations lend to standard words—or even to entire passages, like the defense of peace that Sterne plagiarizes and reinstates as Toby's apologetical oration defending war.[61] I do not wish to reiterate these arguments here. Instead, I mean to emphasize the ways in which Sterne's language follows Johnson's standardized spellings only to resist Johnson's standardized meanings and the implications that this resistance has for our assumptions about the printed word as necessarily stable or legible.

Cibber emphasizes his sole ownership of the language of his texts and the meaning of his identity by misspelling words or misusing grammar, transforming the common "horse" into the Cibberian "Harse." Sterne achieves a similar effect by imbuing ordinary words with extraordinary implications. In doing so, he challenges not only the assumptions of legibility and stability by which we might interpret his book and the characters (including his own) that that book promises to reveal. He challenges also the guarantees made by Johnson's *Dictionary* that the meanings of a printed word remain stable and legible no matter in which book they appear. Sterne's experiments with the conventions of the printed word destabilize not only the characters within *Tristram Shandy* but also the characters within any printed book utilizing its words.

Instead of deriving the meanings of these words from the standardized spellings or universal meanings imposed by a growing numbers of dictionaries like Johnson's, readers of Sterne's narrative must depend instead on meanings particular to Sterne himself. These readers must, in other words, judge the words within Sterne's narrative based on the byline on its cover—and on their knowledge of the elaborate performances of self with which that byline came increasingly to be associated. I want to turn now from how Sterne dismantled the stability of the printed page by emphasizing the body of his book to how Sterne dismantled the stability of the printed page by linking it to the body of that book's author. Scholars have long been aware of Sterne's efforts to promote his book by encouraging readers to associate him with its main characters. Thomas Keymer perhaps goes furthest in his description of Sterne's self-posturings as performance art. Despite such suggestions, however—and despite a growing interest in recent years in Sterne's caperings around his text—most critics have followed Keymer's lead in keeping their discussions of those caperings largely distinct from their analysis of the texts themselves. Instead they honor Johnson's suggestion of the printed book as disembodied, depersonalized, and disconnected from the public persona of its author and insist, with Frank Donoghue, that such performances "bear only a tangential relationship to the conventional concerns of Sterne criticism."[62]

Yet throughout *Tristram Shandy* and his other works, Sterne plays with the ways that the meanings of his words change as his own reputation develops. Relevant are not only the bawdy implications that words like "nose" or "clock" take on when reprinted in a book known to be Sterne's or the way that a sentence like "I wrote not to be *fed*, but to be *famous*" transforms from true confession to superficial description as soon as we recognize its author. Relevant, too, is Sterne's insistence on autographing the title pages of later volumes—a move that transforms his printed books from works of art in an age of mechanical reproduction to artifacts that bear the aura of their author's physical presence. And relevant, once again, is the name of Parson Yorick, which angered many of Sterne's readers when it appeared in place of his own byline on the collection of his sermons but which resurfaces again in the "Versailles" chapter of *A Sentimental Journey* (1768). When, in that chapter, Yorick introduces himself to the Count de B——, the count cannot distinguish between the parson who stands before him and the dead jester in the Shakespearean play he's just been reading—a play that now belongs, in a sense, to Laurence Sterne.[63] Just as no decent young lady could wind a clock in eighteenth-century England without blushing, so no well-read eighteenth-century citizen could return to Shakespeare's text without being haunted by Sterne's ghost.

These examples suggest that Sterne's manipulation of his public identity is crucial to "the conventional concerns of Sterne criticism" and to the ways that we interpret his works. So much is clear when we consider the remarks of Sterne's contemporaries, who dismissed the notion that Sterne's biography was irrelevant to his text. It was not that their critical assumptions encouraged them to judge a book by its byline, as one reviewer asserts, but that Sterne's celebrity status made him a special case. "It is true, that in some degree, it is our duty, as Reviewers, to examine books, abstracted from any regard to their Author," acknowledges a writer for the *Monthly Review*, condemning Volumes III and IV in 1761. "But this rule is not without exception: for where a Writer is publicly known, by his own acknowledgment, it then becomes a part of our duty to animadvert on any flagrant impropriety of character."[64] Though the professional critic should regard a text impartially and without the distraction of its author's biography, the *Monthly Review*er implies, a celebrity author demands special consideration. His public persona, already so widely known, can hardly be ignored—and as Sterne dances with and around the characters he creates in his fiction, he demands that his readers and critics take note. The *Monthly Review*er's apology and Sterne's frequent cameos within his novel thus force us to rethink what might constitute criticism's "conventional concerns." Sterne's appearances in London and "throughout the land" were not just a clever marketing technique but were integral to how eighteenth-century readers interpreted Sterne's text.

Or, perhaps more accurately, they were integral to how eighteenth-century critics recognized their inability to interpret Sterne's text, the characters it elucidated, and the celebrity author whose persona it refused entirely to reveal. For it was not only the author of *Miss C——Y* who noted the frustrating inaccessibility of Sterne's texts. "The Spectator somewhere observes, that an author may print a joke but he cannot print a face, which is often the best part of a joke," wrote a contributor to the *Critical Review*, criticizing *Tristram Shandy*'s seventh and eighth volumes, in 1765. "The principal part of the work before us is its manner, which is either above or below criticism; for if it is level with it, it becomes a kind of an impassive object, upon which the artillery of criticism must be discharged in vain."[65] By transforming his text into a mere accompaniment to his "manner" and his novel into an elaborate self-promotion—a self-promotion incomplete without his presence but necessarily haunted by his absence—Sterne disables the "artillery of criticism" and protects himself from the analysis and condemnation to which a celebrity author might otherwise be subject.

Tristram Shandy and Sterne's other works thus answer the same question that Cibber's overexpressions in the *Apology* sought to address: that is, how to meet the spectators' demands "to be let into the whole secret from first to last, of everything which concerns" the celebrity without giving these same spectators too much fodder to feed their "artillery of criticism."[66] And though Sterne's efforts begin with a strategy that very much resembles Cibber's overexpression (and often alludes directly to it), his defense against his critics takes a few twists and turns away from Cibber's in its journey from the fop's wig to the printed word and from the stage to the page. These twists and turns include an emphasis on the materiality of the printed page that defies Samuel Johnson's claims for its stability. They include, too, copious references to the author's body that defy Johnson's claims for the printed page's universality. And they include, most pointedly, an insistence that the meanings of the printed words inside a book depend on the performances enacted outside, around, and because of that book—that, in other words, it is impossible to divine a celebrity author's private self as apart from or somehow truer than his public reputation since we cannot help but judge a book by its cover.

The materiality of the printed page and its inseparability from the materiality of the author's performances come together in the marbled page of Volume III, which Sterne describes (facetiously?) as "the motly emblem of my work."[67] Sterne links the page explicitly to its black and white companions—and to the illegibility that they denote—when he predicts that his reader "will no more be able to penetrate the moral of the next marbled page . . . than the world with all its sagacity has been able to unraval the many opinions, transactions and truths which still lie mystically hid under the dark veil of the black one."[68] (In most early editions of *Tristram Shandy*, the marbled page was not black and white but multicolored; nevertheless, its patterns depended on a *Chiaro Oscuro* contrast between the "dark strokes" of the murkier pigments and the "principal lights" of the brighter ones.)[69]

Many scholars have remarked on the ways that these contrasting colors call attention to the materiality and the conventions of the printed book. Like Sterne's "I wrote not to be *fed*, but to be *famous*," however, the marbled page also underlines the extent to which the secrets we find buried in a book's meaning or which we interpret as clues to the inner lives of its characters depend on the adornments on its surfaces. The marbled stone that the page calls to mind achieves its distinctively contrasting colors through the exposure of overlapping layers: the colors come to light when the stone is cut away to reveal the web of different elements buried within its interior. The effect of the marbling on a printed page, however, is accomplished through the manipulation of surfaces: differently colored pigments are dropped into a tray of water, where their oily substance allows them to float; the paper to be marbled is then placed in the tray and removed after it has absorbed the pigment but before it can sink below the water's surface. Like the methods that Sterne employs to describe both his fictional personae and the authorial persona from which they seem inseparable, the marbled page he celebrates as "motly emblem of my work" seems to offer the reader a cutaway view of a body that, like Yorick's character, "lye[s] open" before him.[70] In actuality, it is yet another potent reminder that the reader is limited to the very surface of Sterne's pages.

Keymer discusses the marbled page as turning Sterne's book "inside out," embedding in its pages and labeling as its central "emblem" the decorated paper that eighteenth-century conventions of bookmaking usually pasted just inside a book's cover.[71] I have argued throughout this chapter that Sterne's celebrity and the references to that celebrity that he scatters slyly throughout his text accomplish a similar feat. They tempt us to read the name on the book's cover as a clue to the meanings of the words the book contains; or, conversely, to read the words within Sterne's fiction as clues to his private life. Leading us through such a labyrinth of confessions and concealments, self-references and self-erasures, Sterne constructs his own, more complex version of his censurers' self-protective cloak of "grave" countenances—a pun that the marbled page's resemblance to a tombstone seems designed precisely to evoke.

According to John Croft, the brother of Sterne's patron and the writer of a short biography of the author published in 1795, Sterne declared he was "mortgaging his brains" to his bookseller when he sold the first volumes of *Tristram Shandy* in 1759.[72] The story is plausible, for Sterne uses similar language in a letter addressed to Catherine Fourmantel in 1760: "There is a fine print going to be done of me," he writes, referring to a painting by Sir Joshua Reynolds intended for the frontispiece of *The Sermons of Mr. Yorick*; "—so I shall make the most of myself, & sell both inside & out."[73] Sterne's language cheekily recalls the language of his female contemporaries, who, as Catherine Gallagher writes, created "fictional nobodies" who could be bought, sold, and circulated within a literary marketplace while their authorial counterparts remained inaccessible and undefiled.[74]

Unlike the "nobodies" that Gallagher discusses, however, Sterne's characters remain inseparable from and incomplete without the body of their author—an author who, as his determination to sell himself "both inside and out" suggests and as his recognizability as a celebrity ensured, was always somehow present within his texts. Rather than deny or divide this presence as Gallagher's women writers do, Sterne exaggerated it. In doing so, he made ever less distinct the line between the fictional nobody and the authorial somebody—or, more accurately, he transformed his authorial somebody into an extratextual everybody (embodying Yorick and his author at once).

There is, of course, a third character whom Sterne habitually embodied and whom his printed pages cleverly expose only to obscure. Tristram Shandy seems to be at the center of Sterne's self-representations, as he is at the center of the narrative that bears his name. Yet as that narrative and those self-representations continue, the story of Tristram and the promised elucidation of his character are continually deferred. In their place we find only blank spaces: the asterisks replacing the words he prefers not to pronounce, the excised details that the critic must complete in his or her own imagination, and, of course, the white page that refuses to print the character of the Widow Wadman and invites the reader, instead, to "paint her to your own mind."[75] These blank spaces, I will argue, constitute yet another strategy by which Sterne will address the invasive inquiries of his readers by transforming his critics into collaborators and his spectators into integral parts of the spectacle they now find difficult to critique.

TRISTRAM'S "INVISIBLE COCK": THE CRITIC AS COLLABORATOR IN TRISTRAM SHANDY'S AUTOBIOGRAPHY

I began this chapter with an analysis of the hobbyhorsical methods of characterization that, I argued, Sterne borrows from Cibber and for which he finds an apt metaphor in the black page—a page whose inky darkness might signify the abundance of printed words that comprise the portrait of poor Yorick. Necessarily paired with such "dark strokes" in the methods of characterization that Sterne employs, however, are the "principal lights," suggesting the white spaces that the reader must fill in with his or her own "figure"—the missing details of the text that must be supplied by extratextual means. These extratextual means include not only the performances of the book's author, as I argued in the previous section, but also the critiques and imitations of *Tristram Shandy* that flooded London periodicals and pamphlets as soon as the book's popularity became apparent. Though scholars have long been aware of these works, few have taken seriously their influence on Sterne's writing of *Tristram Shandy*. I want to suggest in this final section, however, that such works were central to Sterne's construction of later volumes and to the defenses of Sterne's privacy that these volumes would deploy.

For as eager as Sterne's original readers were to read Yorick as a stand-in for his author, they were even more eager to read Tristram himself as a thinly veiled version of Laurence Sterne. It was a confusion that Sterne did little to discourage. Christening his work after the model of contemporary autobiographies and publishing his first two volumes without his name on the title page, Sterne fooled many of his readers into regarding Tristram Shandy as the true author of the work. In the first review of the narrative, published in the *Monthly Review* in 1759, William Kenrick identified the author of *Tristram Shandy* as "the droll Mr. Tristram Shandy" himself and praised his adaptation of the increasingly popular autobiographical form.[76] Later readers realized the mistake but nonetheless played along with Sterne's implication of Tristram as the true author—or, at the very least, assumed that Tristram's adventures consisted of the true-life tales of Laurence Sterne.

Identifying Tristram as a stand-in for Sterne, however, hardly helps to reveal the author's true self: if one trait defines Tristram for the first four volumes, it is his conspicuous absence from the work that bears his name. The first two volumes famously devote so much time to Tristram's family history that Tristram never seems to get around to being born. Even the third and fourth volume fall short—or, more accurately, run long: Tristram finally arrives into the world, but the reader is sequestered from the rooms where his birth and christening are actually taking place and confined to the parlor where Toby, Trim, and Walter idly await his arrival. The copious details that defer the arrival of Sterne's hero bear some resemblance to the overexpressive techniques evident in Sterne's portrayal of Yorick. But in Volume V, Tristram's descriptions of his family history are brought to an abrupt halt when a malfunctioning window comes crashing down on his exposed penis, and our lack of access to Tristram's person gives way to an almost embarrassing overexposure. Not insignificantly, this overexposure facilitates Tristram's entry into autobiography: it is at this moment that he rejects his father's *Tristrapoedia* and determines, as he says, "to wr[i]te the chapter myself."[77]

I want to linger on the moment that Tristram takes over as his own biographer as the moment at which Sterne removes the final barriers between character and narrator, the objective "me" and the subjective "I," the voice of

Tristram Shandy and the voice of Laurence Sterne. By melding Sterne and Shandy, this episode joins the bodies within the text to those outside it and, as it does, portrays the autobiography that Tristram is writing as well as those in which he is written as at once printed and embodied. Yet even as Sterne here continues his insistence on the printed work's materiality, he builds upon this strategy by portraying the body at the center of the performance as an absent one and the characters at the center of the text (alphabetic characters, fictional characters) as necessarily incomplete.

To describe Tristram's autobiographical impulses as constantly deferred within his narrative is not, of course, to imply a dearth of life-writing models within *Tristram Shandy*. If Yorick's hobbyhorse is his missaddled steed, the hobbyhorses of Uncle Toby and Tristram's father Walter are their obsessive attempts at life-writing. Significantly, these attempts map neatly onto the distinctions between the printed self and the performed self that I mentioned in the previous section. Toby's attempt is an autobiography that uses the family's bowling green to stage elaborate simulations of the Battle of Namur, begun so he can demonstrate to anyone confused by his military jargon exactly how he came by the wound in his groin. Frustrated by the inadequacies of mere words (and even of printed maps), Toby elects to reenact his war experience in elaborate and embodied performances.

If these war games suggest Toby's attempts to return to an ephemeral past that can never be exactly recalled, Walter's *Tristrapoedia* represents a text written, much like Johnson's *Dictionary*, to last into and to set rules for the future. The *Tristrapoedia* is Walter Shandy's massive dissertation on how he will raise and educate his only surviving son, and Tristram notes its importance to the man who, he reports, "gave himself up to it with as much devotion as ever my uncle *Toby* had done to his doctrine of projectils."[78] Yet like Johnson's *Dictionary*, which fails to embalm the living language that continues to grow and change without it, Walter's story fails to keep up with Tristram's life. Page by page, the printed biography of the future becomes an outmoded romance about an idealized childhood that Tristram never actually lived.

It is possible to consider these two forms of biography in terms of Sterne's earlier description (and dismissal) of biographies written either "in the *Camera*" or "*against the light.*"[79] In other words, the "flatly white-wash'd" pages of Walter's *Tristrapoedia* present their subject not as he is but as he should be, and the "besmear'd" and hobbyhorsical battlefields of Toby's war games enact over and over the fateful accident that deformed their subject into what he must remain.[80] Neither model is particularly empowering for the subject, for

Tristram is no more the author of his life as it is presented in the *Tristrapoedia* than Toby is the author of his, doomed as he is to repeat but never to revise his inevitable and endlessly iterating fate.

Tristram's accident with the window sash, however, halts Walter's composition of the *Tristrapoedia* and dampens the exuberance of Toby's war games. As it does, it transforms Walter's narration of Tristram's future and Toby's narration of his own past into an autobiography of the present that is at once printed and performed, experienced by the same hero who records it. "'Tis my own affair," Tristram declares of the incident. "I'll explain it myself."[81] Sterne's language here is particular. Upon learning of Tristram's accident from his manservant, Walter declares, "I thought as much," and starts for the nursery to examine the damage done to his son. "One would imagine from this," Tristram narrates, "that my father before that time, had actually wrote that remarkable chapter in the *Tristrapoedia*, which to me is the most original and entertaining one in the whole book;—and that is the *chapter on sash-windows*, with a bitter *Phillipick* at the end of it, upon the forgetfulness of chamber-maids.—I have but two reasons for thinking otherwise."[82]

The first reason, Tristram explains, is that if Walter had predicted the accident in his *Tristrapoedia*, he would have taken the precaution of fixing the sash window before it came crashing down on his son's manhood. But this explanation is, Tristram writes, "obviated under the second reason, which I have the honour to offer to the world in support of my opinion, that my father did not write the chapter upon sash-windows and chamber-pots, at the time supposed,—and it is this.——That, in order to render the *Tristrapoedia* complete,—I wrote the chapter myself."[83] The accident that threatens Tristram's manhood, then, also makes him a man, narrating his male anatomy into being at the same time that it is destroyed. This same incident also awakens Tristram's autobiographical voice, allowing him the freedom to "render" his life story "complete" by allowing him to "wr[i]te the chapter myself."

With this episode, Sterne introduces two peculiarities about Tristram's autobiographical performance that become central to his own strategy of protecting his private life and increasingly public body from his critics' dissections. First, the story recasts autobiography as not only a printed but also, crucially, an embodied performance—as both the story of a life and an event within that life. The window that injures Tristram's body and inspires his story malfunctions because Toby and Trim have robbed it of its sash. And Toby and Trim have robbed it of its sash because the sash contains materials that Toby will use in the war games that constitute his own autobiography. In other words, the fact that Toby's autobiography becomes both an event in Tristram's life and a mark upon his body suggests that autobiography is an embodied medium, made possible by its subject's presence and occupying time in his life. As he has suggested throughout his idiosyncratic text, Sterne here depicts autobiography not only as a life story recorded on a printed page but also as a performance staged in real time, an event in and of itself.

Sterne's suggestion of Tristram's autobiography as an embodied medium leads to the second peculiarity of this episode within *Tristram Shandy*. Despite—or indeed because of—its overexposure, the body at the center of the text is not and cannot be fully reproduced. It is perhaps useful here to think back to Sterne's declaration, "I wrote not [to] be *fed*, but to be *famous*"—and to ensure we are thinking of it, Sterne repeats it just before his narration of the window sash episode.[84] "'Tis worth explaining to the world," Sterne writes of his digression about the *Tristrapoedia*'s composition, "was it only for the encouragement of those few in it, who write not so much to be fed—as to be famous."[85] This statement, as we've already seen, emphasizes the extent to which Sterne's meaning depends on our familiarity with the appearance of his body. At the same time, it reminds us of that body's inaccessibility, its irreproducibility on the printed page. In this statement Sterne defines his own body according to its lack of materiality—its lack of "feeding" and thus its lack of the very things that make it a body. Similarly, Tristram defines his entrance into sexual maturity as the loss of (or at the very least significant damage to) the very organ that makes him sexual. Populating his narrative with characters defined by their absences or inadequacies, Sterne exposes Tristram's distinguishing traits as the very traits to which his spectators lack access.

Tristram's supposed initiation not only as the narrator of but also as a character within his tale contains many more gaps beside the one in Tristram's breeches, and these gaps highlight the frustrating inaccessibility of the body most crucial to defining Tristram's character—that is, the body of Laurence Sterne. Not only Sterne's emaciated body and Tristram's sexual maturity but every object at the center of Tristram's story lacks the very things that make it what it is. "'Twas nothing," Tristram explains of his accident with the window sash. "The chamber-maid had left no ******* *** under the bed:——Cannot you contrive, master, quoth *Susannah*, lifting up the sash with one hand, as she spoke, and helping me up into the window seat with the other,—cannot you manage, my dear, for a single time to **** *** ** *** ******? I was five years old.——*Susannah* did not consider that nothing was well hung in our family,——so slap came the sash down like lightening upon us;—Nothing is left,—cried *Susannah*,—nothing is left—for me, but to run my country.——"[86] As Sterne's editors have long recognized, the number of asterisks in the first and second blank spaces correspond to the number of letters in the words that might fill those blanks: "chamber pot" or "pissing pot" (in the first set of asterisks) and "piss out of the window" (in the second). By excising these words from his text and replacing them with asterisks, Sterne tricks the reader into supplying the missing letters and thus places any blame for the text's vulgarity squarely on the reader's shoulders.

But the asterisks are only the most obvious blanks in the episode, and other holes in the narrative only increase the reader's complicity in its creation. Tristram's injury occurs, after all, as the result of a chambermaid's conspicuous absence from his chamber. He responds by promising a "chapter upon sash-windows and chamber-pots" that will (we presume) describe a sash window defined by its lack of a sash, a chamber pot worth mentioning only because it is missing from its chamber. Not to mention that the very "chapter upon sash-windows and chamber-pots"—the chapter in which the *Tristrapoedia* transforms from Walter's biography of the future to Tristram's story about his life, the chapter that Tristram claims as "the most original and entertaining one in the whole book"—is not included in the text we have. Like the Shandys' sash window, like Tristram's masculinity, like Sterne's ill-fed body, Tristram's autobiography disappears at the very moment it is articulated. Or, to be more precise, its articulation is inextricably intertwined with its disappearance—for the autobiography, the sash window, the bodies within and attached to the text all become a part of the story only when and because their standard definitions fail.

Into the vacuum created by these failures flood the observations, assumptions and commentaries of Sterne's critics, dissectors, and casual readers, whose new role as collaborators precludes their objectivity as spectators. Sterne's direct evocation of and collaboration with his readers is evident throughout *Tristram Shandy* but becomes explicit, significantly, at the very moment that his own voice both appears in and immediately disappears from the story Sterne relates. Among the much-talked-about but ultimately inaccessible aspects of Tristram's story is the scream he emits at the moment of his accident with the sash window. We might characterize this scream as Tristram's first truly autobiographical utterance, the first time that the text refers to a noise that Tristram the character has made to describe his experience. In the narrative Tristram offers us, however, the scream itself is conspicuously absent. For in place of his own description of his scream Tristram gives us the interpretation of that scream by his spectators:

> Fifty thousand pannier loads of devils . . . could not have made so diabolical a scream of it, as I did—when the accident befell me: it summoned up my

> mother instantly into the nursery,—so that *Susannah* had but just time to make her escape down the back stairs, as my mother came up the fore.
>
> Now, though I was old enough to have told the story myself,—and young enough, I hope, to have done it without malignity; yet *Susannah*, in passing by the kitchen, for fear of accidents, had left it in short-hand with the cook—the cook had told it with a commentary to *Jonathan*, and *Jonathan* to *Obadiah*; so that by the time my father had rung the bell half a dozen times, to know what was the matter above,—was *Obadiah* enabled to give him a particular account of it, just as it had happened.[87]

Eccentrically though not uncharacteristically, the sound of Tristram's scream is defined by what it is not rather than by what it is. Much as he describes so many aspects of his story, Tristram describes his first autobiographical utterance through its negative: it is a noise that "fifty thousand pannier loads of devils" could *not* have made. With this oblique narration, Tristram redirects our gaze from the sound that he produces in this moment of his autobiographical awakening to the sounds that his spectators produce in reporting this sound. In this way, he deflects the critical gaze from his own autobiographical performances onto the performances of his critics themselves.

Indeed, despite Tristram's declaration, "I was old enough to have told the story myself," the story takes an amazingly circuitous route from Tristram to his reader. The sound of Tristram's voice reaches us only through the mediation of his spectators' voices: Susannah, as Sterne tells us, translates Tristram's scream into her own shorthand in order to relate it to the cook, who adds her "commentary" before passing it on to the servant Jonathan, who tells it to Obadiah, no doubt adding some embellishment of his own. By the time that it reaches Walter the account is so "particular" that it casts some doubt on whether it relates Tristram's accident "just as it happened." Instead of following Tristram's experience of the accident and the scene that builds around him, the reader follows the story itself as it is translated and embellished, through the twisting corridors of Shandy Hall and the interpretations of servants like Susannah, who has already once proven herself a "leaky vessel."[88] Each time the story is told, we get further and further from the body to whom the injury happens and the voice of the character supposedly being defined. As the story passes from one interlocutor to the next, Tristram sidles out of the spotlight and refocuses the reader's attention instead on his spectators. The more Tristram is spoken of, the further we get from knowing who he is. In this way, he—and the author who impersonates him—remains determinedly private even at the center of the public gaze.

Our journey away from Tristram and his author does not conclude with the story that Walter receives from Obadiah. Further contributing to the dubiousness of the story that Walter hears as a story that will reveal Tristram—and to the dubiousness of the story that Tristram tells as a story that will reveal Sterne—is the fact that the scream not heard 'round the world seems to originate not with Tristram, or with Sterne, but with one of Sterne's most notorious imitators. *The Life and Opinions of Jeremiah Kunastrokius* was published shortly after the unprecedented success of Volumes I and II of *Tristram Shandy*, in 1760; and it purported to present the full autobiography of a character Sterne had mentioned only in passing. Its appropriations of Volumes I and II include a discussion of the spelling of Kunastrokius's name that resembles Sterne's discussion of Yorick's name while capitalizing on the bawdy connotations of "Kunastrokius." More significantly, however, *The Life and Opinions of Jeremiah Kunastrokius* shares important similarities with Sterne's tale of Tristram's accident—despite the fact that this tale doesn't occur until Volume V of *Tristram Shandy*, published five years after *Kunastrokius* appeared.

The only scholar to have examined such imitations at length, Rene Bosch, has argued that Sterne responded to his imitators by rejecting their suggestions for the continuation of his story. But this chronology suggests that, much as Tristram diverts attention from his inaudible scream by reporting on its reporters, so Sterne manages criticisms of *Tristram Shandy* by parodying his parodists. These clever imitations of his imitators in this episode and throughout *Tristram Shandy* complicate, once again, the relationship between cruel critic and helpless author as well as between unseen spectator and spectacular celebrity. By recasting his critics as collaborators and incorporating their critiques into his narrative, Sterne frustrates attempts to dissect and to appropriate the character of Sterne as well as the character of Tristram and the printed characters of the narrative that bears his name.

One of the most obvious links between *Jeremiah Kunastrokius* and *Tristram Shandy* is both narratives' interest in the difficulties of translating verbal performances into printed text. In *Jeremiah Kunastrokius*, as in *Tristram Shandy*, these performances take the form of a scream: "Yah! Yah! Yah!" Kunastrokius protests, against his nurse's efforts to restrain him: "'——Why Nurse, what the Pox are you at—you have pinn'd on this Clout so, that it pricks me to the Quick.—There again!—Yah!' There is nothing in the World more difficult to express, than the Articulation of a Scream upon Paper; you must therefore imagine, every one of those *Yah's* to be an exquisite Outcry, and that my Nurse is all this while coaxing me, and fondling me into a good Humour."[89] Sterne's refusal to represent Tristram's scream offers an ironic acknowledgment of the observation that "there is nothing in the World more difficult to express, than the Articulation of a Scream upon Paper." The scream missing from the printed "paper" of Sterne's text evokes a verbal utterance outside of the text, linking the printed page to the embodied performance that it depends upon but cannot possibly "express."

Among the chorus of voices that Sterne describes in place of Tristram's scream, then, are not only the voices of Walter's servants but also the voices of *Tristram Shandy*'s imitators, whose interpretations of Sterne's text he works back into the text itself. The episode suggests a much closer—and a much cleverer—reaction to imitators like "Kunastrokius" than previous scholars have acknowledged. Tristram's character becomes impossible to appropriate not because Sterne's ongoing story rejects all attempts to appropriate him but, rather, because *Tristram Shandy* foregrounds these attempts. By incorporating imitations of *Tristram Shandy* into the narrative itself, Sterne shares his spotlight as celebrity author with the critics who have attempted to dissect him. He also shares his vulnerabilities. After the publication of Volume V of *Tristram Shandy*, anyone who criticized Sterne criticized also Sterne's critics like the author of *Jeremiah Kunastrokius*, upon which the most inflammatory parts of Volume V were based. In imitating these imitators, Sterne refocuses our gaze from what *Tristram* means to what the public has said about what *Tristram* means; and in delving further and further into a close reading of Sterne's narrative, we only find ourselves further and further away. Like his declaration, "I wrote not to be *fed*, but to be *famous*,"[90] Sterne's imitation of his imitators seems to offer up the language that will lead us to his inner self while in fact offering up only the language of his public, a public as clueless as we are about what that inner self contains.

In the midst of the confusions that Sterne creates between original and imitation and between creator and critic, the tools that readers relied upon in order to distinguish a "celebrated author" from a mere hack—and to judge Sterne's work as either brilliant or derivative—become obsolete. As more and more critics and imitators appropriated Sterne's style and as Sterne's style appropriated these appropriations, many learned readers—both in Sterne's day and in our own—admit their inability to distinguish the spurious editions from those that Sterne wrote.[91] The same *Critical Review*er who had praised Volumes I and II of *Tristram Shandy* in 1760 as "a humourous performance, of which we are unable to convey any distinct ideas to our readers" and who had referred those readers instead to "the work itself" had no such qualms about his ability not only to define but also to parody Volumes VII and VIII.[92]

While the parody hardly spares Sterne's personal identity, it makes evident one important accomplishment of overwrought prose and extratextual performances. "Well, says my uncle Toby," the parody begins:

> Corporal, did you see that same cock——Cock, cock, said my father—What cock?—-Here my mother took a large pinch of snuff——Why, the invisible cock, said my uncle Toby—Did you pay for seeing it, said my father? (gaping over the table)——Yes, and please your honour, that I did——and where was he? Said my mother (taking up a stitch in my father's stockings)——Why in a box, and please you, madam (replied the corporal)——And you really saw him, said uncle Toby (taking the pipe out of his mouth, and shaking out the ashes)—Lord bless your honour's soul (said the corporal) how could I see him, did not I tell you he was invisible?–Did the man tell you so before you paid the money, said my father, knitting his brows!——Yes, yes, replied the corporal—Then, Trim, said my father, you was not cheated; for if you paid your money for an invisible thing, how couldst thou see it?[93]

Nearly as diverting as *Tristram Shandy* itself, this parody succeeds by imitating the very strategies of self-presentation (and self-erasure) that Sterne so skillfully employs: like Sterne's frequent repetition of the word "nose," the reviewer's determined repetition of the word "cock" transforms it from the dictionary-approved appellation of a barnyard animal to a bawdy reference to the male anatomy.

Lest we miss the joke—or its application not only to the text but also to its celebrity author—the parodist concludes the episode with a final hint: "We are afraid the purchasers of these two volumes are pretty much in the corporal's situation. The author has pretended, from his commencement of authorship, neither to wit, taste, sense, nor argument,——*Videri vult et est.* His purchasers have bought the sight of his invisible cock."[94] Here the parody seems to commit the critical violation that celebrity autobiography seeks to disable, peeking between the lines—and between the legs—of the author-celebrity to expose the inadequacies buried there. But the parodist fails—and thus Sterne's autobiographical performances succeed—in two important senses. First, the parodist's comparison of Sterne's printed book to a mountebank performance—in particular, a performance in which that makes "invisible" the very objects it promises to reveal—suggests once again the ways in which the text's dependence on extratextual performances defies the stability and legibility that Samuel Johnson and others attributed to the printed page.

Second, the parodist must finally come to the conclusion that, for all the foolishness he might assign to the author of *Tristram Shandy*, the real fools are his readers: those who, like poor Corporal Trim, have "paid [their] money for the sight of an invisible thing." To define a man by what he lacks—or to read a word as what it isn't—is as foolish an enterprise as thinking you've seen something invisible when in fact you've seen nothing at all. Like the author of *Miss C——Y's Cabinet of Curiosities*, this parodist recognizes Sterne's seeming self-exposure as a tale read by an idiot, signifying nothing. And with this recognition comes the dissolution of the systems by which any work of art is valued—as personal property, as intellectual property, and as either good art or bad. If, in other words, Sterne's distinct style allows him to inflate not only his prose but also his prices—to sell nothing for more money than he could sell anything by passing that nothing off as a spectacularly invisible something—by what standards can we value or evaluate his performances? Sterne's strategy may not have protected his identity or his art from being imitated or appropriated. But at the very least it seems to have disrupted the systems through which that identity, that art, is commodified.

We have come a long way from the inky excesses of the black page to the blank canvas of the white, from the death of poor Yorick to the emasculation of Tristram, and from an author who declares himself throughout his narrative to an author who pushes responsibility for that narrative onto his critics. These strategies share, however, a common ancestor in Cibber's overexpressions, whose illegibility they emulate and whose features they imitate, comment upon, or react against. And just as Sterne's white page works to set off his black page, so too the asterisks, holes, and blank spaces that define Tristram's entry into autobiography depend on the excesses and periphrases of Yorick's death in creating their clever *Chiaro Oscuro*.

CONCLUSION: "ALL *BE-TRISTRAM'D*"

Sterne's experiments in applying overexpression to the increasingly standardized printed page challenged celebrations of the printed book's legibility, universality, and stability at the same time that they discovered new ways to preserve and pass down overexpression and its offshoots for future generations. One anonymous pamphleteer, claiming to represent the community of clockmakers whose products Sterne had sullied with his double entendres, complained vociferously of the confusion that accompanied Sterne's idiosyncratic use of the printed word. "Our manners and speech at present," he wrote in his pamphlet of 1760: "are all *be-Tristram'd*. Nobody speaks now but in the *Shandean* style: the modish phraseology is all taken from him, and his equally intelligible imitators. . . . The directions I had for making several clocks for the country are counter-manded; because no modest lady now dares to mention a word about *winding-up a clock*."[95]

The pamphleteer's complaint gets to the heart of the three overlapping methods that, as this chapter has argued, Sterne would use to shield his private self from a growing throng of critics: his incorporation of Cibberian overexpressions into his narrative, his translation and transformation of these overexpressions into printed pages that take on the illegibility of performance, and his reconfiguration of his critics as collaborators on a work they can no longer judge impartially. Against Johnson's strict separation between a language "suffered to spread" on the lips of its idiosyncratic speakers and that preserved (if only partially) in print, the self-proclaimed clockmaker complains that *Tristram Shandy* has infected not only Britons' "speech" but also their "manner." Against James Boswell's later celebration of his mentor as having "Johnsonized the land" and its language, the clockmaker laments that even the standardized words in Sterne's book have taken on a "*Shandean*" meaning that precludes the legibility that their printed medium promises. And as if all that weren't enough, the clockmaker continues, Sterne's unprecedented influence has changed the meanings not only of the words inside his printed book but also the meanings of all printed words, including those of the critics who seem now mere pawns in his increasingly elaborate plot. Cibber's unmistakable drawl might have tricked a few gullible fops or parliamentarians into adopting the *Lingua Cibberiana*, but with the unprecedented success of *Tristram Shandy*'s first two volumes, all of England seemed at risk of being "*be-Tristram'd*."

A good thing, too, that it was. In the years leading up to *Tristram Shandy*'s publication many of the assumptions and traditions that had contributed to overexpression's invention seemed to be fading away. Cibber died at the end of 1757, just as Sterne was beginning the preliminary work that would lead to his popular book. With him died the declamatory acting style that, even toward the end of his career, had come to seem exaggerated and insincere. And though people still read and remembered the *Spectator* essays that had popularized the unseen observer as the symbol of cultural authority for a generation of Englishmen and Englishwomen, the sentimental novel—which Sterne would both praise and parody in his *Sentimental Journey*—was gaining in popularity. Both on the stage and on the page, in other words, the values of objectivity and reason seemed to be giving way to those of sympathy and sincerity, and the sharing of one's self seemed no longer the liability that it had once been. Both championing and embodying these values was David Garrick, the actor who had taken over Cibber's old post as Drury Lane manager in 1747 and who had introduced Sterne to London's celebrity circles in 1759. My turn to Garrick and his successors in the remainder of this book seems to mark an important turn in the story of overexpression and its offshoots that I have been telling until this point. But it also, more significantly, marks a continuation of that story, despite the changes in acting and writing style that sentimentality wrought. By examining overexpression's later iterations in the continuation of this book, I hope to demonstrate both its endurance and its continuing impact on the self-presentation of the modern self.

CHAPTER 4

The Fate of Overexpression in the Age of Sentiment

David Garrick, George Anne Bellamy, and the Paradox of the Actor

On or about October 19, 1741, theatrical character changed. Or so the critics claimed. It was on that evening that David Garrick debuted on the Drury Lane stage, usurping Cibber's old role of Richard III (and using Cibber's—not Shakespeare's—script). Audiences declared they'd never seen anything like it. Where Cibber stood still to declaim the speeches of the villain-king, Garrick strutted and fretted across the stage. Where Cibber seems to have held his hands just so—as in the engraving of his Lord Foppington by John Simon (figure 4)—Garrick trembled, stumbled, and looked wildly about him—if the rippling fabrics of Hogarth's *David Garrick as Richard III* (figure 2) are any indication. Garrick's contemporaries and his historians credit him with introducing a new, more "natural" style to the eighteenth-century stage, one that applied the tenets of sentimental literature to the art of acting. Exemplified by the novels of Garrick's friend Samuel Richardson, sentimentality celebrated the raw emotionality and unself-conscious nakedness of feeling that Garrick's performances seemed to embody.

Yet at the same time that he was hailed as the stage's harbinger of "authentic" emotion, Garrick also drew praise for his professionalism. Thomas A. King credits Garrick with spearheading the "so-called professionalization of the commercial theater in the eighteenth century, the reconstruction of playing as the acquisition of commercially valuable skills practiced at a distance from one's personal or 'authentic' embodiment."[1] These two qualities seem paradoxical: where the sentimental actor wears his heart on his sleeve, the professional actor segregates his private emotions from his public appearances. Where the sentimental man exhibits heightened and sometimes erratic emotion, the professional man exemplifies consistency, diligence, and the ability to produce the same emotion night after night. I am not the first to remark on the paradoxical nature of Garrick's dual identities as man of feeling and consummate professional, for they are the qualities that inspired Denis Diderot's description of Garrick in *Paradoxe sur le Comedien* (1830), a text to which I will return later in this chapter. What is unique about my approach here is my contention that Garrick's ability to embody such a paradox owed much to the techniques of autobiographical performance introduced by Cibber and popularized by Sterne. By revising these techniques according to the tenets of sentimentality, I will argue in this chapter, Garrick was able to satisfy his audiences' demands for powerful emotion onstage while rarely allowing that emotion to taint his private life. Understanding Garrick's performances in this way helps us to understand both the precedents for his interactions with his public and the influence these interactions had on how later celebrities would manage the distinctions between privacy and publicity.

I am calling Garrick's particular brand of autobiographical performance the overexpression of sentiment, and its effectiveness hinges on a distinction I would like to make between *earnest* and *mimetic* performances.[2] The concepts are not difficult to define: an earnest performer is one who produces real actions or emotions (a person who cries because he or she is sad), while a mimetic performer is one who imitates real actions or emotions (a person who cries because he or she is pretending to be sad). These concepts are, however, much more difficult to distinguish, and trying to determine whether Garrick was using tricks of makeup, costume, or acting technique to fake the emotions he displayed onstage and when he "really" felt them (as well as what it means to "really" feel) is not part of my project here. It seems much more useful to trace the distinction between earnest and mimetic performances to the spectator's assumptions when the performance begins.

In this context, the distinction between an earnest performance and a mimetic one, far from being futile, seems fundamental. The critic who approaches a performance with the assumption that it is earnest (as eighteenth-century critics might regard a mountebank's tricks or as today's spectators might approach a reality television show) values it for what seems unbelievable: did that *actually* happen? Did she *really* say that? The critic who approaches a performance with the assumption that it is mimetic, however, values it for how closely it approximates reality, and we say an actor in a play (a mimetic performance) is talented when she can convince us she really feels the emotions she represents or that she really is the character she portrays, though we know her to be someone else. The more a mimetic performance resembles an earnest performance, the more we praise its creators for their technical knowledge and professional skill. Yet the performer who appears too earnest is often said to be naive or unprofessional—to lack the necessary distance from and control over his or her craft.

The eighteenth-century critic's judgment depends, most fundamentally, on his or her ability to discern a mimetic performance from an earnest one; it is from this discernment that all other critical judgments stem. Those who deem as earnest what is merely mimetic are portrayed as gullible at best and corruptible at worst, the Catherine Morlands and female quixotes of eighteenth-century novels. Those who mistake earnestness for mimesis, on the other hand, also put themselves at risk, as the theatrical-turned-actual marriage of John Gay's *The What D'Ye Call It* makes clear. Performers who can create confusion between an earnest performance and a mimetic one, then, have the potential to disable their spectators' critical apparatus and to cast their interpreters as fools. This chapter will argue that this is precisely what Garrick did. In particular, he exaggerated the sentimental tropes that marked behaviors as earnest until they began to appear mimetic. By blurring the borders between the body thought to betray his emotions and the costumes that covered this body up, Garrick's overexpressions disabled their spectators' attempts to discern what is really felt from what is realistically feigned. These overexpressions help to explain why so many of Garrick's spectators and critics (Diderot most famously) spent so much time debating whether his performances were too emotional to be faked or too exaggerated to be true.

Far less successful at preventing her critics' interpretations and appropriations was Garrick's protégée, George Anne Bellamy, who published her own autobiography, *An Apology for the Life of George Anne Bellamy*, in 1785. Though she employed strategies that seem similar to Garrick's, her spectators read all of her performances—no matter how theatrical—as entirely earnest. In the second half of this chapter, I attribute this difference to eighteenth-century spectators' tendency to read women's performances as always more earnest than men's—a tendency that is reproduced in modern critics' assessments of both Bellamy and Charlotte Charke. This tendency stems from a hesitance to regard women as professionals with technical skills, or to separate their public roles from their private lives. It also forestalls an overexpressive strategy that relies on precisely this distinction. Bellamy registers this failure throughout her autobiography, but not until Bellamy's sentimental successor, Mary Robinson, did any woman discover a solution. I examine Robinson in my final chapter.

Even as it looks ahead to chapter 5, this chapter also looks backward to chapter 2—most notably in its use of the same central prop: the wig. In this case, the wig in question is one that Garrick wore in his performance as Hamlet, rigged to stand on end at the pull of a string after the entrance of the Ghost. Most scholars have read in Garrick's wig an illustrative—if a somewhat ridiculous—enactment of sentimental expression and its insistence on the body as a legible surface upon which emotions appeared as symptoms. But if the wig was a bid for credibility, it seems odd that it should be greeted—both in Garrick's time and in our own—with incredulity, prompting Todd Andrew Borlik, in a recent article, to describe it as most likely "apocryphal."[3] I am less interested in whether or not Garrick's wig existed than in why (assuming it is fact) it should so often be read as apocrypha, or why (assuming it is apocrypha) it should so often be read as fact. For as we shall see, similar confusions between earnestness and mimesis pervade several of Garrick's self-representations, suggesting that some of his most famous devices, rather than attempts at believability, were instead strategies for illegibility.

I use this common prop of the wig to suggest a through-line from Cibber's autobiographical performances to Garrick's. This through-line is crucial because, at first glance, the rise of sentimentality appears to obviate the need for such performances. Cibber aimed to hide the actor's emotions from his public in an age that saw every spectator as a persecutor, while sentimentality seems to celebrate the opening of the body to feeling and to being seen. By exploring how forms of overexpression persisted even as audiences were forming new assumptions about how best to act onstage and in the public sphere, I mean to promote the influence of these strategies as looming larger in eighteenth-century culture than its appearance in Cibber's autobiography or Sterne's parody alone might suggest. In this chapter, in other words, I make the case for overexpression not as a novelty but as a growing tradition crucial for our understanding of how celebrities—in the early eighteenth century and beyond—perform themselves to, for, and among their publics. Exploring the variations on this tradition in the sentimental performances of David Garrick and George Anne Bellamy offers us not only a deeper understanding of the many paradoxes in Garrick's (too often overlooked) autobiographical performances, but also a deeper understanding of how public personae protected their private lives across several revolutions in acting style.

THE PERSISTENCE OF OVEREXPRESSION IN A CULTURE OF SENSIBILITY

The revolutions in acting style that replaced Cibber's declamations with Garrick's gesticulations weren't quite as dramatic as theater history often portrays them. Understanding Garrick's and Bellamy's emotive performances as descendants of Cibber's foppish ones, however, requires a more nuanced understanding of sentimentality as it came to govern mid-eighteenth-century aesthetics. Such an understanding requires, too, a more nuanced understanding of the relationship between sentimentality and what I am calling earnest performance. I want to explore this relationship briefly before turning directly to Garrick's and Bellamy's performances in order to answer the question of why—despite the rise of an aesthetic style that seems to reward legible bodies—Garrick and Bellamy should strive for illegibility.

It is tempting to read sentimentality as a movement toward earnestness—in other words, to interpret its celebration of unbridled emotion as a condemnation of bodies that disguise or perform emotions without truly feeling them. The bodies within sentimental literature are portrayed as surfaces upon which interior emotions manifest themselves as if without their subject's permission or consciousness. "In the novels of the mid-eighteenth century," writes John Mullan, "it is the body which acts out the powers of sentiment. . . . Tears, blushes, and sighs—and a range of postures and gestures—reveal conditions of feeling which can connote exceptional virtue or allow for intensified forms of communication. Feeling is above all observable, and the body through which it throbs is peculiarly excitable and responsive."[4] Sentimental literature, according to Mullan, celebrates spontaneous displays of emotion as key to demonstrating one's fitness for society, and it assumes a direct correspondence between interior feeling and the display of that feeling through a body believed to be legible. Accordingly, the tenets of sentimentality seem to value earnest performance over mimetic performance and to call for an acting style in which the actor truly feels—rather than simply representing—the emotions he displays onstage. They seem also to make techniques of autobiographical performance like overexpression obsolete. If the display of emotion and the revelation of one's interior self make a literary character like Yorick or a celebrity like Garrick not less but more fit for eighteenth-century society, what use is there for the obfuscation of identity that such techniques accomplish?

Mullan suggests an answer to this question when he describes the "postures and gestures" of the sensible and sentimentalized body not as signals but as "symptoms"—a word that hints at sentimental literature's problematic hierarchy of the spectator feeling over the feeling body on display. Like a medical symptom, the expressions of the sensible body are physical, visible, and unpremeditated; their authenticity is guaranteed by the assumption that the body that exhibits them cannot help doing so. But the earnestness of the sensible body neither defies convention nor resists categorization. Just as the science of medicine is based upon the supposition that all bodies experiencing the same disease will exhibit more or less the same symptoms, so too the literature and art of sensibility assumes that interior emotions are manifest in much the same way regardless of the particular body that displays them. This assumption works, in many cases, to disempower that body, portraying it as a passive object that doctors (or readers) are invited to interpret and diagnose. To exhibit emotions earnestly is to relinquish control of those emotions, surrendering them as symptoms that only another can interpret, understand, or articulate.

Both of the celebrities with which I am concerned in this chapter register the hierarchical relationship between spectator and sentimental victim that, like the relationship between doctor and diseased, robbed the victim of his or her ability to narrate his or her life. George Anne Bellamy describes the examinations of the English public into the private virtue of its actresses as "an ordeal almost equally hazardous to that used of old as a test of chastity."[5] And Garrick suggests the similarities between the sentimental victim, the helpless patient, and the spied-upon celebrity in a poem he composed in 1765, *The Sick Monkey*. Tellingly, the poem appeared just as Garrick's fame—and the dissections of and dissertations upon his performances that accompanied this fame—were reaching their height. Arthur Murphy blames such dissections for Garrick's trip to France in the summer of that year—a trip that Garrick publicized as a kind of grand tour but that Murphy suspects he undertook because "his temper was soured by the injuries he had received."[6]

Published on the eve of Garrick's return to London, *The Sick Monkey* portrays its celebrity author as an ape made sick by the critical commentaries his fame invited. The poem adopts the familiar language of dissection and diagnosis to accuse the spectators who, following the dictates of a sentimental tradition that reads all illness as psychosomatic and the diseased body as a template upon which to read the soul, assert their power by treating the celebrity as a patient.

> Pug sickens, mopes, and looks like death,
> Speaks faintly, and scarce draws his breath;
> Some call it Megrim, some the Spleen;
> Words often us'd that little mean:
> But Scandal, with her face demure,

> Hints it is heat of blood,
> By which is understood,
> *An old Amour*:
> In short, they ransack all diseases,
> And give him that their fancy pleases.[7]

The poem hints at the sense of helplessness shared by the celebrity—notated and narrated by public "Scandal"—and the sentimental victim—poked, prodded, and diagnosed by his or her spectators. At the intersection of celebrity culture and sentimental literature, Garrick suggests, is a public body whose flaws might be either dismissed as symptoms of disease or denounced as signs of degeneracy, either pitied as side effects of "the Spleen" or condemned as the lingering vestiges of "*An old Amour*." Any celebrity who displays his body must submit to the invasive examinations and potentially degrading diagnoses of a public driven less by science than by "that their fancy pleases."

Garrick's poem suggests an important corollary to an understanding of sentimental literature (or sentimental acting) as celebrating legible bodies or earnest performance: the sentimental hero might exhibit emotion to demonstrate his or her fitness for a sentimental society, but he or she forfeits subjectivity the moment that this emotion becomes too evident, the moment that the body becomes too transparent. Barbara Benedict argues that the stylistic devices of sentimental fiction serve to distance the reader from the sentimental victim, precisely in order to "reign the reader back from identifying heedlessly" with the character.[8] "The true sentimental perspective," she explains, "resides in the view of the spectator, the reader of scenes of sensibility who also sees the whole picture."[9] Even a sentimental tradition that purportedly encourages extreme displays of emotion rewards subjectivity and authority not to the sentimental spectacle but to the sentimental spectator, one who feels sympathy on behalf of others but who resists becoming the object of sympathy herself.

The perceived vulnerability of the sentimental victim suggests one reason that strategies that attempt to conceal or dissolve the very emotions sentimentality promises to reveal might have persisted in the middle to late eighteenth century. Another (and related) reason is the superiority of the spectator over the spectacle that the literature of sentimentality inherited from early eighteenth-century works like *The Spectator*. Despite the obvious contrasts between the sentimental hero whose emotional expressiveness admits him into society and the coffeehouse critic whose emotional reserve guarantees his objectivity, both models share an implicit elevation of the discerning and dissecting subject over the dissected object of the gaze. When Thomas Davies wishes to confirm Garrick's status as the greatest actor of his age, he does so not by identifying Garrick as an expressive performer but rather by comparing him to the most celebrated empiricist of the previous generation: "Mr. Garrick shone forth like a theatrical Newton," Davies declares; "he threw new light on elocution and action."[10] And in a telling scene from Bellamy's *Apology*, the actress narrates her elevation in status in terms of an elevation from sentimental victim to sentimental observer of the scene before her.

The hierarchy of observer over observed emerges most clearly in this climactic scene of Bellamy's autobiography, when the actress—too poor to eat and too proud to beg—walks to the edge of Westminster Bridge and prepares to throw herself into the Thames. As she describes the scene in language adopted from the sentimental tradition, Bellamy suggests that subjectivity and authority in this tradition belong not to the spectacle but to the spectator, one who feels sympathy on behalf of others but who resists becoming the object of sympathy herself.[11] She begins by positioning herself as the spectacle of the reader's gaze—if of no one else's—as she stands on the lower level of the bridge and contemplates her fate. "Here pause a moment, and admire with me the strange vicissitudes of life," she instructs the reader. "Behold your once lively friend, reduced from the enjoyment of ease, affluence, esteem, and renown in her profession, to the most desperate state that human wretchedness will admit of—a prey to penury, grief, contumely, and despair—standing tiptoe on the verge of this world, and impiously daring to rush, *unbidden*, in to the presence of her Creator—I shudder at the recollection—Let me draw a veil across it, and proceed."[12] The "pause" in Bellamy's narration as a subject coincides, significantly, with her positioning herself as a spectacle that the reader must "behold." Here she is a sentimental victim, but one whose extreme emotions exclude her from society and whose attempts to take her own life appear rather less sympathetic than "impious." In order to reestablish herself as a member of society and as a narrative subject, Bellamy must remove herself from the object of the gaze by closing the curtain on this theatrical moment. She must "draw a veil across it" in order to "proceed."

It is Bellamy's resumption of the position of spectator that allows the continuation of her life, the continuation of her *Life*, and her return to the society she seeks to occupy. "I was suddenly roused from my awful reverie," she writes, "by the voice of a woman at some little distance, addressing her child; as appeared from what followed, for they were neither of them visible."[13] As Bellamy listens, the woman explains to the child that she can feed neither it nor its father, who lies dying at home. She ends her explanation with an imprecation to "my God!" and the pious prayer, "*But thy almighty will be done.*"[14] "The concluding words of the woman's pathetic exclamations communicated instantaneously, like the electric spark, to my desponding heart," Bellamy continues:

> I felt the full force of the divine admonition; and struck with horror at the crime I had intentionally committed, I burst into tears; repeating in a sincere ejaculation, the pious sentence she had uttered, "*thy almighty will be done!*"
>
> As I put my hand into my pocket, to take out my handkerchief in order to dry my tears, I felt some halfpence there which I did not know I was possessed of. And now my native humanity, which had been depressed, as well as every other good propensity, by despair, found means to resume its power in my mind. Impelled by its pleasing influence, I hastily ran up the steps, and having discovered my hitherto invisible monitress, gave them to her.[15]

The passage overflows with the familiar tropes of the sentimental novel: extreme emotions; "sincere ejaculation[s]"; verbs like "struck with horror," "burst into tears," and "hastily ran up the steps," which emphasize the spontaneity of the body's movements and the implied earnestness of its actions. But also important to the sentimental structure of the passage is the hierarchy it creates, as Bellamy's "hitherto invisible monitress" steps from the shadows to take form as the scene's primary spectacle, and Bellamy transforms into her spectator. This repositioning accompanies not only Bellamy's literal ascension from the lower level of the bridge and "up the steps" to its raised pathway but also a metaphorical ascension from the depths of despair to the height of sociability and to the "native humanity" that this sociability requires.

Bellamy confirms her rising position in the hierarchy by giving her few remaining coins to the woman and abandoning her suicidal intentions. Then, she revisits the scene of her attempted crime in order to measure the distance between her old role as sentimental victim and her new, improved role as sentimental spectator. "I now returned to the place where the impious scene was to have been acted," she writes, "and humbly adored that Being, who had by such an eventual circumstance counteracted it; and for the first and last time in my life, felt a sensation of happiness from finding there were persons in the world more wretched than myself."[16] From an immodest woman inviting her audience to "behold" her melancholy scene to a pious person who "humbly adore[s]" her creator, Bellamy now emphasizes her role as a spectator qualified to reenter her society—and a spectator capable of sympathizing with (rather than descending to the level of) the "persons in the world more wretched than myself."

Bellamy's journey from suicidal victim to sentimental benefactor suggests that performances that prevent the public from "beholding" the emotions of a private individual still have a place, even within the sentimental aesthetic upon which Bellamy is clearly drawing here. To maintain her subjectivity while demonstrating her sensibility, even the sentimental subject must portray herself as a spectator who feels for others more demonstrably than she feels for herself. She must strike a delicate balance between heartlessness and helplessness, between a healthy susceptibility to emotion and a destructive passivity in the face of adversity.

Garrick and Bellamy attempted to strike this balance by disrupting the sentimental assumption that such symptoms were impossible to fake and by blurring the distinction between earnest and artful emotion upon which sentimentality relied. Their spectacular disappearances often took the form of costumes indistinguishable from their bodies or of performance styles that allowed them to occupy the roles of spectator and spectacle at once. These performances began as versions of the strategies that Cibber had introduced and that Sterne had popularized and parodied. As their fame grew, however, both Garrick and Bellamy began to incorporate the tenets of sentimental literature into their autobiographical performances to create a style unique to their era and its assumptions about emotional display. By exaggerating the symptoms and emotions that sentimentality portrayed as earnest until they seemed merely mimetic, they attempted—and Garrick seems to have succeeded—to suggest a private life while at the same time challenging spectators' attempts to read that real life into performances that seemed, instead, merely realistic.

AGAINST NATURE: DAVID GARRICK'S EARLY INTEREST IN OVEREXPRESSION

In many of his self-representations and his engagements with his critics, Garrick portrays criticism as a violation of the celebrity's body. At the same time, these works propose a solution that allows Garrick to escape, transform, or defy that body and the clues it seems to offer to a sentimental audience. The great actor's early performances betray an interest in aping the overexpressive disguises that Cibber introduced. His first professional role, as Aboan in Thomas Southerene's *Oroonoko*, for instance, required him to cover his face in a mask of black makeup. For his London debut months later he chose Cibber's old role of Richard III—a choice that, according to Leigh Woods, "may have been influenced by the severity of the physical transformation required of those who undertook to play the hunchbacked king, and by Garrick's desire to hide himself in the role."[17]

Garrick also suggests his debt to Cibber's strategies in *The Meeting of the Company*, an afterpiece that he wrote in 1774 and that joins the impressive collection of self-referential pamphlets, plays, puffs, and prologues for which Garrick was celebrated in his lifetime but to which (with the exception of his ironic *Essay on Acting*) today's scholars rarely refer.[18] *The Meeting of the Company* deserves attention not only for its vociferous complaints against the critics (complaints that Garrick's biographer Arthur Murphy described, in 1801, as the actor's "ruling passion").[19] It deserves attention also as one of Garrick's most sustained and explicit articulations of the overexpressive strategy that, by 1774, he had come to adopt and to adapt in his own performances of self.

A backstage drama that follows the misadventures of a company of Drury Lane actors (played by the actual company of Drury Lane actors) as they prepare to rehearse a new play, *The Meeting of the Company* suggests two strategies for avoiding the critics' barbs. Patent, the bustling and business-minded theater manager whom audiences have long recognized as a parody of Garrick, suggests that actors maintain strict professional decorum. "If the Fools of our Profession, would have more Sensibility on the Stage, & less off it They might Strut their hour without fretting," Patent declares. "Let 'em never play the Fool but when they ought to do it—be as fine Gentlemen as they can in their business, & never assume the Character out of it—& the Newspapers won't hurt 'em."[20] This separation of the actor's personal life from his professional performance is one that scholars like King have identified with Garrick and to which they have credited the increasing respectability that actors enjoyed in Garrick's day.

How, though, might an actor hope to maintain such distance from his audience members when his celebrity invites wild speculations—stated as proven fact—about his private life or his public body? In answer to this question Garrick proposes a second strategy, less discussed in recent work about the actor but no less enthusiastically adopted by the actors Garrick portrays in the play. This strategy Garrick associates with Bayes, the authoritarian but untalented playwright whose work is to head the bill that night. Bayes's name recalls not only George Villiers's parodic portrayal of Dryden in *The Rehearsal* (1672) but also Colley Cibber, to whom the appellation had been most recently applied—and to whose overexpressive strategies Bayes's advice bears an uncanny resemblance.

Those players wishing to avoid their critics' complaints, Bayes suggests, should simply exaggerate their performance into illegibility: "Be in extremes in Buskin, or in Sock / In action Wild—in attitude a Block! / From the Spectator's Eye, your faults to hide, / Be either Whirlwind,—or be petrify'd." Bayes recommends, further, that in order to "Extort applause" actors must "Distort *Yourselves*"—an instruction that calls up the ghost of Cibber's deformed king even as Bayes's suggested distortions of language ("Bawl, / And when you're out of breath—pant, drag, & drawl" [21]) contain echoes of Cibber's drawn-out "My Kingdom for a *Harse*!"

Despite Garrick's repeated dismissals of Cibber's acting style (and despite Bayes's obvious function as the object of ridicule in this play), *The Meeting of the Company* implies a lineage between Cibber and Garrick in their shared attempts to avoid "the Spectator's Eye" by taking their own autobiographical performances to "extremes."[22] Sure enough, as Bayes continues his instructions, the tricks and trappings he recommends come more and more to resemble those for which Garrick himself was known, until a final catalog of necessary props makes the resemblance unmistakable: "To heighten Terror—be it wrong or right, / Be black your Coat, your handkerchief be white, / Thus pull your hair to add to your distress, / What your face cannot, let your Wig Express."[23] In the contrast Bayes celebrates between the actor's "black . . . Coat" and white handkerchief, eighteenth-century audiences might have remembered an infamous bit of stage business in which Garrick, as the black-clad Hamlet, would "take out a white handkerchief" and "twirl it round with vehemence."[24] It was the one gesture of which Davies disapproved—for, he wrote, "The conforming to a uniform method of action makes the whole appear a lesson got by rote rather than the effort of genuine feeling."[25]

In Bayes's "pulled hair," moreover, audiences might have recalled Garrick's controversial decision, as Macbeth, to enter the stage after the murder of Duncan with his wig awry and untied—a decision that *The Connoisseur* described in 1754 as "absurdly ridiculous: for who can forbear laughing, when he finds that the player would have us imagine, that the same deed, which has thrown all that horror and confusion into his countenance, had also untwisted one of the tails of his periwig?"[26] And finally, in Bayes's instructions to "Let your Wig Express" "what your face cannot" Garrick's spectators might have called up Garrick's famous (and possibly apocryphal) rigged wig, one of the most talked-about features of his role as Hamlet. Like Lord Foppington's, the wig in Bayes's description seems at times to frame and at times to distract from the actor's face: whether it illustrates or disguises the emotions that the actor feels, Bayes does not say.

I will return to Garrick's curious wig in the next section of this chapter, but for now I want only to stress the level to which Bayes's engagement with his critics resembles Cibber's. Despite his disagreements with Cibber's style of acting, Garrick seems in *The Meeting of the Company* to represent himself as an inheritor of Cibber's style of autobiographical performance—one who, like his predecessor, has resolved to "Be in extremes" in order to "hide" his "faults" from the "Spectator's Eye."[27] Yet Garrick's strategies differed from Cibber's in important ways—ways suggested by Davies's critique of Garrick's "vehement" handkerchief-twirling as a "uniform method of action [that] makes the whole appear a lesson got by rote rather than the effort of genuine feeling."[28] At the heart of Davies's complaint is his expectation that Garrick should exhibit earnest rather than mimetic emotions onstage, and his disappointment that in this case Garrick's actions seemed memorized rather than spontaneous. Crucially, however, Davies attributes this inauthenticity not to Garrick's stiffness—not, in other words, to Garrick's insufficient performance of the organic style for which he was known. Instead, it is the vehemence of Garrick's action that arouses Davies's suspicion: his action seems insincere because it is *too* passionate, not because it is not passionate enough. This excess of passion leads Davies to question his own assumptions about which emotions Garrick is feeling and which he feigns. In the next section of this chapter, I discuss this "vehemence" as central to Garrick's complex autobiographical performances. Like his business with the handkerchief, these performances seem removed from the actor's "true" emotions and private self not because of an insufficient but rather because of an exaggerated display of sensibility.

RIGGED WIGS AND "PAPER KINGS": DAVID GARRICK'S EARNEST PERFORMANCES

One year before *The Meeting of the Company* debuted at Drury Lane, Garrick's friend Suard sent him a copy of a short essay that had appeared in France earlier that year and that promised to unlock the secrets of Garrick's performances. In the letter that accompanied the essay, Suard solicited Garrick's response, but Garrick seems not to have complied.[29] It is unfortunate that he did not, because when it was published in its complete version in 1830 the essay—Denis Diderot's *Paradoxe sur le Comedien*—became one of the most well-known and oft-cited works of acting theory to come out of the eighteenth century. Years later Garrick would criticize Madame Clairon—Diderot's favorite actress and Garrick's costar in the *Paradoxe*—as lacking "those instantaneous feelings, that Life blood, that keen Sensibility, that bursts at once from Genius," and most scholars have interpreted this critique to indicate Garrick's rejection of Diderot's principles.[30] Yet Diderot's description of the actor's technique in the *Paradoxe* bears some resemblance to Bayes's description of the proper way to avoid the critics in *The Meeting of the Company*; and it echoes, too, the imagery and language that Garrick used to describe his acting techniques in his 1744 *Essay on Acting* and other autobiographical writings and performances. I turn now to Diderot's influential essay as offering a description of Garrick's acting style that underlines its debt to overexpression. Diderot's *Paradoxe* will serve as a kind of interlude between Garrick's citation of Cibber's style of autobiographical performance in *The Meeting of the Company* and the actor's attempts to theorize his own autobiographical performances in *The Essay on Acting*.

The progression here is not a chronological one: Garrick's *Essay* appeared in 1744, thirty years before *The Meeting of the Company* and coinciding with a new production of *Macbeth* that Garrick feared would startle his conservative critics. Diderot didn't begin his *Paradoxe* until 1769, writing in response to and in refutation of a pamphlet by Antoine Sticotti entitled *Garrick, ou les acteurs anglais*. The most complete version of the *Paradoxe*—and the one to which I will be referring—was published long after both men had died. Instead of moving in chronological order, I move in an order of lessening abstraction to address the problem of how a celebrity like Garrick might maintain both his credibility as a sentimental actor and his respectability as a seasoned professional while hiding his "faults" from "the Spectator's Eye."[31] As we shall see, Diderot will take up this problem posed by *The Meeting of the Company* and will offer a metaphor for the actor's sentimental body that Garrick, employing similar language in his *Essay*, will use to mime the physical symptoms of earnest emotion and exaggerate them into acts whose earnestness his audience members could not gage.

The question with which Diderot begins is one implicit in Davies's critique of those who perform "by rote": how does an actor play one character on one night and a completely different character on the next night if (as the doctrine of sentimentality seems to suggest) the actor actually experiences the emotions he represents? Garrick provides Diderot with a prime example, for (as Diderot notes), his performances were consistently praised for their naturalness even as his celebrated stage trick—thrusting only his head through the opening of a curtain and exhibiting a rapid succession of emotions by manipulating his facial expressions—belied their supposed earnestness.

To explain Garrick's versatility, Diderot puts forth the revolutionary suggestion that great actors do not really feel the emotions they purport to feel in the moment they purport to feel them. For Davies, this suggestion might denigrate the actor to the status of ape, one who merely repeats the "lessons got by rote."[32] For Diderot, however, it elevates the actor to the status of artist—or, more accurately, to the disinterested authority of a seasoned professional. In other words, the sort of actor that Diderot idealizes is precisely the sort of actor that the autobiographical performances I have been examining throughout this book arise to construct: an actor who lives his life at the center of the spotlight while somehow resisting his role as the object of the gaze. "It's the same with a play as with a well-ordered society, where everyone sacrifices some of his original rights for the good of the whole," Diderot explains, describing a public stage as a kind of microcosm of the public sphere. "Who will best appreciate the extent of this sacrifice? . . . In society, it will be the just man; in the theatre, the actor who has a cool head."[33]

Diderot recommends that the actor who wishes to keep "a cool head" should practice manipulating, exaggerating, and imitating the symptoms of each emotion—a practice that resembles the overexpression of sentiment with which Garrick maintained his status as a speaking subject. Curiously, the performance style that Diderot here endorses seems a perfect reversal of the strategies adopted by Cibber, Charke, and Sterne: while these celebrities don prosthetics that come to stand in for their bodies, Diderot's *comedien* wears a body that appears as a prosthetic, depicting as a costume what is merely flesh and bone. This reversal signals the new primacy that the body had assumed over and above the actor's costume in creating character on the sentimental stage. In order to conceal his private life from the public gaze, Diderot's *actor anglais* must go beyond putting on an exaggerated costume or a billowing wig. He must expand into illegibility the surfaces of the body itself.

The surfaces of the body, which in sentimental literature seem stuck fast to and always illustrative of interiority, become, in Diderot's metaphor, clothes that don't quite fit. Speaking of the onstage state of his favorite French actress, Madame Clairon, Diderot writes, "Just as sometimes happens in our dreams, her head touches the clouds, her hands seek out the bounds of the horizon; she is the soul within a great lay figure enveloping her; her experiments have clothed her in it."[34] The natural body that Cibber or Charke might enhance with stage properties or costumes Diderot portrays as a costume itself—a costume of flesh and bone in which the actor's identity is "clothed" but beneath which that identity cannot precisely be discerned.

Thus the symptoms that the body might exhibit are nothing more than illusions, a "sublime piece of clowning" tantamount to a jester's oversized shoes. "The actor has spent a long time listening to himself," the philosophe asserts,

> and he's listening to himself at the very moment when he moves you, and all his talent consists not in feeling, as you supposed, but in giving such a scrupulous rendering of the outward signs of the feeling that you're taken in. His cries of pain are marked out in his ear. His gestures of despair are memorized and have been prepared in a mirror. He knows the precise moment when he'll take out his handkerchief and the tears will flow: expect them at that word, that syllable, no sooner and no later. The tremor in the voice, those halting words, those stifled or lingering sounds, that trembling in the limbs, that shaking of the knees, those swoons, those furies: pure imitation, a lesson learnt in advance, a show of pathos, a sublime piece of clowning.[35]

Recasting the "tears," the "trembling in the limbs," and the "swoons" that guarantee the sentimental body's earnestness as mere "show" and the flesh on which they are displayed as yet another element of the actor's costume, Diderot transforms the actor himself from sentimental spectacle into spectator—both the spectator who is "listening to himself" and the spectator who watches his audience being "move[d]" by his performance. The actor becomes a puppeteer operating the "wicker mannequin" of his body from afar—and from beyond the audience's gaze.[36] And he does so not by minimizing his body but rather by expanding it into and exhibiting it as the great puppet that Diderot names. Diderot's *Paradoxe* thus provides clues as to how overexpression not only survived the transition from Cibber's declamatory to Garrick's sentimental style of acting—but, what's more, how the sentimental actor came to co-opt the assumptions of sentimentality as tools of this strategy. By exaggerating his body until it becomes a "mannequin," Diderot suggests, the *actor anglais* disables his audience's ability to distinguish his body from his costume and his "true self" from the character he portrays.

Despite Garrick's later protestations against the technique of Madame Clairon, his own descriptions of his acting style in his 1744 *Essay on Acting* bear an uncanny resemblance to Diderot's theorizations in the *Paradoxe*. In

Garrick's complexly self-referential essay, the image of the actor's body as a puppet surfaces as a strategy not for describing the project of the gifted actor but for protecting the identity of the English celebrity and disabling his critics' attempts to dissect him. I turn now to Garrick's essay in order to trace its similarities to Diderot's *Paradoxe* and to draw from these similarities an articulation of Garrick's overexpression of earnestness. As we shall see, Garrick's autobiographical performances borrowed principles from those of his predecessor Cibber and his friend Sterne while drawing upon the language of sentimentality to adapt his strategy to emergent theories of performance.

The *Essay* constitutes Garrick's most pointed (if not exactly his most direct) address to the critics who followed him through the waxing and waning of his celebrity. Davies remembers that when Garrick "first acted Macbeth, he was so alarmed with the fears of critical examinations, that, during his preparation for the character, he devoted some part of his time to the writing a humourous pamphlet upon the subject. He knew that his manner of representing Macbeth would be essentially different from that of all the actors who had played it for twenty or thirty years before; and he was therefore determined to attack himself ironically, to blunt, if not to prevent, the remarks of others."[37] The *Essay* adopts the tone of an unfavorable critic bent on "dissect[ing]" Garrick's performance as Macbeth.[38] Yet into his ironic commentary Garrick tucks insights that seem sincere, so that the *Essay* seems to oscillate dizzyingly between Garrick and his imaginary critic and between earnestness and irony. If Garrick's purpose was, as Davies claims, "to blunt, if not to prevent, the remarks of" the "critical examinations," he seems to have succeeded beyond his wildest dreams. Scholars from Garrick's day to our own have been divided on where Garrick's voice ends, in the *Essay*, and where his critical spectator's voice begins. This confusion applies not only to the language of the *Essay* but, as Garrick's manipulation of the wig suggests, to the body that language describes—a body that seems at times nothing but a costume.

Garrick's ironic tone makes close reading the essay a tricky business, and in doing so I don't want to lose sight of this tone, or to imply that we should interpret Garrick's descriptions of the actor as puppet to indicate (as they do for Diderot) his conception of the proper way to act a tragedy. Instead, I want to suggest that the language and imagery that Garrick employs in his *Essay* serve as a kind of *occupatio*—a literary device in which the speaker articulates an idea by declaring that he or she *won't* articulate it. Whether or not Garrick envisioned the tragic actor as a puppet, he creates in the *Essay* the character of a critic who envisions the tragic actor as a puppet. Any critic who believes the tragic actor is a puppet and attempts, despite this belief, to diagnose the performer's gestures as if they were sentimental symptoms or to discern in the performer's expressions the remnants of an "*old Amour*" exposes him- or herself as a ridiculous figure.[39] For as Ben Jonson's Zeal-of-the-Land Busy argues in *Bartholomew Fair*, puppets have no interiority. Garrick employs the image less as a commentary on the art of acting than as a critique of the work of the critic who attempts to dissect a puppet as if it were a person—or who interprets as earnest what is merely mimetic.

Garrick introduces his critique in two mysterious epigrams that head the *Essay* and that provide clues as to how his critics should read the body he will display onstage. The second I will discuss in more detail later; the first Garrick attributes to "*Tom Thumb*": "*So I have seen a Pygmie strut, / Mouth and rant, in a Giant's Robe.*"[40] Vanessa Cunningham explains that "Garrick was always sensitive about his height, and a recurring theme in *An Essay on Acting* is his physical unsuitability for the part of Macbeth."[41] The consensus of critics from Davies onward is to read the epigram, like Cunningham does, as self-referential.[42] Much like Sterne's "I wrote not to be fed, but to be famous," Garrick's epigram seems here to remind his readers of the uniqueness of his body, a body evoked by though not present in the printed *Essay* as it might be in performance.[43] Such a reminder might serve to emphasize the sudden fame through which that body has become recognizable. Garrick the celebrity, the epigram suggests, can never appear onstage as anything but Garrick the celebrity. No matter how many devices Garrick uses to fool his spectators into believing he is someone else, they will never forget the diminutive actor whose sensible body reveals its secrets even beneath its "giant's robes."

The meaning of the epigram becomes vastly more complex, however, when we trace its origins. The words are not, in fact, a quotation from *Tom Thumb*, whether this refers to Fielding's 1730 farce or any other version of the story. Rather, they paraphrase a line from *Macbeth*, act 5, scene 2, in which Angus refers to Macbeth's new kingship as a "title [that] / Hang[s] loose about him, like a giant's robe / Upon a dwarfish thief."[44] The epigram, like the quotation it adapts, suggests that we will never mistake the "dwarfish" actor Garrick for the great character he plays, any more than Angus will mistake a "dwarfish thief" for a powerful king. But the very fact that so many of the *Essay*'s readers have interpreted the epigram as a self-portrait rather than as a literary allusion suggests that they have already mistaken the border between the self and its disguise, between the "pygmie" and his "giant's robes"—so much so, in fact, that they have mistaken a description of Macbeth's body for a description of David Garrick's. Against a sentimental public confident in its ability to distinguish the body from its costume—and to read the symptoms of that body as windows to its soul—David Garrick has fooled us all by covering his frame in a "giant's robe" that we, seduced by the assumptions of sentimentality and the promises of celebrity culture, have taken for his skin.

The epigram is typical of the doubleness that Garrick maintains throughout the *Essay on Acting* as he struggles both to remind us of his celebrity (evoking his specific body in discussions of his stature, providing brief insights into his philosophy of acting) and to bar our access to that celebrity (effacing his own with his character's identity, burying his voice in the voice of his critic). Mixing up the indicators of earnestness and mimesis, Garrick seems to flaunt while at the same time dissolving his identity. What Garrick is working against here is the literalness of a sentimentalized body whose every movement is interpreted not as deliberate action but as inevitable reaction, not as an expression but as a symptom. The body that the actor exhibits onstage expresses interiority, in Garrick's description, but it is the interiority of the character rather than the interiority of the actor-celebrity who portrays him. That actor-celebrity remains always removed from and always in control of that body, like Madame Clairon sighing and blushing and fainting while "enveloped" in the clothing of her flesh.

And if the body that the actor-celebrity exhibits is nothing but a costume—if the actor himself is a puppeteer manipulating the puppet of his own corpus—the critics' dissections must seem as ridiculous as Zeal-of-the-Land Busy's debate with the puppets of *Bartholomew Fair*. The opening lines of Garrick's *Essay* hint at the superfluity of the critical examination upon which he is (however ironically) about to embark, as they indicate the emptiness of the body that Garrick's critic labors to expose. "In the following Dissection of our *Puppet Heroe*," the *Essay*'s presumed author declares, "I will endeavor . . . to convince my dear *Country Men* and *Country Women*, that they are madly following an *Ignis fatuus*, or *Will of the Whisp*, which they take for *real substantial Light*, and which I shall prove to be only the *Rush-light of Genius*, the *Idol of Fashion*, and an *Air-drawn Favourite of the Imagination*."[45] Anticipating Diderot's later description of the actor's body as a huge wicker mannequin within which the actor's self is concealed, Garrick here describes his onstage self as a "*Puppet*" whose body consists of cloth and paper rather than of flesh and bone. He is at once both larger than life and lacking any real life at all.

It is impossible, of course, to overlook the irony in Garrick's tone here; for if we can detect Garrick's own voice someplace within the *Essay* it is surely not in the critic's description of the actor as a mere "*Idol of Fashion*." Garrick's imagery resurrects the traditional associations between puppets and political pawns or unsophisticated artists—associations like those that, as we have already seen, Henry Fielding employed in his parodies of Cibber in *The Author's Farce* or that Charke evoked in her presentations of Punch in petticoats. In positioning the actor as a puppet here, Garrick is echoing the language of his most dismissive critics, but he is also pointing out the ridiculousness of dissecting as if it were a body something that is merely a costume. For puppets also signified a body with nothing beneath it, like the skirt covering the unsexed body of Busy's interlocutor. The puppet's body reflects less about the performer who displays it than it does about the critic who attempts to examine or—in Garrick's language—to "dissect" it.[46] Garrick's critic congratulates himself on his ability to expose the performer as a mere puppet—the performer's body as a mere costume—while at the same time he ignores the larger question of why, if the performer's body is indeed a costume, he should bother to "dissect" it at all.

Attesting to the importance of the image of the great actor as little puppet in Garrick's self-representations is the sheer number of times it comes up in discussions around and within his performances of self. In an oft-repeated anecdote, a biographer of Garrick records Samuel Johnson's testy response when Garrick admonished his old friend and former tutor for talking loudly backstage and interfering with the actor's attempts to summon the feelings for his performance. "Pshaw, sir," scoffed Johnson; "Punch has no feelings!"[47] Johnson's retort seems an insulting dismissal of Garrick's tragic performances as Hamlet or Macbeth, the sort of response that his *Essay on Acting* attempted to resist. Yet Garrick himself takes up the very same image, not only in the *Essay* but in two more of his most widely circulated self-representations. One was a 1745 prologue that he wrote and delivered in his production of *Much Ado about Nothing* (timed to coincide with his marriage to Eva Maria Veigel and thus inviting his spectators to conflate the actor with the character of Benedick), in which Garrick describes himself as "fit for nothing—but a Punchinello!"[48]

The other appeared a few years later in *The Fribbleriad* (1761), Garrick's mock-heroic response to a series of essays that the critic Thaddeus Fitzpatrick published against him in *The Craftsman*.[49] As he does in the *Essay on Acting*, Garrick here speaks in the voice of the critic—in this case, Fitzpatrick. "Every *Actor* is a *thing*," the critic proclaims, "A *Merry Andrew*, *paper king*, / A *puppet* made of rags and wood, / The *lowest son of earth* mere mud."[50] Garrick's repeated references to himself as a puppet-performer suggest the accuracy of Johnson's dismissal of him as pure exteriority, as nothing but mimesis. At the same time, Garrick's reclaiming of this same image indicates that this is precisely the representation he hoped to cultivate, in his performances of self if not in his performances on stage.

Garrick's efforts to blur the all-important borders between earnestness and mimesis destabilize attempts by critics like Johnson or Fitzpatrick to read his inner self into his theatrical performances or to understand the emotions he exhibited onstage as clues to his private life. The puppet's body is more than a body—a "wicker mannequin" that surrounds and envelops the actor's "true self"—but it reveals much less than the sentimental body that discovers all of its secrets through symptoms. If Punch has "no feelings"—if the body upon which the spectators are invited to gaze is a costume for rather than a sentimental revelation of the interiority it conceals—Garrick's self-representations ask, what can a "dissection" possibly expose? Garrick's project in these performances of self seems to be to convince his critics to regard the body onstage not as a character's anatomy but as an actor's accessory, a prop or costume that the actor wields with skill—and with full cognizance of the story that it tells.

Garrick's strategy in preventing his critics' dissections by blurring the boundary between sentimental victim and "paper king" seems, to some extent, to have worked. In their descriptions of his performances Garrick's critics admit their inability to distinguish between earnest emotion and mimetic performance or between the actor's body and his costume. This is especially true of one of the most oft-discussed elements of Garrick's performances: the rigged wig he is rumored to have worn in his wildly popular production of *Hamlet*. When Garrick pulled a string in the pocket of his coat, so the legend goes, the hair of his wig stood on end, allowing him to express with astonishing detail—or with ridiculous exaggeration—his character's terror at encountering his father's ghost. The wig seems, then, a perfect illustration of the emphasis that sentimental audience members placed on the apparently involuntary reactions of the body to emotional stimuli. Among theater historians, its mythology is often repeated with a certain hushed tone and twinkling eye reserved for the most delicious of theatrical anecdotes; and any scholar trying to make a case for Garrick's relative "naturalness" onstage must take it into account. Most have explained it away by assuming that the eighteenth-century idea of naturalness simply didn't accord with our idea of naturalness today.

Garrick's contemporaries, however, seem nearly as incredulous in their descriptions of the wig's "naturalness" as these more recent historians. Few modern scholars have considered this incredulity in taking the wig's mythology as fact, but it suggests that, far from a bid for naturalness, the wig may instead have been a prime example of how Garrick's autobiographical performances dismantled the tools that his critics used to interpret them. There are only two sources for the story of the wig: an 1826 autobiography by the actor Frederick Reynolds, who claims to have met Garrick's wigmaker; and a playful poem by Samuel Pratt, written on Garrick's retirement in 1776, that accuses the actor of favoring bells and whistles over acting technique. Neither was published during Garrick's career onstage, and both express some skepticism at the anecdote's truth. After describing his meeting with Garrick's wigmaker, for instance, Reynolds writes: "Whether this story was related by the facetious perruquier, to puff himself, or to hoax me, I will not pretend to decide." Despite the wigmakers' testimony, Reynolds admits he "did not see Garrick's hair rise perpendicularly."[51] (Tellingly, Georg Christoph Lichtenberg, in an otherwise detailed account of Garrick's performance as Hamlet, makes no mention of the wig.)

Pratt's description is more scientific in its details, but its form treats the anecdote more as bon mot than as bona fide, as easily a metaphor for Garrick's heightened sensibilities as a statement of fact. Much as Garrick ironically adopted the voice of his critic in his *Essay on Acting*, Pratt adopts the voice of Garrick, offering his advice to the young actors who will succeed him upon his retirement from the stage: "'Twere well indeed, if, when [the Ghost has] come, / With dext'rous dash of hand, or thumb, / You caus'd the hair, to stand on end; / As that would much the horror mend."[52] Pratt's reduction of Garrick's technique to simple instructions throughout the poem casts some doubt on the truth of his description, as does his ironic appropriation of Garrick's voice. Indeed, the payoff of the poem itself is to suggest that few critics can tell the difference between tears that flow from genuine feeling and those that are merely the trappings and the suits of woe. "I would not have you then despair," Pratt's Garrick comforts his successors, "Tho' Nature, should her blessings spare, / Tho' some of you, should feel no more, / Than DUNSTAN's giants o'er church door: / Sheer art, may move a man about, / And who's to find the secret out."[53] What won't be felt might be faked, Pratt implies, and even the most discerning critics won't detect the fraud if the costumes, like Garrick's great wig, are skillfully rendered. "Much, much, dear folks," he intimates a page later, "depends on dress."[54]

Pratt's suggestion that Garrick's acting "technique" is the result of elaborate costumes and clever gimmicks casts some doubt on the sincerity of his anecdote about the wig. Despite its mocking tone, Pratt's poem seems to have proven true in one sense at least. Since the poem's publication critics and historians of Garrick's performances have been unable to agree on whether the emotions he displayed onstage were earnest or mimetic. It is not my intention to weigh in on this debate here. But the mere fact that we have been having such a debate for nearly 250 years testifies to the effectiveness of Garrick's strategy. Whether his fright was so sincere that his hair stood on end or whether his acting was so realistic that it merely seemed to, his efforts paralyzed his critics' ability to distinguish between the two and thus to read his public performances for insights into his private life.

Garrick's rigged wig shares this ambiguity with several props, costumes, and anecdotes left over from several of Garrick's best-known performances, many of which make cameos in Bayes's advice in *The Meeting of the Company*. Garrick's most famous scene as Macbeth, for instance, has inspired a familiar debate over whether the symptoms his body displays constitute costumes so artful they seem authentic, or a body so authentic it must be artifice. In his dialogue with Lady Macbeth (played by Hannah Pritchard) after the murder of Duncan, Murphy notes, Garrick wandered about the stage with unwashed hands while "his complexion grew paler and paler every moment."[55] Was Garrick's pallor the physical manifestation of genuine feeling, the feat of a highly sensible body somehow willed to feel the terror of a fictional character? Or was it merely an illusion that Garrick achieved, as a critic for *The Connoisseur* suggests, by wiping away his makeup during his break behind the scenes?[56] (Zoffany's 1768 painting, *David Garrick and Mrs. Pritchard in "Macbeth"* (figure 8), depicts the scene but offers few clues to the authenticity of Garrick's pallor.) Such skepticism reverses Partridge's naive celebration, in *Tom Jones*, of acting so artificial it must be artistic. Garrick's performances, conversely, seem so real they must surely have been rigged.

It is precisely this confusion between earnestness and mimesis, between exposure and disguise, that Garrick seems to labor toward in *The Meeting of the Company* and that, when he achieves it in *An Essay on Acting*, allows him to be seen without being examined, to display a body without exposing it to his spectators' dissections. Not through the diminution but precisely through the exaggeration of his body and his symptoms does Garrick achieve illegibility. Not by denying his "pygmie" stature but by draping it in "giant's robes" does he defy the grammar of sentimentality.

If it might seem odd to unravel the threads of Garrick's "giant's robes" and arrive at the great white wig of Lord Foppington, it did not seem so to Garrick's contemporaries. In a farcical poem entitled "A Bone for the Chroniclers to Pick" (1758), the penny poet William Shirley adopts the voice of "Jemmy," a frustrated prompter trying to convince Garrick to bolster the thinning

8. Johan Zoffany, *David Garrick and Mrs. Pritchard in "Macbeth"* (1768). © The Garrick Club / The Art Archive at Art Resource, NY.

crowds at Drury Lane by composing a play himself. "To stifle your Genius for writing were Folly," Jemmy urges Garrick:

> Already, believe me, you half-rival *Colley*.
> Push on your Endeavours, and all Men will hope
> To see you soon equal to *Shakespeare* and *Pope*.
> Half-rival! Says *David*,—by G—d, Sir, 'tis fine!
> The Writings of *Colley* sure equal not mine.
> I'm *Dryden* for *Prologues* the Chroniclers cry:
> And that *Shakespeare* I've *mended* can any deny?
> Whilst in *comic*, there's *Chalkstone* was judg'd by the *Pit*
> To excel all e'er drawn both for Humour and Wit.
> And as for *Sublime*, let each *Pope*-praising Elf
> Compare him with what I have wrote on myself.[57]

The *Colley* to which Shirley twice refers here is, of course, Colley Cibber, Garrick's predecessor in the management of Drury Lane and the inspiration (according to Shirley) for Garrick's bombastic and overblown style on page and stage. In an explicit comparison between the two actor-managers, Shirley suggests that they share not only a peculiar style of writing but also an egotistical desire to write about themselves (as well as an egotistical confidence in their own poetic skills). And if Cibber's sentences are overblown, they are nothing compared to those of Garrick, whose style exceeds even that of his overexpressive predecessor.

In noting the differences between Cibber's declamatory and Garrick's sentimental styles of acting on the stage, we must be careful not to overlook the similarities of their self-presentations on the street, in the papers, and in the autobiographical writings that at once offered up and covered up the secrets of their private lives. These similarities suggest that the question of how to protect one's private life from the public gaze was as urgent—if not more so—after the rise of sentimental literature and theater as before it. They suggest as well a more complex relationship between the sentimental self and its spectators than influential narratives of the rise of the novel or descriptions of Garrick's naturalness have acknowledged. The transparent selfhood that Garrick's supporters praised in his stage appearances or that *Pamela*'s readers celebrated in their heroine might have made Garrick and Pamela famous, but it did not protect them from the invasions, violations, and misinterpretations leveled at them by their readers and spectators. Even after the introduction of sentimentality to the English stage, in other words, the truly modern self belonged to those who could seem almost earnest without leaving themselves exposed.

The oscillation between earnestness and mimesis that critics like Diderot acknowledge in Garrick's stage performances and the debt to Cibber that commentators like Shirley attribute to his autobiographical works suggest that the great actor was precisely this sort of self. Yet what was perhaps most infuriating to these critics was not the influence that Cibber's overexpressions had on Garrick's autobiographical performances, but rather the influence that these autobiographical performances threatened to have on the generations of young actors who would create selves as slippery and as singular as Garrick's. "You observe," complained the *Theatrical Examiner* in 1757, "all the young actors start, jump, and Garrickize, which is the true reason there is none of them tolerable, and that the public so soon let them fall from the pinnacle they are at first set on."[58] The neologism proclaims the uncategorizability and illegibility of Garrick's style even as it suggests the solidification of that style into a recognizable tradition of autobiographical performance. If all theatergoers had become well versed in the *lingua Cibberiana,* if all readers had been "be-Tristram'd," so all of England would come, one day, to "Garrickize."

In the final section of this chapter, I turn to the autobiographical performances of one of these "Garrickizing" young actors, George Anne Bellamy, who was an early protégée of Garrick and who enjoyed brief fame for her portrayals of doomed virgins and sentimental ingénues. In 1785, Bellamy published an autobiography whose title, *An Apology for the Life of George Anne Bellamy*, references Cibber and whose prose more than once alludes to Sterne. While Garrick achieved both professional success and personal esteem in his skillful application of Cibber's strategies, his protégée Bellamy adopts what I will describe as overexpressive methods but fails at staving off her critics' stares. Here, I ask why this might have been, and also suggest some ways that Bellamy presages the more complex devices invented by Mary Robinson, whose performances and autobiography I will examine in depth in chapter 5.

THE FAILURE OF OVEREXPRESSION IN *AN APOLOGY FOR THE LIFE OF GEORGE ANNE BELLAMY*

Like many of Garrick's autobiographical performances, Bellamy's *Apology for the Life of George Anne Bellamy* indulges her contemporaries' interest in the language of sentimentality as she relates a life that might have seemed—to some of her readers—something less than virtuous.[59] Bellamy describes herself as the illegitimate daughter of a Lord Tyrawley and his beautiful but impoverished mistress who is forced, after his abandonment, to seek a living on the stage. From her narration of this low birth to the last "recapitulation of my errors and misfortunes," Bellamy evokes the tropes of sentimentality again and again to portray herself as a woman more sinned against than sinning.[60]

Bellamy's theatrical career began when her performance in an amateur production before her mother's theatrical friends caught the eye of Garrick, who, she writes, "observed that I was much more in earnest than the [other actress] who had been accustomed to theatrical amusements."[61] She played a variety of roles as a member of the Drury Lane company, but she excelled in the part of the sentimental ingénue. One critic preferred the great "variety" of her Juliet to Susannah Cibber's in the rival productions of *Romeo and Juliet* that dominated London's two stages (and countless newspapers) in 1750.[62] (Cibber played opposite Spranger Barry and Bellamy opposite Garrick him-

9. Benjamin Wilson, *David Garrick and George Anne Bellamy in "Romeo and Juliet", Act V, Sc. 3* (1753). © Victoria and Albert Museum, London.

self.) "When she finds that *Romeo* has overheard her" in the balcony scene, the critic explains, "the surprise, the sudden change of voice, and flutter of spirits so natural on that occasion, are finely represented by Miss *Bellamy*, while Mrs. *Cibber* continues to ring on her usual tone."[63] Benjamin Wilson's 1753 painting of the tomb scene (figure 9) immortalizes Bellamy's performance and foregrounds her adherence to the sentimental style. Bathed in white light, Bellamy seems an innocent girl, her reclined posture and waving hand indicating the helplessness of the sentimental victim.

Her actual life was decidedly less innocent, though perhaps no less tragic. Punctuating her sporadically successful stage career were several descents into poverty, as well as a series of affairs with and abductions by prominent men, including West Digges (the rakish actor), John Calcraft (her estranged husband), and George Metham (the father of her child). The structure of Bellamy's *Apology* thus resembles Charlotte Charke's *Narrative* in its wild oscillations between love and loneliness, soaring prosperity and desperate poverty. But Bellamy herself suggests that her influences originate with Colley Cibber, whose title she adapts, and with Laurence Sterne, whose prose style she praises as both the inspiration for and the aspiration of her own. "Oh Sterne!" she exclaims, after one too-hasty resolution causes her to regret her sentimental impulsiveness. "Had thy recording angel but obliterated with a tear of pity this vow, this hasty vow, and thereby erased it for ever from the eternal register of mortals deeds, I might still have been happy.—But ah! It was not to be done."[64]

Bellamy's seemingly contradictory yearnings for self-preservation and self-erasure—her desire for a "recording angel" who will nonetheless "obliterate" the mistakes of her past—echo the language we've encountered in other works by celebrities eager to be remembered but anxious that such memories might imprison them in identities that they can't revise or control. Accordingly, she signals the perpetuation of the very paradox that gave rise to the strategies of autobiographical performance that I have been examining here: the simultaneous desire to keep an account of themselves and the fear that such an account will subject them to the invasions and misinterpretations of their spectators and readers. To this paradox Bellamy offers a solution that, like Garrick's, adopts and exaggerates the language of sentimentality until it reveals not her inner emotions but their inaccessibility. The "recording angel" that Sterne imagines and that Bellamy here recalls enacts the "obliteration" of Bellamy's past mistakes not through the suppression of sentimental emotion but rather through its excess. It is with a "tear of pity"—that exemplary symptom of the sentimental body—that the recording angel will wash away Bellamy's faults. By feeling too much the sentiments of Bellamy's story, the angel will drown the ink of Bellamy's pages with her tears; and by expressing too keenly the emotions of her life Bellamy might cause the yearned-for erasure of her life's record.

In this episode as throughout her autobiography, Bellamy echoes Garrick in exaggerating the language and gestures that mark the body and its emotions as earnest only to question the earnestness or the readability of this body and the identity it suggests. Examining such performances as descending from Cibber's overexpressions—performances that allow the body to avoid scrutiny by seeming to bare all—helps to make sense of Bellamy's odd narration of the Kelly Riots of 1747, in which a theatergoer she refers to as Mr. Kelly incited a riot in Dublin's Smock Alley Theater (where Bellamy was employed for the summer) to protest the new rule barring patrons from the green room. The episode reveals several similarities between Garrick's overexpressions of earnestness and those that Bellamy describes, both of which divert the sentimental spectator's stares by blurring the boundaries between actor and puppet or between corpus and costume. Yet the same strategies that, for Garrick, reinforce the separation of his professional character and his private emotions fail to protect Bellamy from spectators like Kelly, who attempt to invade her private rooms and her private life.

Bellamy portrays Kelly, tellingly, as a brusque and burlesqued version of Mr. Spectator. He might even seem an exaggerated parody of the same disembodied, disinterested, and discerning spectator that Habermas describes as the ideal participant in the bourgeois public sphere. Like the members of the public sphere, who gather with their newspapers in the coffeehouses of London, the members of Kelly's cohort convene in "Lucas's Coffee-House" near the Dublin theater.[65] Like these members, too, Kelly longs to gaze upon the hidden interiors of the celebrities in his midst as he longs to penetrate the inner rooms of the stage and its actors. "The house was so much crowded," Bellamy explains of the events that instigated the riot, that Kelly, "finding himself inconveniently situated in the pit, got over the spikes which divide that part from the stage. This removal received marks of approbation from many of the audience, who by no means approved of the new regulation, which debarred them from coming behind the scenes."[66] First attempted by Cibber and finally achieved by Garrick, the "new regulation" that banned spectators from the stage and scenes signaled an increasing interest—culminating in the darkening of the auditorium in the mid-nineteenth century—in the spectator as an anonymous figure allowed to see without being seen.[67] But it also widened the gulf between the spectator and the spectacle and made the backstage activities of both stage machinery and stage actors all the more intriguing to intrusive spectators like Kelly for being all the more difficult to discern.

Kelly's attempts to mount the stage are foiled, Bellamy continues, by Smock Alley's actor-manager, Thomas Sheridan, who bars the spectator's access to his theater's inner recesses. Undaunted, Kelly finds an alternate route into the backstage spaces where the theater keeps its secrets. He "ma[kes] his way to the green-room" and then "pursue[s]" Bellamy toward her dressing room, where he "attempt[s] to force the door."[68] In her description of Kelly's pursuit, Bellamy betrays the vulnerability of an actress to whose inner rooms—and to whose inner self—her spectators feel entitled. Sheridan, she notes, is similarly vulnerable to attack, yet he manages to escape Kelly's threats through a trick that will seem, by now, quite familiar. After Sheridan suppresses Kelly's initial outburst on his first night at the theater, the audience members return to their seats, and, writes Bellamy, "The play proceeded till we were come to the first scene of the last act, when an orange or apple was thrown at Mr. Sheridan, who played the character of Aesop, and so well directed, that it dented the iron of the false nose he wore, into his forehead."[69] Sheridan ends the play unharmed.

The false nose that protects the theater manager from his spectators' protestations here seems an apt—if an odd—metaphor for the overexpressive method exemplified by Cibber's false wig or Tristram's protuberant proboscis. Against the assumption of the body as a legible surface upon which the self might be read—and ridiculed—Sheridan exhibits a body whose surfaces are malleable and muddled. It is a body that, at once more than a body and no real body at all, is inaccessible to his spectators' anatomizing gaze (not to mention their "well-directed" projectiles).

The fight doesn't end with this first attempt, however; and if Bellamy's description of Sheridan's initial defense seems to recall the strategies deployed by Cibber, Sterne, and Garrick, her narrative of Kelly's second attack makes the resemblance unmistakable. For even larger—and even odder—than the false nose that protects Sheridan on this first night is the enhanced body that takes the brunt of Kelly's barbs when he returns the next day. This time, Kelly is bolder than ever in invading the private rooms of the theater—and the private parts of its personnel. "They broke open every door in the house, to find the *offender*, as they called him," Bellamy writes. "These dastardly ruffians broke open the wardrobe, and as they could not find the manager, they revenged themselves upon the stuffing of Falstaff, which they stabbed in many places."[70] Here again Bellamy emphasizes the theater's spectators as violators, breaking open "every door in the house" and invading even the wardrobe in pursuit of their prey. When they cannot find Sheridan, however, they revenge themselves on an empty costume, an enhancement of the body that has come to stand in for the body itself. Like Bayes offering up his wig as a substitute for his face in *The Meeting of the Company*, Sheridan frustrates his spectators' attempted anatomization by presenting a body that is at once more than a body and nothing more than a costume. Overexpression works as well for Sheridan, she implies, as it did for Garrick.

And yet it seems not to work for Bellamy herself. When the same spectators that threaten Sheridan turn their attentions to Bellamy, she seems uncertain what to do. "In their researches" on the second night, Bellamy explains, Kelly and his gang "did me the honour of a visit. But apprehending them, in my fright, to be leaders of the mob, and finding that the rioters were determined to leave no part of the theater unsearched, instead of returning thanks for their politeness, as I should have done, I answered with some acrimony, 'that my room was an improbable place to find the person they wanted, as I certainly should not undress, was there a gentleman in it.' . . . And I don't know whether I should have escaped further insult, had I not, in a resolute tone of voice, ordered them to quit the room. To this at length they consented, upon being permitted to lift up the covering of my toilette, to see whether the manager was there."[71] Bellamy's reference to the dressing room into which the rioters have burst as the private place where she might "undress" (provided there is no "gentleman in it") hints at the extent of the rioters' violation. They seek access not only to Bellamy's private rooms but also to her body.

Bellamy chases them away, but her description of her defense leaves some ambiguity about the effectiveness of her escape. She writes that they are satisfied only when they are "permitted to lift up the covering of my toilette, to see whether the manager was there." The two possible meanings for the word "toilette" here paint Bellamy's encounter with Kelly either as a close call or as a complete surrender, depending on which meaning we choose. Presumably "toilette" refers to the dressing table within which Bellamy stores her puffs, powders, patches, Bibles, and billet-doux. In this sense, her offering up her "toilette" instead of her "undress[ed]" body seems a strategy similar to the one she attributes, a page later, to Sheridan: unwilling to surrender her body to her pursuers, she surrenders instead the inanimate accessories and accouterments that adorn and enhance that body. Like Sheridan's false nose or Falstaff's fat, Bellamy's "toilette" substitutes the enhancements of the body for the body itself and thus deflects her spectators' interest in the "real" self they seek.

Yet there is a second way of interpreting the word "toilette" that makes Bellamy's blurring of costume and corpus seem far less effective at staving off Kelly's attack on her person. In the eighteenth century, "toilette" might mean the piece of furniture used to store a woman's dress and accessories, but it might also signify the "dress, costume, 'get-up'" itself.[72] In this sense Bellamy's statement that her pursuers quit her rooms only after being permitted "to lift up the covering of my toilette, to see whether the manager was there" takes on a more sinister (and more sexual) implication. Bellamy suggests here that, far from preventing her pursuers' access to her person, she invited it, allowing them to lift up the "toilette" covering her body to gaze at the body itself. Not only that, but her hint that Kelly and his gang might discover "the manager" under her skirts suggests that the access to her person and to her privates that they enjoy is open to everyone. The double meaning of *toilette* thus evokes the same confusion between corpus and costume that haunts discussions of Garrick's rigged wig, or that protected Sheridan's body from Kelly's projectiles. Yet rather than stressing her immunity, as it did for

Garrick and Sheridan, this ambiguity emphasizes Bellamy's vulnerability to spectators who might as easily be accessing the body inside her clothes as the clothes inside her bureau. Like Charke in her donning of her father's wig, Bellamy borrows the same tools of overexpression that worked so well for her male colleagues only to find that they fail to protect her from her spectators.

But why? How might we account for the failure—or at least the precariousness—of Bellamy's autobiographical performances when compared to the similar strategies of the men around her? Why does overexpression seem so much more effective for the men of this study than for the women?

My suspicion is that these questions are best answered by a detailed inquiry into how eighteenth-century audiences interpreted men's performances differently from women's—an inquiry far beyond the scope of this book. Instead, I want to offer here a few observations about how Bellamy's autobiographical performances differ from those of her male colleagues, and to speculate on what these differences might reveal about the relationship she imagined between the female celebrity and her curious spectator. For as she registers the failure of overexpression in her own performances of self, Bellamy seems to attribute that failure to her audience's tendency to read men's costumes as disguises or distractions and women's costumes as earnest expressions. We might consider, for instance, one of the strangest episodes of Bellamy's *Apology*—an episode that, tellingly, turns around a familiar prop: the wig.

In the fifth and final volume of her autobiography, Bellamy abandons her post at Covent Garden Theatre to follow a former lover to Holland. (Accompanying her on her journey is "Miss Betty Cibber, who had been left me as a legacy by her grandfather, Colley Cibber"—a coincidence that Bellamy seems to call up to invite her readers to speculate on what other "legacies" Cibber left her.)[73] Before she can reach Holland, however, Bellamy is intercepted by another former lover, the actor West Digges, who is also eager to rekindle their affair. She abandons Calcraft and agrees to follow Digges instead—but only under the condition that he not take her into Edinburgh. This city, where Digges is employed as an actor, is too close to home, she fears, and not far enough from the spectators, creditors, and jilted lovers who threaten to apprehend her. Digges agrees to the condition, so Bellamy is surprised when she discovers that he has not only "decoyed" her into that very city but—still worse—has settled her in a boardinghouse directly across from the theater, where she will be most easily recognized and most enthusiastically importuned to make an appearance. "I no sooner made the discovery," Bellamy writes, "than I took a pair of scissors, and cut my hair off, quite close to my head, to prevent my being solicited to appear in public."[74] We might regard Bellamy's haircut as the antonym to overexpression. Eager to unmark herself in the midst of those who would make her into a spectacle, she discards her most spectacular feature: the blond hair for which she is known and admired.

But attempts at modesty rarely work for the already famous, and Bellamy's efforts to disguise herself by disguising her most recognizable feature prove unsuccessful. "The English papers having announced my absence," she explains, "it was conjectured, that the new-comer at Miss Coustone's [boardinghouse] was the very fugitive that had recently deserted her situation at Covent-Garden. The next day, Mr. Bates, joint proprietor of the Edinburgh theatre with Mr. Dawson, and acting manager, acquainted Mr. Digges, that it would be useless to open the doors, unless he could induce me to appear on the stage. . . . Our journey had been expensive. I had but little money left, and Mr. Digges less; for the bills I had upon Holland, were of no use to me here. In this situation, there was no other alternative but my conforming to Mr. Bates's wishes."[75]

Bellamy articulates the paradox that has plagued so many of the celebrities in this study: to appear before the public is to encourage her sharpest critics and to invite her creditors; to refuse to appear is to surrender the funds that might allow her to pay those creditors. Cornered, Bellamy agrees to take the stage—but not before altering her appearance once more. "The loss of my hair was the greatest bar to my appearance," she writes. "However, for the first time, I had recourse to false; and, as I had not even necessaries, I was obliged to have clothes made at a great expence. But my success was so much beyond expectation, that I was very well enabled to do this. Curiosity induced families to come from all parts of the country."[76] At first glance, Bellamy's strategy seems to resemble Garrick's or Sheridan's: foiled in her attempts to unmark herself by changing her appearance, she decides to enhance it, donning clothes of "great expence" and slipping into a big wig to appear as herself.

But Bellamy's wig seems in important ways a reversal of Garrick's. To start, Garrick's wig works by blurring the line between earnestness and mimesis. It is this blurring that accounts for the sense of betrayal in the reactions to these works by the actors' readers and reviewers, who declare their inability to discern actor from character or body from costume and so to interpret the celebrity's "true self." The audience that Bellamy describes, however, seems either unaware of or unconcerned with her betrayal in donning a wig to play herself. Instead, she implies, they accept her long blond hair as a part of herself—either because it is a part of her body or because, even if it is a wig, it represents or somehow expresses that body. We might notice a parallel here with how contemporary critics regard Charke's transvestitism: her man's clothes might contradict the shape of the actual female body they obscure, but they nonetheless express the inner desire for a man's body, or for a woman's love. In both cases, the clothes that appear on a woman's body (long blond wig or cocked-up cap) are read as earnest expressions of that woman's "real" self, while those that appear on a man's body are disguises for or distractions from that self. Clothes might make the man, these readings suggest, but they expose the woman.

This suggestion might help to explain why so many of Bellamy's backstage anecdotes center around her battles with another actress over a coveted costume, which takes on a significance above and beyond its ability to flatter its wearer's figure and becomes instead, it seems, a signifier of her taste and virtue. Her expectation that her spectators will read her clothes as expression rather than disguise is evident, too, in the odd and ambiguous frontispiece that adorns all five volumes of the fourth edition of Bellamy's *Apology*, published in 1786. The print portrays Bellamy in her green room, removing a grinning mask to reveal her grinning face behind it (figure 10). The trope is a familiar one: we might recognize it from Cibber's promise to gratify "the Curiosity of his Spectators to know what he was, when in no body's Shape but his own"[77] and in the title of *Miss C——Y's Cabinet of Curiosities*, which never actually reveals the contents of its *Green Room Broke Open*. In the pages that follow, Bellamy's crude portrait suggests, we will be granted access to the self beneath the costume.

Except that, curiously, the face that Bellamy exhibits appears identical to the face she has just removed—or, perhaps, the face she is about to put on. Is Bellamy suggesting the futility of trying to distinguish face from mask and exposing the foolishness of the critic who dissects the puppet-king's body to try to understand his self? Or does the frontispiece represent her, instead, as the spectator sees her: a woman whose costumes and coverings earnestly resemble—or at least accurately represent—the self that lies beneath?

This second possibility offers one explanation for why so many of the men in this study seem to be successful at deflecting the stares of their spectators while, for so many of the women, overexpression fails. As I have argued, Garrick confused his spectators by dissembling the boundaries between costume and corpus, earnestness and artfulness, public and private. For Bellamy, the same strategies failed because her spectators—or rather, the ideal spectators she imagines and describes in her autobiography—refused to recognize these boundaries to begin with. In attempting to overexpress her identity, in other words, Bellamy repeatedly encounters a spectator eager to read all of her

10. Frontispiece to *An Apology for the Life of George Anne Bellamy*, 4th ed. (1786). © National Portrait Gallery, London.

overexpressions as earnest expressions and to interpret every element of her performance—costume pieces, body parts, tears, gestures, and makeup—as governed by her inner desires. While Cibber's delights in the frustration of his spectators and Garrick grins at their confusion, Bellamy seems only to register the impossibility of evading spectators primed to read all of her performances—no matter how unreal—as revelatory.

CONCLUSION: A RETURN TO STERNE'S RECORDING ANGEL

At the beginning of my discussion of Bellamy's *Apology*, I mentioned her allusion to Sterne as an example of what I have been calling, throughout this chapter, the overexpression of sentiment. Recalling the mistakes of her past, Bellamy inserts an apostrophe to Sterne and "thy recording angel" who might "obliterate" her hasty vow "with a tear of pity."[78] By imagining an angel who might erase her past life through a profusion of sentimental emotion, Bellamy evokes the ways that performances like Cibber's, Garrick's, and Sterne's exaggerate their most seemingly revealing features until those features can no longer be read. It is interesting, however, that Bellamy couches her most obvious example of overexpression in an allusion to Sterne: in order to create the overexpressive elements of her own life story, Bellamy must borrow the characters of a male contemporary. Her dependence on Sterne's angel—or on Sterne's ghost—to tell her own story confirms what the wig she dons in Edinburgh and the mask she removes in her frontispiece have already suggested: that an autobiographical strategy that scrambles corpus and costume in order to secure the celebrity's right to self-definition cannot succeed for a woman whose costume and corpus are already indistinguishable and whose public persona, no matter how exaggerated, will always be read as an extension of her private self.

Until now this book has focused largely on successful examples of spectacular disappearance. Cibber's bent body, big wig, and blotted pages inspired his would-be interpreters to give up any attempts to glean his meaning and reduced them instead to mimicking his idiosyncrasies. Sterne's black page and pseudonymous sermons didn't exactly silence his critics, but they destroyed his critics' confidence in their power to interpret his prose. Garrick's rigged wig and clever quips, somewhat more successfully, cemented his status as the greatest—and the most professional—artist of his age. Bellamy's *Apology*, however, provides an early example of an overexpressive autobiography that fails. Perhaps more interestingly, it seems, in its wistful call for Sterne's "recording angel" or in its admiring description of Sheridan's false nose—to register that failure.

But where, exactly, does this leave the female celebrity, whose opportunities for making a living outside of the public eye are even more limited than those of her male colleagues but whose relationship to privacy is so much more vexed? Was there any version of overexpression—or alternative to overexpression—that arose to address the needs of women who had come, more and more, to share the lifestyles of eighteenth-century England's rich and famous? The answers to such problems were, it seems, imperfect, and none of the autobiographical performances by women in this study achieved the popularity of Cibber's *Apology* or the professionalism of Garrick's persona. Yet one woman did manage to turn her brief stint on the stage into a lifetime of fame and fortune—and, at the same time, to project a private persona that remained, both in her day and in ours, frustratingly enigmatic. This woman, the actress, courtesan, and poet Mary "Perdita" Robinson, was one of the most controversial figures of the late eighteenth century; and her elusive and elliptical performances of self are the subject of my next and final chapter.

CHAPTER 5

The Memoirs of Perdita and the Language of Loss

Mary Robinson's Alternative to Overexpression

In the opening pages of this book, I described the black page of *Tristram Shandy* as the emblem of overexpression. Since then the page clouded by too many words has come to stand in for the elaborate costumes, overwrought gestures, and purple prose of the eighteenth-century celebrities who deflected invasions of their privacy by presenting what Colley Cibber described as "this *Chiaro Oscuro* of my mind": autobiographical performances so clear they were obscure.[1] But this *Chiaro Oscuro* is incomplete without the white page that follows and counters the black in Sterne's narrative. While the black page marks a death, the white page proclaims a love affair (or perhaps merely a flirtation) between Uncle Toby and the Widow Wadman. While the black page prints words too numerous to elucidate the character its writer imagines, the white page prints no words at all—and invites the reader to imagine the character he would prefer. And while the black page records the life of a man, the white page alludes to that of a woman. The man in question is known for defying, again and again, the death that his page's blackness proclaims, and he is resurrected in Sterne's text much as his name has been resurrected from Shakespeare's. The woman in white, conversely, never seems to materialize: as Sterne's story progresses we learn little more than her name—and this name is not even her own but lent her by a former husband, long dead before our story begins.

I introduce the Widow Wadman and her white page not only as a counterpoint to the black page that has guided so much of this study but also as a useful tool for imagining an eloquent alternative to overexpression that emerges in the autobiographical performances of Mary Robinson. An actress, poet, and royal courtesan, Robinson is perhaps better known as "Perdita," "the lost one." Her nickname derives in part from the role she played in *Florizel and Perdita*, David Garrick's adaptation of the *Winter's Tale*, when it was staged in 1779; and in part for the role she played in the gossip columns after the Prince of Wales (later King George IV) wooed her with a note addressed from "Florizel" to "Perdita" and delivered backstage. (Robinson was middle class and married, but no matter.) The affair lasted two years, but the celebrity it generated clung to Robinson for over two decades, as did the name that, as Emily Hodgson Anderson has eloquently written, identifies its subject by effacing her.[2]

The same might be said of many of Robinson's autobiographical performances, all of which define their subject according to her absence. In this chapter I explore the elliptical phrases Robinson inserts into her poetry, the portraits that depict her turning away from the viewer, and the *Memoirs* that she left famously (and conspicuously) incomplete. As Sterne's white page suggests an antonym and an antidote to the black, these works offer an antonym and antidote to the overexpressive performances practiced by Robinson's predecessors. While Cibber's, Sterne's, and Garrick's performances revolve around a prop that seems too large (a big wig, a black page), hers revolve around a prop that seems too small: a miniature picture that the prince gave her as a token of his affections and that resurfaces, again and again, in the works by and about her. While their performances exaggerate a defining trait, Robinson's exaggerate only her absence. Yet it is the conspicuousness of this absence that reveals Robinson's debt to her overexpressive predecessors and that justifies her inclusion in my narrative about a technique of self-presentation that seems in many ways so different from hers. Her strategy, I argue, represents a reaction to overexpression as practiced by Cibber, Sterne, and Garrick—and a partial solution to the failures of overexpression as lamented by Charke and Bellamy.

Here again, the white page serves as a useful emblem for understanding precisely what this solution entails. In previous chapters I noted that overexpression—which, like the black page, makes its subject illegible by exaggerating his or her identifying marks—works differently for women than for men. Chapter 2 pointed out that Charlotte Charke's autobiographical performances failed to earn the charges of illegibility that her father's did, despite their similar features. Chapter 4 suggested that George Anne Bellamy met with similar frustrations because of eighteenth-century audiences' tendency to read women's performances—no matter how outrageous—as reflections of inner desires, and thus to ascribe meanings to words, gestures, and costumes that the actresses themselves mark out as ambiguous. Sterne's white page seems a nod to readers' tendency to make of a woman's writings what they will: recognizing that his male readers will be dissatisfied with any portrait of perfect femininity that he might devise, Sterne invites them instead to "paint her to your own mind."[3]

Sterne makes the offer playfully—and, as David Brewer has pointed out, few eighteenth-century readers took him up on it.[4] But there was a genre that was emerging as Sterne wrote *Tristram Shandy* and gaining popularity as Robinson wrote her *Memoirs*, one that assumed precisely this collaborative relationship between reader and subject. The fashion magazine, evoked by the elaborate descriptions of dress that populate Robinson's autobiography, dismantles the hierarchy of critical spectator over dissected spectacle that the first four chapters of this book have assumed. It presupposes a female reader (unlike Sterne's white page) and presents the fashion icon as an empty vessel over which that reader superimposes her own body, a blank that the reader occupies with her own story. The reader who admires the celebrity as a fashion model cannot also dissect the celebrity as an object of criticism; if she does, she finds that her inquiries tell her less about the celebrity than they tell her about herself, the collaborator who fills in the celebrity's story and the body that fills out the celebrity's clothes.

The second half of this chapter argues that the conspicuous absences that Robinson scatters throughout her autobiographical performances accomplish a similar task, and that in doing so they answer Charke's and Bellamy's calls for a strategy of autobiographical performance more suited to women, one that somehow defies spectators' tendency to read women's performances as always confessional and never professional. It is perhaps thanks to this strategy that Robinson succeeds in gaining some control of her life story where her female predecessors had failed. Even amid the rumors of her affairs, Robinson managed a successful (and highly respectable) career as a writer and editor of the *Morning Post* (a position also held by such luminaries as Robert Southey and Robinson's friend Samuel Taylor Coleridge). She even enjoyed a brief stint as the publisher of a periodical whose pseudonymous persona, the shape-shifting *Sylphid*, seemed a direct descendant of the objective and unmarked Mr. Spectator.[5] Today, critics are more likely to read Robinson's autobiographical performances as evidence of what Judith Pascoe calls her "Romantic theatricality" rather than (as they were for Charke or even for Bellamy) clues to some inner desire.

Throughout this chapter I build on current scholarship that examines Robinson as flitting between a number of predetermined identities, trying on selves as she might try on costumes. But where Pascoe and others have examined the particular selves Robinson chooses, I am more interested in the spaces between these selves.[6] I agree with these scholars that Robinson's works seem not to strive for the stable and legible lyric "I" of Wordsworth's *Prelude*, which sets out in chronologically ordered verses *The Growth of the Poet's Mind* to be perused and preserved for posterity. Yet neither, I would argue, does she perform what Marjorie Levinson calls the Keatsian "not-self: a fetishized, random collection of canonical signatures" that "creates the illusion of ethereality."[7] Instead, we might describe Robinson's autobiographical persona as a not-not-self, co-opting Richard Schechner's identification of the performer as at once actor and character, self and other. Robinson is, similarly, both undeniable and undefinable: a woman recognizable only when she is lost.[8]

This final chapter thus returns us to the place where we began: to the black page as companion to the white, and to these earlier performances as the springboard for Robinson's enigmatic *Memoirs*, begun one hundred years after Colley Cibber first shuffled across the boards as Richard III. But even as they look backward to the ghosts of overexpressions past, Robinson's autobiographical performances also look forward—to the Romantic poets that Robinson undoubtedly influenced and to the search for self central to so much of their work. Considering Robinson's shifting selves as the origins of these later identities offers an alternative history of the Romantic self as constructed not of words but of ellipses and an alternative history of autobiography as a genre striving not for the self's expression but rather for its spectacular disappearance.

LOST AND FOUND: THE LIFE AND CRIMES OF PERDITA ROBINSON

A review of Mary Robinson's life calls up the ghosts of the celebrities that have preceded her in this book, and the similarities between her strategies of autobiographical performance and theirs seem at first more striking than the differences. Robinson was born Mary Darby in Bristol in 1756 (the year before Colley Cibber died). She enjoyed a relatively comfortable childhood until her merchant father abandoned the family for an ill-fated venture in Labrador and the mistress who had accompanied him there. Her mother's resulting financial distresses drove Mary, against her father's wishes, to the Drury Lane theater, where she trained under David Garrick.

But before she could debut she forsook the stage for what she believed was the more respectable choice of marriage to a lawyer's clerk, Thomas Robinson. Unfortunately, she soon found that her husband had misrepresented his finances, and his proclivity for philandering sank the young family into debt. After giving birth to her daughter, Maria Elizabeth, in 1774, Mary Robinson returned to the stage, debuting in George Anne Bellamy's old role of Juliet in Drury Lane's 1776 production of *Romeo and Juliet*. A mild success, she may have continued her performances as the sentimental heroine or as the woman in breeches were it not for the affair she began with the prince in 1779.

Suddenly, Robinson found herself the object of national attention and the subject of satires, parodies, encomiums, and portraits by the era's most celebrated artists—Sir Joshua Reynolds, Thomas Gainsborough, and George Romney among them. Though she continued to appear onstage periodically until 1783, Robinson discovered the prince's patronage and the celebrity it brought her to be far more lucrative than her stage career. She performed onstage less and less frequently after 1779. Yet even after the prince left her in 1781, Robinson continued to appear in London's public places as a maven of fashion and as a mistress to several important men, including the parliamentarian Charles James Fox and the military hero Banastre Tarleton. It was in pursuit of Tarleton—on his way to the continent to escape his debts in 1783—that Robinson took ill, suffering complications from a miscarriage that left her paralyzed from the waist down.

After the accident, newspapers predicted the end of Robinson's relevance as a celebrity and trendsetter. Instead, the former actress continued her public appearances, now aided by a series of lavishly decorated carriages that paraded her through the London streets. During this time she continued to appear in printed books and periodicals as one of the era's most popular authors, developing a career she had begun by publishing her *Poems* in 1775 (a year before her theatrical debut). Though she composed six novels, two plays, an autobiography, and several essays (including a feminist tract greatly influenced by that of her acquaintance Mary Wollstonecraft), Robinson enjoyed her greatest successes as a poet. Coleridge praised her command of rhythm and meter, and recent scholars have traced her influence over other Romantic poets, such as Wordsworth and Keats.

The satirical prints and caricatures that lined newspapers and gossip columns from the beginning of Robinson's affair to the year of her death tend to denigrate these authorial ambitions. Here Robinson appears most often as a sexual object and a royal distraction, but she appears also, more pathetically, as a cripple who might have been a queen. At such moments Robinson's persona seems ghosted by that of Cibber, another actor who wished to play author but settled for a role as deformed royalty. At other moments Robinson's writings take on the attributes of her other overexpressive predecessors: she casts herself as a sentimental heroine in the manner of George Anne Bellamy or as the writer exhausted by her own self-description, recalling Laurence Sterne. Though Robinson's *Memoirs* contains few direct references to other actors' autobiographies, it does describe her proudly as one of Garrick's last protégées. And the Della Cruscan school of poetry, to which her early work belongs, lists Sterne as an important influence (though less for his celebrity than for his sentimentality).[9]

Robinson's relationship with celebrity began much like that of her predecessors, then, and she suffered humiliations and invasions of privacy similar to those about which they complain. The emergence of a full-fledged celebrity industry—in which the celebrity was cast as a mannequin managed, manipulated, and bandied about by a growing population of tabloid writers and caricaturists—only heightened these humiliations. Developments in etching and engraving techniques in the mid-eighteenth century greatly increased the speed and ease of distributing images—including images of celebrities—in periodicals and print shops. "When Hogarth began his artistic practice in London in the 1720s there were only two print shops and a few struggling artisan/engravers," writes art historian Shearer West. By 1790, however, "John Boydell had made a fortune from exporting prints, and the competition among Fleet Street printsellers was fierce."[10] Evidence of this explosion is obvious in the catalog of the British Museum, for instance, which lists seven prints depicting Cibber—only four of which were published during his lifetime—as compared to over thirty prints depicting Robinson.

In many ways the proliferation of such prints facilitated her social and geographic mobility by guaranteeing her profitable attention whenever she appeared in London and a warm reception, too, when she began traveling to France. As if to prevent such mobility, however, many of these prints seem to depict the printmaker's role as harnessing the celebrity whose fame, they suggest, allows her to defy her proper roles as a middle-class woman and as a dutiful wife. In image after image and in text after text, Robinson's caricaturists and unauthorized biographers depict themselves putting her in her place by fixing her on a printed page or imprisoning her within a picture frame. This is the point of the anonymous etching from 1784, *Perdita upon Her Last Legs* (figure 11), in which a now crippled Perdita begs a purse from the Prince of Wales. The old posters on the wall behind them, advertising Robinson's

Perdita upon her Last Legs.

11. *Perdita upon Her Last Legs* (1784). © Trustees of the British Museum.

12. James Gillray, *The Thunderer* (1782). Courtesy of the Lewis Walpole Library, Yale University.

former roles in *Jane Shore* and *Florizel and Perdita*, present a cruel contrast between the actress once known for her dynamism on the stage and her social ambitions off of it and the beggar in the foreground, now paralyzed in her fixed pose and her inescapable poverty.

An earlier print, James Gillray's 1782 etching *The Thunderer* (figure 12), makes the point even more explicit. In the foreground, Robinson's on-again, off-again companion Banastre Tarleton and the Prince of Wales boast about their exploits, while the pub behind them advertises "Alamode Beef, hot every Night." The advertisement's sexual implications come into sharp focus when we glimpse, just above it, a bare-breasted Mary Robinson—legs spread, torso sexually impaled upon a post—serving as the sign of the house. By transforming Robinson from living celebrity into art object, Gillray's print transforms Robinson's publicity as well as her sexuality from tools for social mobility into traps as imprisoning as the signpost that fixes her to one spot.

The trope of the public picture that works against the celebrity's uncontainability by reducing her to an inanimate object was not limited to visual representations of Robinson. In 1784, seventeen years before Robinson would produce her own autobiography, a nearly two-hundred-page book claiming to be the *Memoirs of Perdita* appeared in London bookshops. The book opens, as so many celebrity biographies had before it, with the promise to reveal the most intimate details of Robinson's life—and the most private parts of her body. Even more intriguing than its promise to satisfy the reader's "natural curiosity" about Robinson's sexual escapades is its promise to fulfill the reader's desire to contain, commodify, and control the unruly celebrity as if she were nothing more than a picture.[11] One episode near the beginning of the *Memoirs* describes "Perdita" seducing a visitor to her apartments by transforming herself into an art object. "When disposed to yield the *last amour*," the narrator explains, "she suddenly retreated to her bed-chamber . . . hung round with paintings executed with masterly skill, and calculated to suggest ideas of various modes to indulge concupiscence. She frequently took pleasure to *explain* the several pictures, by throwing herself into the very attitudes they represented, affording such a strange exhibition of *motionless* and *animated nudity*, as fancy can scarce conceive."[12]

The perfect combination of "*motionless* and *animated nudity*," Robinson's body here becomes the ideal art object—real as life but still "*motionless*" and commodifiable—as well as the ideal sexual object—just like a real woman but lacking the voice to protest. Like *The Thunderer* or *Perdita upon Her Last Legs*, *The Memoirs of Perdita* couches its critique of Robinson's sexual exploits in a derogation of her social ambitions. The story depicts its celebrity attempting to "*explain* the several pictures" that adorn her wall, much as the respectable Mr. Spectator or the growing numbers of art or literary critics might explain or interpret a work of art. While Mr. Spectator's credibility comes from his disembodied persona, however, *The Memoirs* portrays Robinson's attempts at credibility as inseparable from her sexuality: she "explains" her pictures not by speaking but by striking a static and sexualized pose. The narrator's description thus neutralizes the threat of the celebrity's always-problematic subjectivity in much the same way that images like Gillray's had: by reconfiguring Robinson as an "*animated*" but inanimate painting that can be bought, sold, reinterpreted, and—most importantly—gazed upon at length.

The author of the specious *Memoirs of Perdita* resembles others in his frequent complaints that Robinson's over-the-top persona and private life exceeded the frames in which her audiences tried to contain her. These works emphasize the paralyzing position into which a growing celebrity industry—with its proliferating prints and pamphlets—had cornered personages like Robinson, but as we shall see they also helped to structure Robinson's particular response. Perhaps the most potent example is Lady Elizabeth Craven's evocatively titled afterpiece *The Miniature Picture*, which opened on May 24, 1780, with Robinson in the starring role as Eliza Camply / Sir Harry Revel. Robinson seems to have frustrated the playwright and a few of her spectators in this performance—one of her last on the Drury Lane stage—by letting her own celebrity upstage the role she played. What Craven describes as Robinson's refusal to conform, however, seems to me to be an early example of the sort of autobiographical performance that Robinson employed throughout her life to defy her spectators' attempts to contain her. In this performance and the scattered materials it left behind, we might glimpse a number of the elements that will recur throughout Robinson's self-representations: her spectators' desire to contain her by reducing her to an inanimate and commodifiable object; a persona that exceeds and upstages the roles or the frames into which Robinson's spectators try to fit her; and a series of unanswered questions and ellipses that this persona, despite or because of its excesses, appears only to highlight. By beginning with Robinson's spectacular disappearances from and surrounding her performance in *The Miniature Picture*, we might better understand her similar disappearances from the printed pages of her poetry collections and posthumously published *Memoirs*.

By the evening of *The Miniature Picture*'s debut, speculations about Robinson's extramarital affair with the Prince of Wales were already filling the gossip columns of London newspapers. The dearth of information surrounding the affair only piqued the public's interest—an interest that almost certainly influenced Richard Brinsley Sheridan (Drury Lane's manager at the time) in his decision to stage Craven's play with Robinson in the starring role. The title, which refers to a portrait that Robinson's character gives to her lover as a token of affection, could not help but bring to the minds of eighteenth-century spectators the "miniature picture" given to Robinson by the prince.[13] And to ensure this association, the play was staged as an afterpiece to Garrick's *Florizel and Perdita*, with Robinson reprising her famed role as the lost princess.[14]

At least one of Robinson's spectators appreciated the implications of the play's title and its placement on the program: "The address of the plot, which is the chief merit of the piece, and some lively penciling, carried it off very well," wrote Horace Walpole, who attended the play with Craven and her husband on opening night; "though . . . Mrs Robinson (who is supposed to be the favourite of the Prince of Wales) thought on nothing but her own charms, or him."[15] Such attentions were not lost on the prince himself, who later wrote that "every tender speech she ought to have addressed to Prince Florizel, [she addressed] to me."[16] Though she doesn't mention in her *Memoirs* her delight in flaunting the intersections between her private life and her public performance, Robinson seems to have attached some significance to her role in Craven's play. Her repetition of it a few days later, on May 31, was her last appearance at Drury Lane before she left the stage to take up with the prince, and it is one of only a few roles earning a special remark in the *Memoirs* she composed twenty years later: "The last character which I played," she writes, "was Sir Harry Revel, in Lady Craven's comedy of 'The Miniature Picture.'"[17]

The Miniature Picture seems an appropriate companion piece to *Florizel and Perdita* in more ways than this one. Garrick's play ends, much like Shakespeare's, with a woman's awakening from stone, as a statue representing the long-lost queen Hermione turns out to be Hermione herself. But *The Miniature Picture* works hard to shut down this threat of a willful woman's coming to life, which Garrick's play unleashed. It engages constantly with the relationship between an animate woman and her inanimate representation as an art object, and it introduces the objectification of a woman in a painting as one possible strategy for controlling both her sexual appetite and her individual will.

The play invites an implicit consideration of the extent to which a living woman might be exchanged for or contained within a static portrait in its manipulation of the miniature picture of its title, the prop that sets the play in motion. The living woman in this case is Eliza Camply, who disguises herself as a man in order to test the devotion of her lover, Mr. Belvil. Belvil's affections seem to have cooled since Eliza gave him her miniature as a token of her love, and she is horrified to discover, upon assuming her disguise as Sir Harry Revel, that Belvil has surrendered her miniature to a notorious coquette, Miss Loveless. As the miniature makes the rounds among the play's dramatis personae, multiple characters complain that the living Eliza seems so much more difficult to describe, to know, and to own than the Eliza contained within the miniature picture. "I have seen her," Miss Loveless admits of Eliza, whose miniature she now examines; "but she blushes so much at every thing, and at nothing—and her countenance alters from one moment to another into such a variety of expressions, that I really never could decide any thing about her."[18]

Remarks like Miss Loveless's recall eighteenth-century anxieties about all living celebrities' tendency to overflow their static representations. They seem particularly appropriate in describing Robinson, whose image had just begun to circulate throughout and beyond London.[19] The "variety of expressions" exhibited by the animated Eliza, like the variety of identities inhabited by the actress portraying her, frustrates her spectators' attempts to describe her according to a single model—or, for that matter, to "decide any thing about her."[20] As her image circulates, so too does its original, as Eliza trades identities and travels widely to get what she wants. Like the circulation of Robinson's image, the circulation of Eliza's comes to stand in for her freedom and for her irreducibility to conventional roles.

The Miniature Picture counters this threat of the woman's uncontainability by reversing the image of the statue turned to flesh, cementing the subject's body and identity in a work of art that properly belongs to a single person. "I say," remarks Eliza-as-Harry, gazing down at the miniature of herself that she has just finessed from Miss Loveless's hands; "Miss Loveless gave me this; and I really think it like Eliza—but in her grave looks though."[21] The pun here—"grave" as serious, but also "grave" evoking both a graven image and a posthumous memorial—revises Miss Loveless's earlier complaint against Eliza's unrepresentability by uniting the image of the celebrity to an image of death. The word's echo of "graven image" calls up the language of idolatry, suggesting the play's concern with England's growing cult of celebrity. Yet at the same time that it evokes, the term also buries the celebrity beneath a memorial representation—a "grave"—distinguished by the silence and the stillness of those it memorializes and by its rootedness to a single place. The miniature picture and *The Miniature Picture* represent Eliza/Robinson only to stifle her power to represent herself. In doing so, the play reduces the threat of the willful woman and of the unpredictable celebrity who insists on her subjectivity against such attempts to cast her as a symbol.

Ultimately, Craven's script downplays these "grave" representations as the proper way to tame or to claim a woman, settling instead on the marriage contract as the representation best suited to limit Eliza's circulation and to keep her will in check. Eliza draws an important comparison between the portrait and the bridal bed in the final scene, as both she and her picture are returned to their rightful owners. "Here is then at last returned to me the copy of a very foolish original," Eliza remarks when the miniature is safely in her hands; "and were the fate of it to be well described in a modern play, I fancy it would teach many giddy girls like myself not to part with the one until the other was secured as fast as a lawyer and parson could bind it."[22] Like the "grave looks" of the portrait, the marriage contract controls the willful woman by binding her "fast" to a single document, a single role as wife. A third term extends such attempts to contain the female to attempts to contain the celebrity performer, as Eliza mentions the "binding" powers not only of the miniature picture and the marriage contract but also of the "modern play." Arrested within these representations, Eliza goes from being a woman whom giddy girls like Miss Loveless can't quite "decide anything about" to being an example they should follow.[23] She goes from being an "original" who controls her self-representation as she performs her story to being a type: easily categorizable, limited to the lines that someone else has written for her and the role that she has been assigned.

But Eliza's sudden metatheatrical reference here serves to highlight the difference between the play's willful but ultimately willing heroine and its unruly star. Unlike Eliza, Robinson could not be tamed or contained by a marriage contract: her affair with the prince had persisted, as her audience members well knew, despite her vows to her husband. Neither could she be tamed or contained by a "modern play" like *The Miniature Picture*, as the anxieties about her unpredictability, littering her spectators' commentaries, make abundantly clear. It is Robinson's excessive persona that distracted Walpole from "the address of the plot" and the plight of its central character and diverted his attention instead to "Mrs Robinson (who is supposed to be the favourite of the Prince of Wales)" and who "thought on nothing but her own charms, or him."[24]

Walpole's complaint that Robinson's own identity overflows from and interferes with that of the character she performs echoes Miss Loveless's objection to a personality impossible to fit into a portrait. It echoes, too, the preface that Craven attached to the printed version of *The Miniature Picture*, published in 1781. "The Author publishes [this play] at the Request of several of her Friends," she declares, "who saw it mis-represented on the Stage, at Drury-lane; as she chuses to submit Faults which are really her own, to the Judgment of the World, rather than be accused of those which she never committed."[25]

Implied in both Walpole's and Craven's statements is their frustration at the uncontrollability of an actor's live performance—and the sense that only by arresting a character in the inanimate medium of print can the author control that character as "her own." Robinson distracts from Craven's printed script, in other words, by being too much herself. But in upstaging the character she plays with her own celebrity, Robinson fuels her spectators' curiosity about her private life without answering their questions or clarifying the wild rumors then circulating about her affair. Her appearance as Eliza / Sir Harry only emphasizes the performance's several conspicuous absences: the conspicuous absence of the prince she is "thinking on" and whose persona eclipses that of her onstage lover, Belvil; the conspicuous absence of the prince's "miniature picture," evoked but not directly referred to by the play's title; and the conspicuous absence of an untold story (the still-fuzzy circumstances of Robinson's affair) alluded to but never clarified by the plot of Craven's play. These ellipses, highlighted though unresolved by Robinson's appearances in *The Miniature Picture*, recall Robinson's moniker of Perdita, which names her by calling attention to her absence. Even as her performance in Craven's play moves questions about her personal life to the forefront of the audience's imagination, it marks the answers to those questions as inaccessible.

Or, perhaps more accurately, it moves the burden of these questions to the purview of the spectator. The greatest absence from Craven's printed script is the performance that it inspired but—framed by Craven's preface—explicitly rejects as a "mis-represent[ation]." In place of this misrepresentation, Craven implicitly invites her readers themselves to reimagine or even to restage the play she now puts in their hands in much the same way that Sterne invites his readers to imagine the face of the Widow Wadman in the space that he has left. In the second half of this chapter, I argue that it was precisely this seeming inclusion of the spectator in the creation of the spectacle that allowed Robinson to escape her spectators' definitions while seeming to invite them. First, I want to examine the poetry that served as Robinson's introduction into published self-representation and that pointedly chastises Robinson's spectators for assuming they can imprison her in a static portrait or in a steady gaze. If others' representations of Robinson try to imprison her mobile body and changeable identity in printed pictures or modern plays, her own representations of herself attempt to capture through print the ephemerality of performance. In the elliptical phrases and blank spaces that characterize so much of her poetry and prose, Robinson points up her own absence and makes it nearly as conspicuous as Cibber's deformed body or Sterne's overwritten characters. But where her predecessors offer too many words Robinson offers only blank spaces—disappearing at the very moments that we imagine her to be within our reach.

POETRY AND THE ELLIPTICAL SELF-REPRESENTATION

Robinson published her first volume of poems in 1775, before her acting career began, and she continued to publish poetry—most of it piecemeal, in periodicals like the *World* or the *Morning Post*—throughout her lifetime. *Lyrical Tales* is perhaps her most famous collection, known for the affinity with Wordsworth and Coleridge's *Lyrical Ballads* (1798) that its title proclaims. But it is in her collection *Poems*—published in two volumes, the first in 1791 and the second in 1793—that Robinson deals most directly with her role as English celebrity and its relationship to her role as English author. In "Stanzas to a Friend Who Desired to Have My Portrait," published in the second volume of *Poems*, Robinson teases her readers with promised access to her portrait, her person, and her private life—only to expose that access as always already impossible and her person as always already departed. The poem seems in many ways a direct response to the caricaturists, spurious biographers, and playwrights who had attempted to arrest or contain Robinson's identity by representing her as a commodity. It seems, more indirectly, a response to the overexpressive representations that preceded hers. Like her predecessors, Robinson begins with the promise of revelation and—rather than disguising the links between her poetry and her well-known biography—seems to flaunt them. But where Cibber and Sterne frustrate the critic's interpretations by preventing him or her from getting a word in edgewise, Robinson leaves too many ellipses in her story and too many spaces between her words. In doing so, she exposes her narrative as one that the reader has imagined—and thus one that reveals less about her life than it does about the reader's own prejudices.

Read by Robinson's contemporaries as an apostrophe to Banastre Tarleton, the poem's lines evoke also the image of the prince—as well as his miniature picture—as they rebuke the (presumably male) reader for his desire to arrest and own the speaker's portrait. "My PORTRAIT you desire!" the poem begins:

> and why?
> To keep a shade on Mem'ry's eye?
> What bliss can REASON prove,
> To gaze upon a senseless frame!
> On looks eternally the SAME,
> And lips that NEVER move?[26]

Part of the thrill of the poem, as Robinson no doubt recognized and as the first stanza confirms, lies in its exploitation of what Joseph Roach calls "public intimacy"—the celebrity's ability to address a wide and diverse public while seeming to address each member of that public specifically and privately.[27] The "you" of the first line includes not only the unnamed "Friend" whom the "Stanzas" claim to address but also the teeming public who actually read these stanzas. Robinson savvily draws this public into the poem through an allusive and elusive title, which promises a glimpse of the more famous affair of which the "PORTRAIT" has so often served as synecdoche.

By the time that the reader reaches the first line, however, Robinson has already begun to admonish him or her for mistaking effigy for individual and for trying to arrest or encompass a living, present celebrity within "a senseless frame." The poem thus indicates a more complex relationship to celebrity than scholars have attributed to Robinson in their descriptions of her later works as either "infected by the nineteenth-century woman writer's abhorrence of autobiographical relations" or exemplifying a brash "tendency for self-publicity."[28] Rather than trying to downplay or delete the private details of her tryst with the prince or the recognizable features captured in prints like *The Thunderer* or spurious biographies like *The Memoirs of Perdita*, Robinson flaunts them. She encourages her public to fill in the gaps in the poem with the rumors surrounding its celebrity author's life. Yet such encouragement serves only to emphasize the gaps in this story and the absence of the subject who supposedly occupies its center.

Such is the case with the first six stanzas, which describe in titillating detail Robinson's celebrated "looks" (l. 5)—her unforgettable "lips" (l. 8); her "eyes, so gentle" (l. 10), and her famous "features" and "form" (l. 20)—only to dismiss these features as empty attempts "To keep a shade on Mem'ry's eye" or to arrest a living celebrity in a static portrait. Such is the case, too, with the remaining thirteen stanzas, in which Robinson seems to offer her private thoughts for the reader's perusal. Having rejected the portrait as a reductively physical and static representation of the subject by her spectators, Robinson suggests that the reader come to know her instead through "The PICTURE OF MY MIND."[29] It is tempting to regard the "frank CONFESSION" that the poet promises in the remaining stanzas as simply providing another static representation through which her public might read, interpret, and appropriate the celebrity's private life—albeit one composed of words rather than appearances and initiated by Robinson rather than her detractors.[30] If the reader cannot own Robinson by possessing her image, such a representation promises, the reader might own Robinson by purchasing her *Poems*.

Two related puns in the final two stanzas of the poem, however, undermine this promise and transform the poem from commodification of identity to dissolution of identity. "Such is my PORTRAIT," Robinson declares in the penultimate stanza, after regaling the reader with a catalog of her (often contradictory) self-characterizations; "now believe; / My pencil never can deceive, / And know me what I paint."[31] Though the stanza asserts the legibility of Robinson's poetic "PORTRAIT" over the painted portrait that her "Friend" covets, the phrase "now believe" casts some doubt on the authenticity upon which the surrounding lines insist. Is Robinson reassuring the reader that her "pencil never can deceive"? Or is she creating belief as the first stanza's portraitist creates character, willing into being a representation with no referent, an illusion sustained only by "the PAINTER's skill"?[32]

The final line of the phrase contains a similarly ambiguous command in its imputation to "know me what I paint"—an elliptical phrase that, paradoxically, signals the unknowability of the "me" Robinson offers in her poetic portrait. Certainly the word "paint" strikes a discordant note with Robinson's assertions of authenticity. For one thing, it violates the dichotomy that the earlier stanzas set up between the painted portrait as unfaithful to its living subject and the contrasting authenticity of the "LASTING sketch" rendered in poetry and "in pencil."[33] What's more, the word calls to mind the image of the woman who "paints"—whose beauty emanates not from nature but from the commodities that transform her imperfect, aging, or wrinkled body into a smooth and unblemished canvas.

The implied ellipsis in the phrase reinforces this ambiguity. While Robinson writes only "know me what I paint," she assumes the reader will understand the phrase as "know me *to be* what I paint." The implied ellipsis creates a sentence that is, in a sense, the antonym to Cibber's overflowing clauses and overladen prose: here, the sentence that the reader understands contains more words than the sentence he or she actually sees printed on the page. Yet the conspicuous absence of Robinson's words has much the same effect as the conspicuous superfluity of Cibber's: both obscure their subject's image more than they clarify it. Robinson invites us to read the phrase not as a command to the reader to read the poet into her poem but rather as a warning to the reader not to mistake this poem as anything more than a representation. For at the same time that it invites the reader to "know me [to be] what I paint," Robinson's elliptical line suggests also that there is "no me [in] what I paint." If there is "no me" here, the portrait must originate instead with "YOU"—the reader / lover whom the poem addresses and who creates the poem's subject from his or her desire to "believe."

Lest we miss the pun between "know" and "no" that makes such a reading possible, Robinson repeats and reverses it in the final stanza of the poem, in lines that again employ the figure of the ellipsis. And as if to signal the strategy that her ellipses react against, Robinson includes in these same lines a version of the *Chiaro Oscuro* imagery introduced by Cibber and elaborated upon by Sterne. "Now contemplate a picture true," Robinson instructs her reader:

> With KINDNESS ev'ry VIRTUE view;
> And all that's WRONG explore:
> If YOU the brightest tints defend,
> The darkest shades I'll TRY to mend;
> The WISEST CAN NO MORE![34]

Ostensibly, Robinson employs the *Chiaro Oscuro* combination of "brightest tints" with "darkest shades" to emphasize once again the authenticity of a self-portrait that neither exaggerates the good nor minimizes the bad but includes with "ev'ry VIRTUE" a fair measure of "all that's WRONG." It is telling that her language and line divisions demarcate the "brightest tints" as the purview of the reader (that is, the doubled reader contained within Robinson's "YOU" and containing both private lover and public admirer). The "darkest shades" belong, conversely, to the speaking "I." Such a demarcation calls up Sterne's combination of the "principal lights in your own [that is, the reader's] figure" with the "dark strokes in the [writer's or character's] HOBBY-HORSE."[35] Like Sterne's self-portrait, the allusion suggests, Robinson's depends as much on what the reader "believe[s]" as it does on what the writer is or expresses. This formulation fosters at the same time that it frustrates the reader's attempts to interpret the writer's character, inviting him or her to explicate and to "explore" the identity that the writer displays but reminding him that these explications might bear little resemblance to the "true picture" that he strives to capture.

The elliptical phrasing at play in the final line of the poem confirms the illegibility and irretrievability of the writer's "true picture" even as it adapts Cibber's *Chiaro Oscuro* metaphor to serve Robinson's particular purpose. Reversing the no/know pun of the previous stanza, Robinson's "The WISEST CAN NO MORE" indicates either the completeness or the incompleteness of the portrait she offers. The difference depends, once again, on where we place the ellipsis. If Robinson intends the missing words to occupy the middle of the phrase, she implies that the portrait is whole: the wisest can *do or hope for* no more than she offers in the self-representation before us. If we move the ellipsis to the end of the phrase, the same line might imply not wholeness but holes in the portrait the poem offers: the wisest can know more *than what is indicated here*—in other words, there are additional self-portraits that this one does not even begin to discover.

Again the implied ellipsis transforms the poem from true confession to guarded evasion and emphasizes both the relationship with and the contrast to overexpression. While overexpression exaggerates the celebrity's presence, the language of Robinson's poem highlights its many absences: the absences not only of the words that might complete and clarify Robinson's sentences but also of the subject whose image those words promise but fail to elucidate. Much like the earlier "know/no me what I paint," this later pun's yoking a word signifying discovery ("know") with a word signifying negation ("no") lures the reader with promises of knowledge at the same time that it negates the very knowledge it promises, the very "me" it seems to introduce. The presence that the poem references without reproducing becomes a palpable absence, a face haunting the white spaces between Robinson's words but never coming fully into focus.

And in the midst of these absences the reader of Robinson's portrait, like the reader of the Widow Wadman's, is invited to fill in the blanks—to commit the very appropriations that robbed Charke of her gender-neutral pronouns and the very misinterpretations that transformed Bellamy's big wig into a true expression of herself. Instead of resisting such appropriations, Robinson embraces them—but she deploys her ellipses as potent reminders that the reader's own appropriations and misinterpretations are not what he or she craves in an autobiographical performance, and that these appropriations and misinterpretations offer much less satisfaction than the confessions, secrets, and self-reflections that such an autobiographical performance promises. In performances like Robinson's, confessions are always elliptical, self-reflections always absent, the subject they promise to represent, like Perdita, always already lost.

As she produced more and more of these printed self-representations in her later years, this loss came to seem more and more a defining aspect of Robinson's identity. In the autobiography that she began six years after "Stanzas to a Friend" was published, Robinson offers another "portrait" that serves not to re-create the presence but rather to proclaim the absence of its subject. Here, however, her absence accrues not in the spaces between the words, but in the words themselves. Language, in Robinson, seems only to dissolve an identity or an understanding, never to recover it. *The Memoirs of the Late Mrs. Mary Robinson, Written by Herself* appeared just as the great age of the confessional autobiography was dawning: Robinson probably began work on her *Memoirs* in 1799, seventeen years after Jean-Jacques Rousseau published his *Confessions* and one year after Wordsworth began the *Prelude*. In its confessional tone and in its focus on her family rather than her professional life, Robinson's *Memoirs* seem to have more in common with the works of these contemporaries than with the earlier works of Cibber or Sterne. Yet while Wordsworth described his *Prelude* as a method for discovering or creating a stable self through imagistic poetry—and while Cibber used his *Apology* as a method for misdirecting his critics through purple prose—Robinson both theorizes and deploys language as a method for proclaiming her own absence. Against histories of Romantic autobiography that describe it as striving toward self-discovery, Robinson's *Memoirs* offer a complex counterexample of the Romantic autobiography as a mode of self-erasure.

THE MEMOIRS OF THE LATE MRS. MARY ROBINSON AS MEMENTO MORI

The actors' autobiographies that I've examined so far in this book all begin with a beginning. Cibber begins his *Apology* with an acknowledgment of his follies and with a description of his father's career. Bellamy begins hers with the life of her grandmother. Sterne begins his pseudoautobiography of *Tristram Shandy*, most famously, with the moment of Tristram's conception. Robinson begins her *Memoirs* with an ending: with the destruction of the once beautiful monastery, "which was never repaired or re-raised," in which she was born.[36] As scholars like Alix Nathan and Jacquelyn Labbe have pointed out, Robinson here employs the Gothic tropes of death and decay so familiar to the literature of her day. Yet while the Gothic ultimately proclaims the persistence of memory and the refusal of lost things to stay lost—be they buried secrets, forgotten histories, or deceased relatives—Robinson's *Memoirs* asserts the irretrievability of the past. "Alas!" Robinson writes later, lamenting her decision to take up a career as an author. "How little did I foresee that the day would come when my health would be impaired, my thoughts perpetually employed, in so destructive a pursuit! At the moment that I write this page I feel in every fiber of my brain the fatal conviction that it is a *destroying labour.*"[37]

Robinson refers here to the effect authorship has had on her mental and physical health. But we might also apply her description of her "*destroying labour*" more widely, for indeed Robinson both portrays and deploys language in her *Memoirs* as a destructive force, useful only in marking—and, in some instances, helping to create—an absence. Robinson learns to read, for example, by "learning epitaphs and monumental inscriptions" on the graves that abut her childhood home, as words come to stand for the absence of those they name.[38] Her only daughter—who will grow up to complete the *Memoirs* as an epitaph for her mother—acquires language in much the same way. The episode—one of the most intimate scenes of family life in the *Memoirs*—serves to articulate Robinson's conception of language as a kind of ellipsis, naming only what is lost.

Like the scene of her birth and her own introduction to reading, Robinson's description of her daughter's first words overflows with the imagery of the Gothic. Robinson sets the scene not in a ruined monastery but rather within the equally inhospitable walls of Newgate Prison, where Thomas Robinson's debts have confined him and where Mary's wifely duties have obliged her to follow him. While in jail, the author passes the time by writing poetry and strolling through the prison yard, often carrying her infant daughter. "It was during one of those night walks that my little daughter first blessed my ears with the articulation of words," she writes. "The circumstance made a forcible and indelible impression on my mind. It was a clear moonlight evening; the infant was in the arms of her nursery maid; she was dancing her up and down, and was playing with her; her eyes were fixed on the moon, to which she pointed with her small forefinger. On a sudden a cloud passed over it, and the child, with a slow falling of her hand, articulately sighed, '*All gone!*'"[39]

Like the know me / no me pun in "Stanzas to a Friend," the knowledge that Robinson promised in the first half of the passage is accompanied in this second half by its negation: the first spoken words that her daughter learns "articulately" describe what is not there. Yet while the absences and ambiguities in "Stanzas to a Friend" snuck into the spaces between words, emerging from the second meaning of "no" implied but not visible in Robinson's language or from the implied ellipsis in her sentences, this absence is proclaimed by the words themselves. The only names worth learning, the only words worth remembering, Robinson implies, are those that name things and people already "*All gone*." Recording these lives in printed words doesn't preserve them or make them legible but only reminds us of their absence. And as we add more words—as "*gone*" becomes "*All gone*," for instance—this absence only becomes more marked. This addition of a word that makes the subject's absence more conspicuous is key to Robinson's strategy and what ties her to her overexpressive predecessors even as it distinguishes her from the "disappearing" performers who, according to Phelan, harness the political power of their ephemeral art form to prevent their spectators' commodifications. Unlike Cibber, Robinson deploys such words to name absences rather than to exaggerate her presence into uninterpretability. Unlike Phelan's performers, however, she achieves these absences by inviting the curiosities and commodifications that seduce her spectators into desiring her portrait or paging through her *Memoirs* for the secrets of her private life. When they do, they discover not secrets but blank spaces to be filled in by their own imaginations.

Of course, the greatest absence within *The Memoirs of the Late Mrs. Mary Robinson* is the absence of the late Mrs. Robinson herself, who died before she could complete her work and whose death interrupts the narrative rather abruptly. At first this absence seems a lamentable accident. Yet certain eccentricities in the text suggest that what at first appears an interruption in the narrative might be its central feature; and what could have been the autobiographer's deepest anxiety—that she be unable to complete her life story before her death—here becomes her cleverest stratagem.

The absence of Mary Robinson from the book that promises to elucidate her is made a foregone conclusion by the work's paradoxical title, which describes the work we are about to read as "*Written by*" the very same Mrs. Robinson it names as already "*Late*." This same absence is made conspicuous once again by the note that interrupts the narrative just before Robinson is set to relate the details of her assignation with the prince. "That she lived not to conclude the history of a life, scarcely less eventful than unfortunate, cannot but afford a subject of sincere regret," it begins, introducing the "Friend" (most likely Robinson's daughter, Maria Elizabeth) who will continue a narrative "regret[fully]" curtailed by the death of its original author.[40] Sincere regret, indeed: Robinson's first-person narrative cuts off just as she is about to describe the most salacious details of her life and loves—the details that mark her indoctrination into celebrity culture and the details for which, after all, we have been reading.

We are provided these details—albeit in an abbreviated and distanced form—through "a letter of Mrs. Robinson, written some years afterwards to a valued and since deceased friend" and reproduced on the pages that follow.[41] Certain details of the letter and the language that surround it, however, suggest that the interruption in the narrative at precisely this moment, rather than a "regret[table]" loss, is instead a cleverly calculated strategy designed to make even more conspicuous Robinson's absence from the story of which she seems to be the center. The truth of how this part of the autobiography took shape is difficult to determine, of course, without the manuscript that remains locked away in the home of Robinson's descendants. But there is some evidence that the letter describing Robinson's affair with the prince, at least, was initially written as part of the autobiography. The details disclosed in this portion of the narrative seem odd for a private letter to a friend, one who, residing "in America," as the note preceding the letter claims, would have had only limited access to the tabloid accounts that the narrative here alludes to and repudiates.[42] And as Hester Davenport, one of the few scholars to have been granted access to the manuscript, notes, certain historical references in the passage suggest it was composed long after 1783, the purported date of the letter.[43] Instead, this part of the narrative seems more in keeping with the autobiographer's public justification of her past behavior for the benefit of her English readers.

This hypothesis is speculative, and proving or disproving the letter's existence as part of the original autobiography is outside the scope of my inquiry here. Whether or not the letter began as a letter to a friend or as part of an autobiography for the benefit of the English public, the effect is the same: like the title's mention of the "late Mrs. Mary Robinson" or the description of writing as a "destroying labour," this break in the narrative reminds us that any effort by the *Memoirs* to reveal or to preserve its subject was always doomed to failure. To believe these words to be written by Robinson and intended for a public readership merely makes this reminder more emphatic.

This interruption also makes its author's absence even more conspicuous. It reveals, for one thing, the author's concerted effort to make her readers aware of her ghostly presence: following the note that announces the author's death, the letter carries the weight of words written from beyond the grave—but written only to remind us of the author's absence. At the same time, it proclaims—against the assumptions of the "culture of posterity"—the written word as a medium for, rather than as a defense against, loss.[44] Describing in the letter a bond of twenty thousand pounds that the prince promised but never paid during their affair, Robinson writes: "This paper was signed by the Prince, and sealed with the royal arms. It was expressed in terms so liberal, so voluntary, so marked by true affection, that I had scarcely power to read it. My tears, excited by the most agonizing conflicts, obscured the letters, and nearly blotted out those sentiments which will be impressed upon my mind till the last period of my existence."[45]

Here as throughout her *Memoirs*, Robinson emphasizes the ephemerality of the written word. The most permanent words of her description are the deeply felt "sentiments" recorded in the prince's letters but also "impressed upon my mind." Describing these words as "impress[ions]," however, Robinson portrays them as marks upon her body—a body whose "latest period of existence," as the title's reference to "*the Late Mrs. Mary Robinson*" reminds us, has already passed. Beyond these "impressions," there is the written word of the prince, who (as Robinson's readers well knew) had refused to fulfill the bond he had "signed" and "sealed with the royal arms." And there are the "letters" of the bond itself, immediately "obscured" by Robinson's tears. In their inseparability from Robinson's body and in their inescapable unreliability, these written words begin to take on the ephemeral quality of performance, disappearing even as their author pronounces them. We might purchase Robinson's book as a commodity and read it for its secrets, such moments suggest, but this purchase will bring us no closer to discovering who "the Late Mrs. Mary Robinson" really is.

Robinson's description of the emotion that "nearly blotted out these sentiments" recalls the "blotted page" that recorded the history of Cibber's Richard in deformed and illegible letters. It contains, too, the ghost of Sterne's "recording angel," whom Bellamy resurrects only to "obliterate with a tear of pity this vow" and "erase it forever from the eternal register of mortals deeds."[46] Bellamy never quite summons Sterne's recording angel, and her vow remains locked on the paper that bears her signature. For Robinson, however, no vows seem lasting—whether they are the promised bond of the Prince of Wales or (more positively for Robinson) the attempts of her critics to contain or circumscribe her. In her elliptical phrases and in her curtailed narrative, Robinson absents herself from the autobiography that bears her name—while calling attention to this very absence. Accordingly, the "blotted" pages of her autobiography seem to dissolve not into the overloaded inkiness of Sterne's black page but into the conspicuous blankness of his white page.

Comparing Robinson's elliptical self-representations to the Widow Wadman's white page goes beyond suggesting a new role for the autobiographical subject as conspicuously absent presence, however. As I have been arguing, it suggests a new role for the autobiographical reader or spectator as well. In the final sections of this chapter, I argue that Robinson's *Memoirs* and the conspicuous absences that litter her autobiographical performances take advantage of a relationship between spectator and celebrity that was becoming more prominent in the second half of the eighteenth century and that depended on the growing number of female readers and consumers beginning to participate in celebrity culture. This relationship was not the hierarchical one of a spectator watching and critiquing the spectacular celebrity. It was, instead, a symbiotic one, in which the spectator fashions himself or—more often—herself after the celebrity's model. And it is a relationship that Robinson promoted in her *Memoirs* not by evoking the media of performance or portraiture, but through suggesting a third, brand-new medium that was changing how female consumers participated in eighteenth-century print culture: the fashion magazine.

THE FASHION MAGAZINE AND AUTOBIOGRAPHICAL EVASIONS AS MASS CULTURE

In the frontispiece that adorns the first edition of the *Memoirs* and several of Robinson's poetry collections, we can glimpse the author gazing back at the overexpressive strategies of Cibber at the same time that she faces forward to the alternative possibilities introduced by the fashion magazine. The illustration reproduces in etched approximation what has become the most famous portrait of Robinson, Sir Joshua Reynolds's *Contemplation*, completed between 1783 and 1784 (figure 13). Robinson did not commission the portrait, and the influence she had over its arrangement and style is a matter of some debate.[47] However, art historian John Ingamells, who wrote one of the first and still one of the most often cited books on the portraits, notes that Robinson is said to have preferred Reynolds's depiction of her to the many paintings that appeared in the years after her stage debut—a rumor that Robinson's choice of the painting as her most frequent frontispiece supports.

Like the autobiography—and like poems such as "Stanzas to a Friend"—"Contemplation" seems to record Robinson on the very precipice of disappearance. It shows the celebrity seated before the viewer but with her head turned in deep profile, her downcast eyes gazing out to the turbulent sea be-

13. Sir Joshua Reynolds, *Contemplation* (1784). © The Wallace Collection, London.

hind her. The technical name for this pose is *profil perdu*, or "lost profile"—a name that, as Anne K. Mellor notes, underlines the absences and enigmas that characterize so many of Perdita's self-representations. The pose and Robinson's bulky updo obscure most of her face, and the expression on her lips is frustratingly inscrutable. Whether her mouth expresses sadness or whether that is a smile playing across her slightly upturned lips—as well as what, precisely, she contemplates during this moment of contemplation—remains unknown, unknowable. Perhaps most frustrating, the position of Robinson's head obscures her eyes, so we can no more understand the emotion they might reveal than we can trace the prospect upon which they gaze. As with so many of Robinson's self-portraits, this one promises to re-create the celebrity's presence but succeeds only in marking her absence.

Yet while her face gazes behind her, Robinson's torso faces forward. The incongruity is striking: it is almost as if a different artist has painted Robinson's body. This may indeed have been the case: in the studio system of which Reynolds was a part, an apprentice would often be employed to paint generic bodies into a number of portraits, leaving the face to be filled in later by the master painter. Paired with Robinson's lost profile, in other words, is a body that might have belonged to any of Reynolds's subjects: shoulders facing forward, hands folded neatly in lap. As if to emphasize the oddness of this pairing, Reynolds has painted a thin black ribbon around Robinson's neck that divides her obscured face from the generic body. Below this ribbon, the only thing that distinguishes Robinson's portraits from the others in Reynolds's studio is the fashionable attire that adorns it and for which Robinson had become known.

The neatly posed and easily transferrable body that anchors Robinson's lost profile—and the black ribbon that sets it off—suggests another function for the celebrity portrait. It becomes, here, not just a metaphorical window to an enigmatic soul but also a display window for the cutting-edge fashions that the celebrity modeled. At the same time that it denies the viewer a position from which to judge Robinson's expression, the painting also encourages the viewer to admire and even attempt to re-create Robinson's look. In this sense, we might interpret the actress's illegible expression in a different light: by refusing to assert the personality of the celebrity-model, it leaves a blank space in which the female spectator might imagine herself.

This promise is precisely that made by the images in fashion magazines, which picture bodies striking enough to set off the clothes they wear while inviting the reader to imagine her own body wearing those clothes (and living the life those clothes represent). Robinson's celebrity depended on the growing popularity of such magazines, which often tracked her style choices and reported them to an eager public. Although the first women's magazines devoted solely to fashion did not emerge until much later, advice about fashion began to appear as early as the turn into the eighteenth century in English periodicals—particularly those marketed in part or exclusively to women. *The Ladies Diary: or, Woman's Almanack* was one of the first; it began appearing annually in 1704. In 1750, the *Diary* included a black-and-white engraving of a fashionable gown at the front of the volume. Such illustrations became a regular feature of the magazine, appearing in every subsequent edition. By 1770, according to historian Beverly Lemire, "A flood of pocketbooks and memorandum books were produced, all with engravings of fashionable figures displayed on the front pages."[48]

Such books not only registered the changes in a literary marketplace increasingly driven by female consumers. They also registered the changes in these readers' engagement with their texts. Instead of presupposing a reader who would maintain an objective distance in order to judge a story aesthetically or morally, fashion magazines imagine a reader who identifies with and puts herself into the place of the subject pictured or described. In this sense fashion magazines work similarly to fiction as Catherine Gallagher describes it, presenting "nobodies" whose subjectivity the reader might occupy.[49] Unlike the characters of a novel, the models in fashion magazines have bodies that the reader can see and must contend with. But the method of reading a fashion magazine (or of gazing at its photos) requires that the reader evacuate the personality from this body and insert her own subjectivity into the clothes and the lifestyle that this body advertises. Oliver Goldsmith makes this point explicit in the caption to a fashion plate he published in the *Lady's Magazine*, a short-lived companion to the more successful *Gentleman's Magazine*, which he published between 1759 and 1763. Next to the picture, labeled *Habit of a Lady*, Goldsmith offers the plate "for the assistance of those in the country who, as they have not the opportunities of seeing the originals, may dress by the figure."[50] Presenting such a "figure" as a model for those in the country, Goldsmith invites the reader to step (quite literally) into the shoes of the image's subject. The subject's body becomes, then, a placeholder for the reader's—a blank space that the reader might refashion according to her "own mind."[51] Yet in doing so the reader also surrenders her ability to critique the celebrity or to pry into her private life: as her reader inserts her own body into the celebrity's clothes and her own subjectivity into the celebrity's story, the celebrity retreats from view. By staging her autobiographical performances as fashion plates, Robinson discovers a new way of preventing her spectators from prying into her private life.[52]

The new relationship between reader/viewer and subject that the fashion magazine helped to fuel suggests a different way of interpreting not only Reynolds's portrait of Robinson but also some of the most remarkable—and some of the most remarked-upon—passages of Robinson's *Memoirs*. These occur when Robinson interrupts the train of her narrative, often stalling its most exciting and most scandalous moments, in order to describe the minute particulars of her appearance. In one instance, she relates her discomfort at the gaze of some strange men she encounters at the Ranelagh pleasure gardens: "Their fixed stare disconcerted me," she writes; "I rose, and, leaning on my husband's arm, again mingled in the brilliant circle. The inquiries followed us; stopping several friends, as we walked round the circle, and repeatedly demanding of them, 'Who is that young lady in the pink dress trimmed with sable?'"[53] A bit later in the *Memoirs*, Robinson pauses halfway through describing her emotional confrontation with one of her husband's mistresses: "She smiled, and cast her eyes over my figure," Robinson writes of her antagonist. "My dress was a morning *dishabille* of India muslin, with a bonnet of straw, and a white lawn cloak bordered with lace."[54]

Previous scholars have argued that in these passages Robinson merely parrots the objectification that her critics and caricaturists cast upon her, "construct[ing] herself as an object of desire for an implied male viewer," in Eleanor Ty's words, and "present[ing] herself as an erotic spectacle . . . for her readers."[55] Yet in including such precise details about the color, cloth, and cut of her outfits, such passages recall not only the paintings that pictured her as an "object of desire" but the fashion magazines then growing in popularity. And in encouraging her readers to approach these passages as "figures" they might "dress by" rather than as spectacles they should judge, Robinson reconceives the relationship between a celebrity and her public until they want no longer to own or to contain her but rather to be her.

In her description of her encounter with her husband's mistress, especially, Robinson harnesses the elliptical prose that so much of her other writings exhibit with the descriptive style of a fashion magazine in order to prevent her reader from appropriating her identity. Her strategy hinges on her use of the word "figure" in her description of the mistress who "smiled, and cast a gaze over my figure." In its most common meaning, "figure" suggests the body beneath Robinson's clothes—and promises that the description that follows will offer the reader access to this body. This promise reiterates those made by so many celebrity biographies and autobiographies, and that is perhaps most vividly illustrated in the autopsy report included in Barton Booth's biography—or in the pornographic *Memoirs of Perdita* to which Robinson's own *Memoirs* seems, in many ways, a delayed response. Crucially, however, the passage never actually describes the body that it promises to reveal. Instead, Robinson slyly replaces the promised description of her "figure" with a minute description of the dress "of India muslin," the "bonnet of straw," and the "white lawn cloak bordered with lace" that obscure that figure.

A second meaning of "figure" furthers Robinson's strategy by suggesting the links between celebrity memoir and fashion magazine that, as we've already seen, invite the reader to insert her own "figure" into the subject's dress and that thus keep the reader's inquiries into the subject's private life or private parts at bay. "Figure" is a word common both to Robinson's *Memoirs* and to the captions on Goldsmith's fashion plates—indeed, to the fashion plates like Goldsmith's popping up in so many late eighteenth-century periodicals—which invite the country ladies to gaze on the illustrated fashions and "dress by the figure." Here "figure" is the image of a sophisticated and fashionable woman that a less sophisticated and less fashionable woman gazes at in order to know how to dress. Portraying Robinson as the original after which another woman might model herself, this sense changes the tenor of Robinson's confrontation with her husband's paramour. The implication is that the mistress is merely following trends that Robinson has originated, and that Robinson herself has already done all of the things—or all of the people—that the mistress now does or will do. The mistress might be appropriating Robinson's look and her lover, the word implies, but there's also a sense that this appropriation is derivative. As the "figure" that the mistress merely gazes upon, Robinson remains in power, the model setting the standard that others must follow.

The genre of the fashion magazine allows Robinson to set up a similar relationship with her reader, who now gazes upon her not as a spectacle to be interpreted and judged but rather as a model to be followed. The reader who puts herself in Robinson's place here accomplishes two goals for the celebrity eager to escape her public's appropriations. First, she forgoes the very interpretations that works like the spurious *Memoirs of Perdita* represent. The reader of Robinson's *Memoirs* might purchase the clothes Robinson wears and even appropriate the styles that she describes here in such great detail. But in her attention to the clothes and accessories that make up the "figure" of Robinson here, the reader overlooks the "figure" beneath those clothes and accessories—the private parts (and the private life) that strategies like overexpression arose to protect. The reader's appreciation of the transferability of these clothes and accessories to her own body depends on her lack of attention to Robinson's body, the particularities of which she must ignore in order to picture her own body and her own subjectivity in the clothes that Robinson describes. Second, then, the reader places herself in the blank spaces Robinson's body and subjectivity once occupied, and as a result offers her own body and her "own mind" as the spectacle she is attempting to decipher. By replacing Robinson's body with her own in imagining this scene, the reader allows Robinson to slip, undetected, into the shadows—without sacrificing the fame and the admiration that fueled her career. In her place stands the reader—once the spectator who must now imagine herself at the center of the spotlight and as the object of the gaze.

CONCLUSION: THE WHITE PAGE AS SPECTACULAR DISAPPEARANCE

Robinson's appropriation of the style of the fashion magazine accomplishes a further task as well. In addition to allowing the celebrity an escape from the spotlight, it teaches the reader to live like a celebrity—and to practice the strategies of autobiographical performance that the celebrity employed. It was a skill that was becoming more and more in demand as the eighteenth century wore on—and as the line between celebrity and citizen became more permeable. Mary Robinson embodied this change, for she seems, among the performers in this book, the most unlikely celebrity. Unlike Charke or Bellamy, she was born not to a theatrical family but within a middle-class home. And unlike Cibber or Garrick—both of whom enjoyed long careers on the stage—her celebrity continued long after the live performances at Drury Lane that first inspired it. With her rise to fame in the late eighteenth century, celebrity and its discomforts had become something that anyone might enjoy—and that everyone must guard against. By claiming their own place in the construction and creation of Robinson's identity—filling in the blanks in her poems and portraits with the subjectivities they envisioned, or following the fashion trends she modeled—Robinson's spectators slowly acquired and began to adopt the self-protective strategies that allowed them to live in a modern world where every life had the potential to be made public.

A curious caricature of Robinson printed around the same time as *The Thunderer* speaks to the newly collaborative nature of celebrity—and foreshadows the ways in which overexpression would spread from the eighteenth-century celebrity to the common man. *Florizel and Perdita*, published anonymously in 1783, depicts the notorious former lovers of its title in twinned portraits (figure 14). On the left, the Prince of Wales, in his royal uniform, is pictured near the insignia of three ostrich feathers that confirm his identity. A vertical line through the center of the page (and through the center of his body) divides his right half from Mary Robinson's left, so that the two faces form a composite image. The sentimentality of the heart shape suggested by the two joined faces is undermined, however, by the smaller images that accompany each portrait. To the left of the prince is the miniaturized

14. *Florizel and Perdita* (1783). Courtesy of the Lewis Walpole Library, Yale University.

image of King George III, shouting "Oh! My Son My Son!" To the right of Robinson is a pedestal labeled "*King of Cuckolds*" and holding a bust of the actress's husband, crowned with horns. The horns balance what looks like another pedestal or a platter holding the busts of three men also rumored to have had affairs with Mary Robinson: Tarleton, the politician Charles Fox, and Fox's then-ally in Parliament, Lord North. The heart shape of the joined faces recalls the heart-shaped card that accompanied the prince's picture and that promised Robinson that her paramour would remain "*Unalterable to my Perdita through life*."[56] In many ways, then, the caricature allows Robinson's spectators access to the very secrets that the interruptions in her *Memoirs* denied them—and ownership of the miniature picture that the prince is said to have given Robinson that night.

The axis upon which the reader's appropriation of the image rotates is the line that divides the prince's half of the page from Robinson's half. A crease following this line in the copies of the image in both the British Museum and in the Lewis Walpole Library at Yale University suggest that the image's original consumers followed the line's directive to fold the image in half. In other words, they recognized it not only as a two dimensional drawing but as what Robin Bernstein calls a "scriptive thing"—a thing that suggests without precisely dictating how its consumer might employ or play with it.[57] In this case, the print invites several activities that allow the consumer to play a part in Robinson's affair with the prince. The more cynical consumer might choose, for instance, to fold the paper with the image to the outside, so that the portraits of Robinson and the prince face in opposite directions. In this arrangement the image might suggest the discord between the two former lovers now unable to see eye to eye. As the folded image is flipped, one side replacing the other, the prince's face alternating with that of his most famous mistress, it refutes (quite literally) the prince's promise to remain "*Unalterable*."

There is, however, another way of handling the image that allows the reader to rewrite Robinson's story with a much happier ending. Folded in on itself, so that the figures of Robinson and the prince face each other, the print allows the consumer to imagine a tête-à-tête conversation between the two lovers. Folded further, conversation becomes copulation, as the images of the two faces, the two bodies, come into contact, one on top of the other. When the consumer partially unfolds the image again, he or she might imagine the two faces melding into a single face, its composite features suggesting the offspring—half-royal, half-common—that the prince's assignations with Robinson threatened to produce. The caricature seems to portray such a narrative as horrifying, calling up the threat of a Britain in the unsteady hands of an insufficiently royal heir apparent. Yet at the same time the drawing leaves room for the intriguing possibility of the spectator in the role of celebrity, manipulating his or her performances in much the same way that he or she has manipulated the ending of Robinson's story.

As the nineteenth century dawned and as technologies of communication improved, the line between spectator and celebrity blurred even further. As it did, overexpressive strategies that held off the celebrity's detractors by blinding them with bodies too overladen with costumes, pages too full of ink, and selves too spectacular to see didn't decline. Rather, they spread. If everyone has the potential for celebrity, after all, everyone has use for overexpression. By the twenty-first century, as I will argue in a brief coda, questions of how to protect oneself from the public gaze spread like one of Robinson's fashions, beginning with the rich and famous only to become a feature of the autobiographical performances of everyday people. As they did, overexpression ceased to be a style of performance used only by a few select celebrities on eighteenth-century stages and became, instead, a key aspect of how one might perform a modern self.

Coda

Overexpression and Its Legacy

Once upon a time, the celebrity was a freak. Whether she was born "abnormally interesting" or had abnormal interest thrust upon her, she tended to stand out in a crowd—and thus to suffer the whispered rumors, the printed gossip, the pokings and proddings and losses of privacy that society reserves for its most visible scapegoats.[1]

Once upon a time the celebrity was a freak but then, instead of shrinking from his freakishness, he learned to embrace and even to exaggerate it until it became the key to his liberation. He wore it in the curls of his wig and in the hump on his back, wrote it into the spellings of his words and the pages of his book; he used it to tell the story of his life. And then, two hundred years later, in one of the most widely viewed artifacts of Western celebrity culture, he brought it back from the dead.

Michael Jackson's *Thriller* became the best-selling album of all time following its release in 1982, and the long-form music video (directed by John Landis) that accompanied the title track transformed the music industry.[2] With its high production values, its technological innovations, and its unmistakable style, the *Thriller* video exemplifies the decadent, late twentieth-century American celebrity culture of which it was a part. In introducing it in the coda to a book about eighteenth-century British celebrity culture, I do not mean to elide the significant differences between those eras. Jackson's early success as a childhood star and his later career as an international idol highlight the twentieth-century celebrity's dependence on an army of publicists, stylists, choreographers, managers, and makeup artists who were largely absence from the eighteenth-century performer's entourage and whose presence complicates the ways in which the celebrity can be said to control his or her own self-presentation. The media technology driving celebrity culture had evolved as well in the two hundred years between Mary Robinson's miniature picture and Jackson's full-color video, broadcast into fans' living rooms immediately and repeatedly at the mere flip of a switch.

Before I address these differences, however, I want to linger momentarily on the similarities between Jackson's performances—most notably those on display in the *Thriller* video—and the autobiographical performances of the eighteenth-century celebrities who came before him. These similarities do not demonstrate (and I do not wish to imply) a direct line of descent from Cibber's *Apology* to Jackson's *Thriller*. Nor do I mean to attribute some universality or timelessness to artifacts that, as the rest of this book has insisted, emerge from a particular historical moment, a particular and culturally conditioned definition of privacy and publicity, and particular (post-Enlightenment and unmistakably Western) assumptions about identity. Instead, I introduce these similarities in order to emphasize the debt that today's (post-Enlightenment, Western) assumptions about privacy, publicity and identity owe to those that emerged in eighteenth-century London. The traces of overexpression that still linger in the artifacts of twentieth- and twenty-first-century celebrity culture teach us the importance of long-past performances—even performances as seemingly flighty and ephemeral as the autobiographical performances of eighteenth-century celebrities—in shaping the culture we inhabit today.

For if we look closely, even the artifacts of eighteenth-century celebrity culture that seem most foreign appear strangely and surprisingly familiar. The practice of including autopsy reports in eighteenth-century biographies like Benjamin Victor's 1733 *Memoirs of Barton Booth*, for instance, seems barbaric until we recall the urgency with which twenty-first-century audiences clamored for the release of Michael Jackson's autopsy report after he died of a drug overdose in 2009.[3] The celebrity status of the eighteenth-century castrati seems similarly unbelievable given twenty-first-century gender norms—and yet Jackson's famously falsetto voice invited comparisons to the castrato not only by Internet conspiracy theorists but also by Dr. Alain Branchereau, a professor at Timone University Hospital in Marseilles, France, who speculated in a 2009 interview that Jackson had been "chemically castrat[ed]" by his use of crypterone, a drug he took for severe acne.[4]

Less surprising but no less revealing is Jackson's interest in the genre of celebrity autobiography that Cibber introduced. In her collection of essays about the pop icon, Margo Jefferson notes that "Michael Jackson read [P. T.] Barnum's autobiography fervently (at least one of the eight versions) and gave copies to all of his staff, telling them, 'I want my career to be the greatest show on earth.'"[5] When he composed his own autobiography, *Moonwalk*, in 1988, Jackson adhered to the conventions of the genre in including a paradoxical plea for privacy within the published story of his life. "The price of fame can be a heavy one," he admits:

> I've been accused of being obsessed with my privacy and it's true that I am. People stare at you when you're famous. They're observing you and that's understandable, but it's not always easy. If you were to ask me why I wear sunglasses in public as often as I do, I'd tell you it's because I simply don't like to have to constantly look everyone in the eye. It's a way of concealing just a bit of myself. After I had my wisdom teeth pulled, the dentist gave me a surgical mask to wear home to keep out germs. I loved that mask. It was great—much better than sunglasses—and I had fun wearing it around for a while. There's so little privacy in my life that concealing a little bit of me is a way to give myself a break from all that. It may be considered strange, I know, but I like my privacy.[6]

Like Cibber and the generations of celebrities that followed him, Jackson clings to the publicity that elevated him from an unhappy childhood and from the poverty that otherwise seemed his fate. Just as steadfastly, however, he clings to the privacy that guaranteed his personhood but that seemed always out of reach in a career in which "people stare at you" and you "have to constantly look everyone in the eye."

Given the resemblance between Jackson's and Cibber's struggles with privacy and publicity, it makes sense that their solutions to these struggles bear some resemblance as well. Jackson describes his sunglasses and surgical mask as costume pieces meant to "conceal" his face, but his awareness of the "strange[ness]"—the freakishness—of his costumes suggests that at the same time that they conceal him they also make him more visible. Over the course of his career this strangeness became in itself a strategy for concealment, a way of removing himself from the categories through which other people—famous or not—were read, labeled, and dissected in the last two decades of the second millennium. Though these categories themselves are arguably unique to Jackson's particular culture, the strategy of concealment-through-revelation that he uses to deploy them—casting himself as a freak in his *Thriller* video as in so many of his autobiographical performances—contains traces of the overexpressions that Cibber and his eighteenth-century successors developed so long ago.

Indeed, far from using the elaborate costumes and heavy makeup of his

Thriller character to conceal his "private self" from the viewing public, Jackson encourages his spectators to interpret the freakishness that defines his onscreen persona as an extension of the freakishness of the actor portraying him. Character and actor first meld into one early in the video, which opens on a private moment between a teenager (Jackson) and his date (Ola Ray), stranded when their car runs out of gas on a dark, deserted lane. When Ray refers to Jackson's character as "Michael," she invites us to read him as a version of the performer whose first name he shares and to read his bashful request that she "be my girl" as a glimpse into—or at least a metaphor for—the private life of our public star.[7] "Michael's" subsequent confession, "I'm not like other guys," seems, then, an admission of the plight of a celebrity, "helpless, and expos'd" (as Cibber termed it) to the burdens of public life.[8] But when the clouds part around a full moon and Michael suddenly morphs into a werewolf, we recognize this fame as inseparable from the monstrous freakishness that makes him "not like other guys." In other words, Jackson deploys the fantastical elements of the video not to distance his private self from his onstage persona. Instead, the video encourages us to interpret its star's freakishness as an indispensable part of his autobiographical performance—a performance as impossible to categorize as it is to ignore.

This oscillation between Jackson's freakish persona and his private self intensifies as the darkened lane gives way to a darkened theater, and we realize that the video we've been watching is a video within a video, viewed with us by a more realistic "Michael" and Ray in contemporary dress. Our relief lasts only briefly, as the two exit the theater to find themselves surrounded by zombies, whom Jackson soon joins in a ghoulish dance of the dead. This mise en abime that structures *Thriller*—a werewolf tale that turns out to be a video within a zombie tale that turns out, by its conclusion, to have been nothing but a dream—becomes less revelatory as it reveals more and more: each installment encourages us to read it as an insight into or a metaphor for Jackson's private life, only to be exposed, moments later, as part of an increasingly elaborate fiction that makes us question whether that private life ever existed at all. "The video plays on the idea: who is the real Michael Jackson?" writes cultural critic Jason King in a recent book about the star.[9] The question haunts the dance that Jackson performs at the video's climax, which emphasizes the uncategorizability of Jackson's autobiographical performances specifically by exaggerating his freakishness.

The dance begins with the zombies, who jerk, shrug, and twitch their way into a circle around Jackson and his companion. After zooming in on Ray's face, the camera follows her gaze to Jackson's face, its features now exaggerated into the bugged eyes, sunken cheeks, and greenish skin of a ghoul. With the start of the beat Jackson joins the other zombies in their dance, and we suddenly recognize the jerks, shrugs, and twitches that once made the zombies particularly freakish as some of Jackson's signature moves. The effect is the opposite to that of, say, the ballerina who makes her long leaps and athletic arabesques appear natural and effortless: here, the zombified makeup and Gothic setting exaggerate the seeming impossibility of Jackson's signature contortions and defamiliarize his familiar body as undeniably monstrous. Highlighting rather than hiding his freakishness, Jackson begins to seem something other than human. And if he is something other than human, we can no more assign a precise gender, age, or race to his famous body than we can to the unreadable bodies of the zombies dancing in his wake.

One signature move in particular captures the pointed illegibility of Jackson's autobiographical performance—as well as the continued relevance of overexpression in the celebrity culture that millennial Anglo-America has inherited, through many a twist and turn, from eighteenth-century England. Approximately twenty seconds into his dance with the zombies, Jackson thrusts his pelvis to the left while cupping his groin with his left hand, biting his lip in an expression of concentration (or titillation?). Variations on this "crotch grab," as it came to be known, are some of Jackson's most recognizable—and most controversial—moves. The crotch grab appeared in videos from *Thriller* and *Billie Jean* (1982) to *Bad* (1987) and *The Way You Make Me Feel* (1987), often accompanied by a high-pitched "Ow!" that animated a gesture of unbridled machismo with the incongruous scream of a girl. By 1993, the crotch grab had become such a trademark part of Jackson's performances that Oprah Winfrey asked him, in an exclusive interview, "Why do you always grab your crotch?"[10] And a 2008 episode of *The Family Guy* featured a Jackson-like performer who takes the move to new heights by shooting his groin with a machine gun, all the time coupling his shots with the recognizable "Ow!"[11]

Behind the tongue-in-cheek tone of Winfrey's question and *The Family Guy*'s parody lurks a genuine bafflement that, I think, marks the endgame of so many of Jackson's performances. Jackson's crotch grab is a marker of identity so obvious as to become unreadable. The gesture itself seems a deixis of Jackson's masculinity: by grabbing the parts of his anatomy that mark him as a man, Jackson makes his manhood obvious to the point of vulgarity. The high-pitched "Ow!" confirms his masculinity by pointing out that Jackson has the parts—and feels the pain—of most men with similar anatomies. At the same time, the "Ow!" suggests damage to or destruction of those parts and of the masculinity that they guarantee. Pairing a gesture that indicates his manhood with the squeal of a girl (or of a castrato), Jackson dons a masculinity so overt that it has come to resemble femininity, an identity so obviously freakish and so freakishly obvious that it has become impossible to read.

Winfrey and the writers of *The Family Guy* aren't the only spectators to have greeted Jackson's autobiographical performances with confusion, and Jackson's gender and sexuality aren't the only aspects of his persona to have sparked such questions. "Was he man, boy, man-boy, or boy-woman?" Jefferson asks, repeating questions that had puzzled fans throughout Jackson's life (and hardly ceased after his death). Was he "mannequin or postmodern zombie? Here was a black person who had once looked unmistakably black, and now looked white or at least un-black. He was, at the very least, a new kind of mulatto, one created by science and medicine and cosmetology."[12] Jackson's twentieth- and twenty-first-century critics struggle and fail to fit their celebrity into the identifying taxonomies of age, gender, race, and sexuality that might make sense of him.[13]

Once upon a time the celebrity was a freak, but *Thriller* suggests some uses for this freakishness as part of an overexpressive strategy that allows the millennial celebrity to sell his story without giving himself away. It also suggests the anxieties of spectators worried that the celebrity's undeniable influence over his fans might transform his freakishness into the fashion. Such anxieties are nothing new: recall, for instance, the critic who speculated that Cibber's drawled "Harse" would spread into a universal "*Lingua Cibberiana*"; or the "clockmaker" who worried that Sterne's bawdy book had forever changed how people would interpret the name of his product.[14] In *Thriller*, these anxieties emerge in the choice of zombies as the monsters who would accompany Jackson in his dance. Unlike mummies, werewolves, or other creatures from the B-horror milieu that *Thriller* evokes, zombies—according to their mythology—aim not only to kill but to convert their victims into monsters like themselves. The final moments of the video, as Jackson reassures Ray that she has dreamed the zombies—only to flash a ghoulish grin at the camera before leading her out of the room—play upon precisely this anxiety. The contagious freakishness that once made Jackson "not like other guys" will spread, the final shot promises, until Ray, until the spectators encouraged to identify with her throughout the video, until all "other guys" become freaks just like him.

The difference between Jackson's zombies and Sterne's Shandyism is that in Jackson's case, the contagion of freakishness seems to have caught on. In October 2006, a group of sixty-two "zombies" met in a community hall in Toronto, hoping to set the Guinness World Record for the largest *Thriller* dance performed simultaneously in one location. They succeeded so well that by the next year "Thrill the World" had spread to eighty cities in seventeen countries, where 1,722 people in zombie costumes danced in unison, brought together by and broadcast to the larger public through social media.[15] The movement's leader, dance instructor Ines Markeljevic, has used websites like Facebook, Twitter, and YouTube to publicize the event, which gains new followers each year. The success of Markeljevic's grassroots organization highlights one of the most important developments that celebrity culture has undergone since the eighteenth century, and that is the ease with which not only anyone but indeed everyone might attain celebrity status simply by manipulating the multiple publics that the Internet and social media have made widely available. In noting this development I am not revealing anything new, and today's pop culture pundits have been quick to point out the myriad ways that social media invites even the most private citizens to record and publicize the most intimate—or most banal—details of their daily lives for hundreds of Twitter "followers" or Facebook "friends" playing the role of fans.

Yet (and again this is hardly a new idea) even as social media satisfies our egotistic desires for fame, it also makes us painfully aware of the "Kicks, Cuffs, and Bastinados" to which the famous have always been vulnerable.[16] This awareness is manifest, for instance, in new policies regarding cyberbullying, in debates over Facebook's ever-evolving privacy settings, and in the worldwide outcry following revelations that the National Security Administration of the United States was tracking citizens' email and phone records.[17] In their struggles to evade such unwanted attentions without forgoing the social connectedness that these media foster, today's citizen-celebrities wrestle with different technologies but with similar assumptions about identity and self-presentation to those that emerged centuries ago. And many of them have developed similar strategies of self-presentation.

In 2010, for instance, artist Adam Harvey launched a series he calls "CV Dazzle" and that consists of a collection of hairstyles, makeup designs, and apparel meant to make the wearer illegible to the facial recognition software often employed in today's security cameras. According to his website, Harvey borrows the name of his series from "a type of World War I naval camouflage called Dazzle, which used cubist-inspired designs to break apart the visual continuity of a battleship and conceal its orientation and size. Likewise, CV Dazzle uses avant-garde hairstyling and make-up designs to break apart the continuity of a face."[18] The name "Dazzle" also suggests the particularly over-expressive qualities of a light so bright as to blind its viewer—or of designs

15. *CV Dazzle* by David Harvey (2010). Used with permission.

that work not by covering a model's face but by making that face appear so freakish as to be illegible to the cameras designed to recognize it (figure 15).

Of course, Harvey's designs are hardly commonplace, and we'd be hard-pressed today to find a CV Dazzle hairstyle in any but the most fashion-forward (or surveillance-averse) crowds. This is not to say that overexpression has yet to spread, as celebrity has, to the masses. We might glimpse it, for instance, in the proliferation of "ironic" facial hair, large glasses, and deliberately clashing patterns among the "hipster" generation, whose penchant for the outdated and the oversized seems to invite the public gaze at the same time that the irony attributed to these fashions warns the gazer from reading them as direct signifiers for the wearer's identity. ("The whole point of hipsters is that they avoid labels and being labeled," writes Julia Plevin in the *Huffington Post*. "However, they all dress the same and act the same and conform in their non-conformity. Doesn't the fact that there is a hipster look go against all hipster beliefs?")[19] Christian Lorentzen, channeling *Thriller*, likens hipsters to "zombies" who resurrect the fashionable bodies of previous subcultures while rejecting their ideological souls.[20] Yet we might also regard them as today's overexpressive performers, their conflicted relationship with mass production and social media exemplified by their simultaneous embrace of LPs and iPods, of digital photos filtered to look like Polaroids; their illegibility as subjects evident in their waxed moustaches and oversized hats.

Once upon a time the celebrity was a freak, but in the three hundred years that have intervened between Lord Foppington's unwieldy wig and Jackson's controversial crotch grab, celebrity culture has shifted with the societies that practice it, with the fashions that allow it, and with the technologies that disseminate it. Constant throughout these shifts is the individual yearning for an identity that might be seen and admired by all but somehow dissected and deciphered by very few. Overexpression offers one path toward such an identity, one strategy to balance the exhilaration of publicity and the freedom of privacy within a modern Western world that seems, paradoxically, to require both. In the "*Chiaro Oscuro* of my mind" that characterized his autobiography of 1740, Colley Cibber articulated a strategy not only for navigating the twists and turns of the burgeoning celebrity culture of eighteenth-century England but also for bearing the burdens and enjoying the rewards of possessing, publicizing, and privatizing a modern self.

NOTES

INTRODUCTION

1. Ian Watt, *The Rise of the Novel: Studies in Defoe, Richardson, and Fielding* (Berkeley: University of California Press, 1957, 2000), 291.

2. C. B. Macpherson, *The Political Theory of Possessive Individualism: Hobbes to Locke* (Oxford: Oxford University Press, 1962, 2011), 3.

3. Dror Wahrman, *The Making of the Modern Self: Identity and Culture in Eighteenth-Century England* (New Haven: Yale University Press, 2004), xi.

4. For the most influential discussions of when and how the modern self emerged, see Stephen Greenblatt, *Renaissance Self-Fashioning: From More to Shakespeare* (Chicago: University of Chicago Press, 1980); Charles Taylor, *Sources of the Self: The Making of Modern Identity* (Cambridge, MA: Harvard University Press, 1989); Jürgen Habermas, *The Structural Transformation of the Public Sphere: An Inquiry into a Category of Bourgeois Society*, trans. Thomas Burger (Cambridge, MA: MIT Press, 1989); Watt, *Rise of the Novel*; Macpherson, *Political Theory*; Michael McKeon, *The Origins of the English Novel, 1600–1740* (Baltimore: Johns Hopkins University Press, 1987); Wahrman, *Making of Modern Self*; Deidre Shauna Lynch, *The Economy of Character: Novels, Market Culture, and the Business of Inner Meaning* (Chicago: University of Chicago Press, 1988); and Richard Sennett, *The Fall of Public Man* (New York: W.W. Norton, 1974, 1976). Scholars of eighteenth-century literature and of the novel in particular (Watt, Macpherson, McKeon, Lynch, Wahrman) have acknowledged that although the sources of the self (to borrow Taylor's phrase) may have emerged during the early modern period, familiar technologies of the private self (such as the realist novel and the secular autobiography as genres that emphasize the self as coherent and psychologically developed) emerged sometime between 1660 and 1800. I don't wish to reiterate these arguments here. I begin this study with Cibber because he was the first to compose a secular autobiography in English. (I define a secular autobiography as one read for its subject's individual qualities and experiences rather than his or her relationship to a religious collective, and structured as a coherent narrative rather than a conversion tale meant to emphasize the subject's distance from his or her former, sinful self.) I conclude with Mary Robinson both because her autobiography marks a somewhat dramatic departure from Cibber's style and because the most influential studies of autobiography suggest that, whatever the sources of the self, the conception of the self and of autobiography changed with the rise of romanticism and the publication of more psychological works like Rousseau's *Confessions* and Wordsworth's *Prelude*. See Roy

Pascal, *Design and Truth in Autobiography* (Cambridge, MA: Harvard University Press, 1989), which argues that a new idea of autobiography emerges during the Romantic period; Felicity Nussbaum, *The Autobiographical Subject: Gender and Ideology in Eighteenth-Century England* (Baltimore: Johns Hopkins University Press, 1989), which concludes with late eighteenth-century works by Hester Thrale; and William Spengemann, *The Forms of Autobiography: Episodes in the History of a Literary Genre* (New Haven: Yale University Press, 1980), which marks a break between the "historical" autobiography of Benjamin Franklin and the "philosophical" autobiographies of Rousseau, Wordsworth, and De Quincey).

5. I am deliberately echoing Jody Greene's language in *The Trouble with Ownership: Literary Property and Authorial Liability in England, 1660–1730* (Philadelphia: University of Pennsylvania Press, 2005), in which she analyzes the predicament faced by modern authors, including Pope, writing after the passage of the Statute of Anne in 1710. As Greene notes, the Statute established writers (rather than printers) as the proprietors of their books and the recipients of the royalties those books generated. While this development allowed authors to claim ownership of their own works, it also made them liable to censorship and libel laws as they had never been before.

6. Joseph Addison, *The Spectator* 1, in *The Spectator*, ed. Donald F. Bond (Oxford: Oxford University Press, 1965), 1:5–6.

7. Colley Cibber, *An Apology for the Life of Colley Cibber, with an Historical View of the Stage during His Own Time, Written by Himself*, ed. B. R. S. Fone (Mineola, NY: Dover, 1968), 136–137.

8. Gender and sexuality, here, are the most obvious examples, as scholars such as Michel Foucault (*The History of Sexuality: An Introduction*, trans. Robert Hurley [New York: Vintage, 1988]), Thomas A. King (*The Gendering of Men, 1600–1750*, vol. 1 [Madison: University of Wisconsin Press, 2004]), and Kristina Straub (*Sexual Suspects: Eighteenth-Century Players and Sexual Ideology* [Princeton, NJ: Princeton University Press, 1992)] have noted. See Wahrman, *Making of Modern Self*, for a discussion of how other aspects of identity became less fluid during this time. Interestingly, Wahrman notes that the exception is geographical origin, which eighteenth-century Europeans regarded less and less as a determining factor in identity.

9. The suggestion of sincerity is what distinguishes overexpression from similar terms like "persona" or "camp." Unlike a persona, an overexpressed identity is never mistaken for a mask concealing identity but always appears—at first—to reveal identity. (For a discussion of the difference between the persona and the "true" character—or what appears to be true character, see Philip Auslander, *Performing Glam Rock: Gender and Theatricality in Popular Music* [Ann Arbor: University of Michigan Press, 2006], 4–5.) Unlike camp, similarly, overexpression never betrays outright irony or deliberate artifice. Essential to overexpression is the spectator's confusion over what aspects of the performance constitute the performer's sincere

attempts to express himself or herself and what aspects of this performance constitute deliberate attempts at disguise. See Susan Sontag, "Notes on 'Camp,'" *Against Interpretation and Other Essays* (New York: Farrar, Straus and Giroux, 1961).

10. Thomas Keymer, *Sterne, the Moderns and the Novel* (New York: Oxford University Press, 2002), 76.

11. Keymer, *Sterne*, 156.

12. Stuart Sherman has written a fascinating account of Garrick's interest in controlling his images in the newspapers of his day; see Sherman, "Garrick among Media: The '*Now* Performer' Navigates the News," *PMLA* 126.4 (October 2011): 966–982.

13. For a wonderful and nuanced exploration of Whitefield's relationship to the theater and to the theatrical celebrities of his time, see Misty Anderson, *Imagining Methodism in Eighteenth-Century Britain: Enthusiasm, Belief and the Borders of the Self* (Baltimore: Johns Hopkins University Press, 2012).

14. Felicity Nussbaum, *The Rival Queens: Actresses, Performers, and the Eighteenth-Century British Theater* (Philadelphia: University of Pennsylvania Press, 2010), 18.

15. This second definition is one invented not in the age of Enlightenment but rather in the electronic age, in which it has come to mean "to destroy (data) by entering new data in its place"—a definition that the *OED* dates to 1951. Nonetheless, the word has always carried the meaning of an excess of writing that results in an exhaustion or a depletion of writing: in 1752, according to the *OED*, Cibber's contemporary Samuel Richardson used it to mean "to exhaust oneself or diminish one's abilities by excessive writing." *Oxford English Dictionary Online*, s.v. "overwrite."

16. Richard Schechner, in his article "Performance Studies: The Broad Spectrum Approach," uses the term "the broad-spectrum approach" to refer to performance studies' interest not only in stage performances but in what sociologist Erving Goffman calls "the presentation of self in everyday life" in his book of that name. Richard Schechner, "Performance Studies: The Broad Spectrum Approach," in *The Performance Studies Reader*, 2nd ed. (London: Routledge, 2004, 2007). The ephemerality of such performances has been a foundational concept in performance studies, theorized by performance scholars such as Peggy Phelan (*Unmarked*), Joseph Roach (*Cities of the Dead*), Diana Taylor, and Rebecca Schneider; and addressed, more practically than theoretically, by theater historian Thomas Postlewait.

17. Peggy Phelan, "Just Want to Say: Performance and Literature, Jackson and Poirier," *PMLA* 125 (2010): 946. In my desire to combine theater history and performance studies I am influenced by a number of scholars working in the field today (including Lisa Freeman Joseph Roach, Felicity Nussbaum, Misty Anderson, Stuart Sherman, and Emily Hodgson Anderson). I am influenced as well by three recent books of theater historiography that have explored both the advantages and the impossibilities of reconceiving theater history as a history of performance practices as well as scripts and stage directions: Thomas Postlewait's *Cambridge Introduction*

to *Theatre Historiography* (New York: Cambridge University Press, 2009), Jacky Bratton's *New Readings in Theatre History* (New York: Cambridge University Press, 2003); and Henry Bial and Scott Magelssen's edited volume, *Theatre Historiography: Critical Interventions* (Ann Arbor: University of Michigan Press, 2010).

18. Joseph Roach, *It* (Ann Arbor: University of Michigan Press, 2007), 1.

19. Leo Braudy, *The Frenzy of Renown: Fame and Its History* (New York: Random House, 1986, 1997), 7.

20. *Oxford English Dictionary Online*, s.v. "fame."

21. Alexander Pope, *The Temple of Fame*, in *The Poems of Alexander Pope*, ed. John Butt (New Haven: Yale University Press, 1963), ll. 69–70, 133–134.

22. Stella Tillyard, "Celebrity in 18th-Century London," *History Today* 55 (June 2005): 23.

23. Ibid., 5.

24. Ibid., 5, 25.

25. I borrow the term "spectacular politicians" from Paula Backscheider's influential work of the same name, *Spectacular Politics: Theatrical Power and Mass Culture in Early Modern England* (Baltimore: Johns Hopkins University Press, 1993), which examines the implications in the late seventeenth and early eighteenth centuries of models of leadership explored elsewhere by Stephen Orgel, Stephen Greenblatt, and Peter Stallybrass and Allon White. "Public representatives" is Jürgen Habermas's term for the spectacular noblemen, noblewomen, and religious figures who controlled society before the structural transformation of the public sphere in the late seventeenth century.

26. Chris Rojek, *Celebrity* (London: Reaktion Books, 2001), 13.

27. Cheryl Wanko, *Roles of Authority: Thespian Biography and Celebrity in Eighteenth-Century Britain* (Lubbock: Texas Tech University Press, 2003), 5.

28. Habermas's account has drawn criticism for being overly general and for not considering significant portions of the European population (women, sexual minorities, ethnic or racial minorities) in its definition of what constitutes a "public." (For a helpful summary of the major schools of such criticism, see Craig Calhoun's introduction to *Habermas and the Public Sphere*, ed. Calhoun [Cambridge, MA: MIT Press, 1992].) While I do not consider Habermas's definition of the public sphere to be all-encompassing, I do find his theories useful in thinking through what eighteenth-century England required for entry into the normative public sphere.

29. Michael McKeon, *The Secret History of Domesticity: Public, Private, and the Division of Knowledge* (Baltimore: Johns Hopkins University Press, 2005), 83.

30. Pope, *Temple of Fame*, l. 361.

31. Addison, *The Spectator*, 1:5–6.

32. Scott Paul Gordon, "Voyeuristic Dreams: Mr. Spectator and the Power of Spectacle," *Eighteenth Century* 56 (1995): 12.

33. Ibid., 17.

34. [Benjamin Victor], *Memoirs of the Life of Barton Booth, Esq., with His Character* (London: published for John Watts, 1733), 23.

35. Quoted in Joseph Roach, *The Player's Passion: Studies in the Science of Acting* (Ann Arbor: University of Michigan Press, 1993), 95.

36. Sterne, *Tristram Shandy*, 66.

37. Shearer West writes, "Journalistic criticism, the print trade and the market for oil paintings all burgeoned in the mid-18th century, just at the time when Garrick was raising the status of the actor and elevating acting to a place beside the other liberal arts. Between 1730 and 1750 a trickle of theatrical reviewing in journals became a flood." West, *The Image of the Actor: Verbal and Visual Representation in the Age of Garrick and Kemble* (London: Pinter, 1991), 2. Paul D. Cannan comes to a similar conclusion in *The Emergence of Dramatic Criticism in England: From Jonson to Pope* (New York: Palgrave, 2006).

38. Roach, *It*, 40–41.

39. Thomas Postlewait has delved into this problem with some depth in "Autobiography and Theatre History," in *Interpreting the Theatrical Past: Essays in the Historiography of Performance*, ed. Postlewait and Bruce McConachie (Iowa City: University of Iowa Press, 1989).

40. Cibber, *Apology*, 6.

41. Ibid.

42. Ibid., 7.

43. The *OED* defines "smear" as "fat, grease, or lard"—all substances removed from the interior of the body (*OED Online*, s.v. "smear").

44. Alexander Pope, *The Dunciad in Four Books* (1743), in *Poems of Alexander Pope*, 4.251.

45. Macpherson, *Political Theory*, 3.

46. Nussbaum, *Autobiographical Subject*, 53.

47. Peggy Phelan, *Unmarked: The Politics of Performance* (London: Routledge, 1993), 148.

48. Jean Baptiste Suard, *London Chronicle* XVII (April 10–18, 1765), in *Laurence Sterne: The Critical Heritage*, ed. Alan B. Howes (London: Routledge and Kegan Paul, 1974), 373.

49. Andrew Sofer, *The Stage Life of Props* (Ann Arbor: University of Michigan Press, 2003), 120.

50. Joseph Roach, *Cities of the Dead: Circum-Atlantic Performance* (New York: Columbia University Press, 1996), 36.

CHAPTER 1

1. There is some question about whether the play debuted in December 1699 or in January 1700. W. van Lennep, E. L. Avery, A. H. Scouten, G. W. Stone, and

C. B. Hogan, eds., *The London Stage, 1660–1800: A Calendar of Plays, Entertainments and Afterpieces, together with Casts, Box-Receipts and Contemporary Comment,* 5 vols. (Carbondale: Southern Illinois University Press, 1960–1968), 1:521. I have followed other scholars in referring to its debut as occurring in 1699.

2. Nussbaum, *Rival Queens*, 51.

3. Cibber, *Apology*, 7.

4. James I. Porter, "Foreword," in *The Body and Physical Difference: Discourses of Disability*, ed. David T. Mitchell and Sharon L. Snyder (Ann Arbor: University of Michigan Press, 1997), xiii.

5. Feminist critics such as Nussbaum (*Autobiographical Subject*), Sidonie Smith (*A Poetics of Women's Autobiography: Marginality and the Fictions of Self-Representation* [Bloomington: Indiana University Press, 1987]), and Phelan (*Unmarked*) have been perhaps most influential in describing autobiography in this way.

6. Maureen Sullivan, preface to Colley Cibber, *Three Sentimental Comedies*, ed. Maureen Sullivan (New Haven: Yale University Press, 1973), x.

7. Cibber, *Apology*, 6.

8. Ibid., 21.

9. Ibid., 22–23.

10. Joseph Addison, *The Spectator* 69, in *The Spectator*, 1:296.

11. Cibber, *Apology*, 23.

12. Ibid., 24.

13. William Shakespeare, *Richard III*, ed. Stephen Greenblatt, in *The Norton Shakespeare*, ed. Stephen Greenblatt (New York: W.W. Norton, 1997), 1.1.1–2.

14. Richard P. Wheeler has influentially read this speech—and Shakespeare's play in general—as exemplifying what he calls a "providential" theory of history, in which the idea that the king is ordained by God plays a prominent role. Wheeler, "History, Character and Conscience in *Richard III*," *Comparative Drama* 5 (1971–1972): 301.

15. Colley Cibber, *The Tragical History of King Richard III* (London: J. and R. Tonson, 1757), 5.

16. Cibber, *Apology*, 19.

17. Shakespeare, *Richard III*, 3.7.214–237; Cibber, *Richard III*, 48–49.

18. Cibber, *Apology*, 1.

19. Cibber, *Richard III*, 60.

20. Ibid., 49.

21. The story is summarized in William Smith, ed., *Dictionary of Greek and Roman Antiquities*, vol. 2 (Boston: Little, Brown, 1870), 439.

22. William Shakespeare, *The Works of William Shakespear*, vol. 4, ed. Nicholas Rowe (London: Jacob Tonson, 1709), n.p.

23. Van Lennep et al., *London Stage, 1660–1800*, 1:400.

24. Cibber, *Apology*, 81.

25. Nicholas Rowe, *Jane Shore: A Tragedy* (London: John Bell, 1791), 58.

26. Ibid.

27. Judith Milhous, "The First Production of Rowe's Jane Shore," *Theatre Journal* 38 (October 1986): 318.

28. David T. Mitchell and Sharon L. Snyder, *Narrative Prosthesis: Disability and the Dependencies of Discourse* (Ann Arbor: University of Michigan Press, 2000), 13.

29. The term "scripts of disability" originates with Carrie Sandahl and Philip Auslander, who use it to describe the disabled person struggling "to become an active maker of meaning, rather than a passive specimen on display. Manipulating and transforming stereotypes are important tactics, since the available 'scripts' of disability—both in daily life and in representation—are frustratingly limited and deeply entrenched in the cultural imagination." Sandahl and Auslander, "Introduction: Disability Studies in Commotion with Performance Studies," in *Bodies in Commotion: Disability and Performance*, ed. Carrie Sandahl and Philip Auslander (Ann Arbor: University of Michigan Press, 2005), 3. Though Richard III does not figure specifically into Sandahl and Auslander's argument, this character has served as the basis for many disability scholars' work on literary portrayals of the "Demonic Cripple," in Leonard Kriegel's words, who, "like Shakespeare's crippled king, . . . must now spend his remaining life resisting categorization. His existence is predicated on the need to become what he believes the world demands he become." Kriegel, "The Cripple in Literature," in *Images of the Disabled, Disabling Images*, ed. Alan Gartner and Tom Joe (New York: Praeger, 1987), 34.

30. Shakespeare, *Richard III*, 5.7.13.

31. Ibid., 1.3.226–227.

32. Lennard J. Davis explains that the category of normality emerged in the eighteenth century, as did the exclusion of the disabled body from this category. Davis, *Bending Over Backwards: Disability, Dismodernism, and Other Difficult Positions* (New York: New York University Press, 2002).

33. Cibber, *Richard III*, 12.

34. Cibber, *Richard III*, 10. These lines originate with Shakespeare's *Henry IV*. Shakespeare, *The Second Part of Henry IV*, ed. Jean E. Howard, in Greenblatt, *The Norton Shakespeare*, 1.1.60–61, 67–69. Cibber adds new meaning, however, by juxtaposing these words with Henry's "What bloody scene has *Roscius* to act?" in the next scene (Cibber, *Richard III*, 15).

35. Cibber, *Richard III*, 15.

36. Ibid., 10.

37. Shakespeare, *The True Tragedy of Richard Duke of York and the Good King Henry the Sixth*, ed. Jean E. Howard, in Greenblatt, *The Norton Shakespeare*, 5.6.10.

38. Cibber, *Richard III*, 15.

39. Ibid., 15, 16, 16.

40. Ibid., 16.

41. Ibid., 17.

42. Shakespeare, *Henry the Sixth*, 5.6.31–84.

43. Shakespeare, *Richard III*, 5.5.136–139.

44. Cibber, *Richard III*, 78.

45. Ibid., 79.

46. The *OED* lists the use of this reflexive pronoun as signaling the individual's return to a "normal condition of mind and body." *OED Online*, 3rd ed., s.v. "himself."

47. Cibber, *Richard III*, 5.

48. Shakespeare, *Richard III*, 5.8.0.

49. Ibid., 5.7.13.

50. Ibid., 5.8.2.

51. Cibber, *Richard III*, 83.

52. Ibid.

53. Though the first four lines of Richard's death speech are original to Cibber, these last he lifts from the first scene of Shakespeare's *Second Part of Henry IV* (1.1.155–160). Cibber did not compose the words about "the first-born *Cain*," then, but his co-opting of them in a different context and in reference to a different character betrays an interest in the metaphor that seems to go beyond the disabled body that Richard shares with Northumberland, to whom Shakespeare assigns these lines.

54. *The Laureat; or, the Right Side of Colley Cibber, Esq.* (London: J. Roberts, 1740), 14–15.

55. Cibber, *Richard III*, 10, 15.

56. Sandahl and Auslander, "Introduction," 3.

57. Julie Stone Peters writes, "By the first decades of the seventeenth century, standard conventions for the dramatic *mise en page* had set in, and most plays resembled one another more than they resembled the particular *Oeuvre* of their authors, generally following national norms." Peters, *The Theatre of the Book, 1480–1880: Print, Text, and Performance in Europe* (Oxford: Oxford University Press, 2000), 56. Elizabeth Eisenstein makes a similar argument about the standardization of the printed book in *The Printing Press as an Agent of Change: Communications and Cultural Transformations in Early Modern Europe* (Cambridge: Cambridge University Press, 1979).

58. Cibber, *Richard III*, 60.

59. Ibid., 83.

60. Porter, "Foreword," xviii.

61. Cibber, *Apology*, 7.

62. *Laureat*, 35.

63. Henry Fielding, *The Author's Farce*, ed. Jill Campbell, in *Broadview Anthology of Restoration and Eighteenth-Century Drama*, ed. J. Douglas Canfield (Toronto: Broadview, 2001), 1804, 1809. Unfortunately, as Judith Pascoe points out so beautifully in *The Sarah Siddons Audio Files*, recovering precisely what an actor's voice

sounded like before the advent of sound recording is impossible, though several scholars have tried to approximate it.

64. Cibber, *Apology*, 33–34.

65. Henry Fielding, *Apology for the Life of Mr. The' Cibber, Comedian* (London: J. Mechell, 1740), 21–22.

66. T. Johnson, *The Tryal of Colley Cibber, Comedian* (London: W. Lewis and E. Curll, 1740), 13. This essay is reprinted (with some deletions) in Fielding's periodical *The Champion*, in the issue dated May 17, 1740. Accompanying it is a damnation of the earlier pamphlet as an unauthorized reprinting. Given Fielding's and his fellow Scriblerians' interest in pseudonyms and in-jokes about the impossibility of claiming any literary work as one's property, however, the damnation is probably facetious. Fielding, *The Champion* (May 17, 1740), in *Contributions to "The Champion" and Related Writings*, ed. W. B. Coley (Oxford: Clarendon, 2003), 423–425.

67. Cibber, *Apology*, 34.

68. Johnson, *Tryal*, n.p.

69. Ibid., 9–10.

70. Addison, *Spectator* 69, 256.

71. *Laureat*, 75.

72. Ibid., 35.

73. Johnson, *Tryal*, 11.

74. Rosenthal discusses Pope's interest in the theater in "Trials of Manhood: Cibber, *The Dunciad*, and the Masculine Self," in *"More Solid Learning": New Perspectives on Alexander Pope's "Dunciad,"* ed. Catherine Ingrassia and Claudia Thomas (Lewisburg, PA: Bucknell University Press, 2000); other critics who write productively of this interest include Aubrey Williams, Valerie Rumbold, and Laura Tosi.

75. Pope, *Dunciad in Four Books*, 4.9–14.

76. Pope, *Dunciad*, 711. Helene Koon identifies the true author of this introduction as Pope's friend William Warburton. Koon, *Colley Cibber: A Biography* (Lexington: University Press of Kentucky, 1986), 164. John Butt, however, suggests that Pope had a hand in many of Warburton's annotations. Pope, *Dunciad*, 710 n. 1. Cibber himself notes that "Pope is so apt to put his own Praises into the Mouth of a fictitious Author, that we cannot be sure whom we are to thank for the Modest Performance" (*Another Occasional Letter from Mr. Cibber to Mr. Pope* [London, 1743], 20). Cibber applies the quote specifically to the "Preface" that precedes Aristrachus's introduction and that is explicitly attributed to Warburton, but his words also cast doubt on the authorship of the introduction that follows. Whether or not Pope composed the introduction, its statements reflect the overexpressive qualities that he attributes to Cibber's prose throughout the rest of the poem.

77. Pope, *Dunciad in Four Books*, 712.

78. Ibid., 3.268.

79. Ibid., 767 n. 20.

80. Cibber, *Apology*, 24

81. Pope, *Dunciad in Four Books*, 713.

82. Ibid., 711.

83. Rawson, "Poetry of the First Half of the Eighteenth Century: Pope, Johnson and the Couplet," in *The Cambridge History of English Poetry*, ed. Michael O'Neill (Cambridge: Cambridge University Press, 2010), 47–48.

84. Ulrich Broich, *The Eighteenth-Century Mock-Heroic Poem*, trans. David Henry Wilson (Cambridge: Cambridge University Press, 1990), 3.

85. Pope, *Dunciad in Four Books*, 713.

86. Ibid.

87. Ibid.

88. Ibid., 714, 715.

89. Ibid., 713.

90. Ibid., 714.

91. Samuel Garth, *The Dispensary: A Poem. In Six Cantos* (London: John Nutt, 1706), 21.

92. *Laureat*, n.p. This description of the mock-epic's distortions of scale survives even in discussions of the genre by today's critics, like Helen Deutsch, who writes that while Pope's earlier mock-epic *The Rape of the Lock* "preserves totality in miniature, that distorted fragment of Parnassus, the *Dunciad*, by its magnifying of contemporary detail into life-size scale, abandons coherent epic wholes for grotesque satiric remnants." Deutsch, *Resemblance and Disgrace: Alexander Pope and the Deformation of Culture* (Cambridge, MA: Harvard University Press, 1996), 176.

93. Pope, *Dunciad in Four Books*, 1.190–196.

94. J. Paul Hunter, "Form as Meaning: Pope and the Ideology of the Couplet," in *Ideology and Form in Eighteenth-Century Literature*, ed. David H. Richter (Lubbock: Texas Tech University Press, 1999), 157. Hunter expands on these ideas in "Formalism and History: Binarism and the Anglophone Couplet," *Modern Language Quarterly* 61.1 (March 2000): 109–129. Wimsatt first proposed his ideas about Pope's couplets in his article "One Relation of Rhyme to Reason: Alexander Pope, " *Modern Language Quarterly* 5 (1944): 323–338.

95. Pope, *Dunciad in Four Books*, 1.1–3.

96. This top-heavy couplet does not appear, significantly, in the 1729 *Dunciad Variorum*, which does not feature Cibber as hero. The earlier version begins with an image similar to that which begins *The Dunciad in Four Books*, but it uses a different syntax that places the third possible rhyme, "sing," within the first line of the initial couplet: "Books and the Man I sing, the first who brings / The Smithfield Muses to the Ear of Kings." Pope, *The Dunciad Variorium*, in *Poems of Alexander Pope*, A.1.1–2. Coming to the "sing" before (s)he arrives at "brings" or "Kings," the reader doesn't recognize it as a rhyme, and thus the effect is lost. Both Hunter and Wimsatt mention the similarly top-heavy rhyme that begins Pope's *Rape of the Lock* as

emphasizing the "barren superfluity" of the mock-epic form, though neither they nor Deutsch discusses the *Dunciad*'s opening couplet directly.

97. Pope, *Dunciad in Four Books*, 1.79–80.

98. Ibid., 4.251.

99. Ibid., 713.

100. Ibid., 718.

101. Ibid., 767 n. 20.

102. Ibid., 4.653–656.

103. Griffin, *Alexander Pope: The Poet in the Poems* (Princeton, NJ: Princeton University Press, 1978), 253.

104. Phelan, *Unmarked*, 148.

CHAPTER 2

1. Charlotte Charke, *A Narrative of the Life of Mrs. Charlotte Charke* (London: W. Reeve, A. Dodd, and E. Cook, 1755), 90.

2. For readings of Charke as a pioneer of feminist autobiography, see Cheryl Wanko's *Roles of Authority*, esp. 71–89; Straub's *Sexual Suspects*, esp. 138–142, and Patricia Meyer Spacks's *Imagining a Self: Autobiography and the Novel in Eighteenth-Century England* (Cambridge, MA: Harvard University Press, 1976), esp. 57–91. Terry Castle (*Literature of Lesbianism: A Historical Anthology from Ariosto to Stonewall* [New York: Columbia University Press, 2003]) has led the effort in exploring Charke's *Narrative* for clues to her sexuality. Erin Mackie ("Desperate Measures: The Narratives of the Life of Mrs. Charlotte Charke," *ELH* 58 [1991]: 841–865), and Sidonie Smith (*Poetics of Women's Autobiography*) read Charke's cross-dressing as an attempt to win her estranged father's affections by becoming the son he wanted. The debate about whether Charke's gender performances are expressions of her psychology seems to have come full circle, with her earliest twentieth-century critics (Sally Minter Strange, "Charlotte Charke: Transvestite or Conjuror?" *Restoration and Eighteenth-Century Theatre Research* 15.2 [1976]: 54–59; Charles D. Peavy, "The Chimerical Career of Charlotte Charke," *Restoration and Eighteenth-Century Theatre Research* 8.1 [1969]: 1–12; and Fidelis Morgan, *The Well-Known Troublemaker: A Life of Charlotte Charke* [London: Faber and Faber, 1980]) arguing that her transvestitism is a ruse; her critics of the 1980s and 1990s (Nussbaum, *Autobiographical Subject*; and Robert Folkenflik, "Gender, Genre, and Theatricality in the Autobiography of Charlotte Charke," in *Representations of the Self from the Renaissance to Romanticism*, ed. Patrick Coleman, Jayne Lewis, and Jill Kowalik [Cambridge: Cambridge University Press, 2000]) arguing that it is a queer expression; and her most recent critics (Wanko and Straub, as well as Danielle Gissinger in "'The Oddity of My Appearance Soon Assembled a Croud': The Performative Bodies of Charlotte Charke and Cindy Sherman," in *The Public's Open to Us All*: Essays on

Women and Performance in Eighteenth-Century England, ed. Laura Engel [Newcastle: Cambridge Scholars, 2009]) arguing that it is a performance designed to expose all gender as performative.

3. Charke, *Narrative*, 94–95.

4. Ibid., 95.

5. Addison, *The Spectator*, 1:5.

6. Wahrman, *Making of Modern Self*, 18. Wahrman's argument that gender and sexuality became essential qualities of selfhood in the eighteenth century is not a new one and, indeed, has been central to eighteenth-century studies since Michel Foucault's historicization of gender in *The History of Sexuality*; his theories of spectatorship and self-policing more generally might also be gleaned from his *Discipline and Punish*. Other influential contributions to this field have been made by Thomas Laqueur, Randolph Trumbach, and Laurence Senelick.

7. *Laureat*, 1–2.

8. Cibber, *Apology*, 137.

9. King, *The Gendering of Men*, 251, 253.

10. Lynn Festa, "Personal Effects: Wigs and Possessive Individualism in the Long Eighteenth Century," *Eighteenth-Century Life* 29.2 (2005): 83. Also noteworthy is a special issue of *Eighteenth-Century Studies* on "hair." Margaret K. Powell and Joseph Roach's article in that issue, "Big Hair," has been especially useful in discussing Cibber's wig in particular and eighteenth-century hair in general as a social performance.

11. Marcia Pointon, *Hanging the Head: Portraiture and Social Formation in Eighteenth-Century England* (New Haven: Yale University Press, 1993), 122.

12. Festa, "Personal Effects," 49; see also Pointon, *Hanging the Head*, 119–122.

13. Colley Cibber, *Love's Last Shift; or, The Fool in Fashion*, in *Three Sentimental Comedies*, 54.

14. Ibid., 55.

15. Laura Brown, *English Dramatic Form, 1660–1760: An Essay in Generic History* (New Haven: Yale University Press, 1981), 114.

16. Colley Cibber, *The Careless Husband*, in *Three Sentimental Comedies*, 156–157.

17. Cibber, *Careless Husband*, 157.

18. The similarities between Brett's character and Cibber's sentimental heroes is striking: in another episode from the *Apology*, Cibber describes his offer to exchange his own clean shirt for Brett's dirty one in order to facilitate Brett's pursuit of his future wife, an episode that recalls Loveless's statement that he has "baulk'd many a Woman in my Time for want of clean Shirt." Cibber, *Apology*, 204–205. Helene Koon cites a rumor that the Steinkirk scene in *The Careless Husband* was based on an interaction between Brett and his wife, but she doubts its truth. Koon, *Colley Cibber*, 48.

19. Cibber, *Apology*, 201–202.

20. Sir John Vanbrugh, *The Relapse; or, Virtue in Danger, Being the Sequel of the Fool in Fashion*, ed. James E. Gill, in Canfield, *Broadview Anthology*, 1487.

21. Ibid., 1488.

22. Catherine Gallagher, *Nobody's Story: The Vanishing Acts of Women Writers in the Marketplace, 1670–1820* (Berkeley: University of California Press, 1994), 34.

23. Ibid., 22.

24. Cibber, *Apology*, 3–4.

25. King, *The Gendering of Men*, 5.

26. Despite Cibber's circumspection, at least some of the autobiography's readers seem to have recognized its benefactor: in his 1968 edition of the autobiography, B. R. S. Fone identifies Cibber's "certain gentleman" as "Henry Pelham (1695?–1754), brother of Cibber's friend, the Duke of Newcastle, and in 1743, prime minister." Fone, introduction to *An Apology for the Life of Colley Cibber*, ed. Fone (Mineola, NY: Dover, 1968), 327 n. 1. Nonetheless, Cibber's insistence on withholding his patron's name invites endless jeers from his critics. In the 1740 parody billed as an autobiography of Cibber's son, Theophilus, the author (probably Henry Fielding) repeats Cibber's refusal to name his patron but portrays it as yet another example of Cibber's kowtowing to a benefactor whose identity was hardly a secret to Cibber's readers. Fielding, *An Apology for the Life of Mr. The' Cibber*, vi–viii. The jest returns again in the front matter of *An Apology for the Life of Mrs. Shamela Andrews*, a sexualized sendup of Samuel Richardson's *Pamela* that has been definitively identified as Fielding's work but which its title page attributes to "Mr. Conny Keyber," a bastardization of Cibber's name. The parody begins with a congratulatory letter written from "The Editor to Himself." Fielding, *An Apology for the Life of Mrs. Shamela Andrews*, in *Joseph Andrews and Shamela*, ed. Judith Hawley [London: Penguin, 1999), 7. Charke begins her *Narrative* with a famous and flattering dedication from "The Author to Herself" (iii–ix), which Sidonie Smith has read as an acknowledgment of the autobiographer's double identity as both the subject and the author of her life. Charke, iii–ix; Smith, *Poetics of Women's Autobiography*, 103–104. Perhaps more prosaically, I consider Charke's dedication to be a reference to the work of her friend Fielding as well as another coded gesture toward her father.

27. Cibber, *Apology*, 1.

28. Ibid., 3.

29. *Laureat*, 7.

30. Cibber, *Apology*, 7.

31. Ibid., 3.

32. Straub, *Sexual Suspects*, 53–55.

33. Cibber, *Apology*, 3.

34. *Laureat*, 2.

35. Ibid., 1–2.

36. Ibid., 2.

37. Ibid., 15.

38. Charke, *Narrative*, 13.

39. In "The Unaccountable Wife and Other Tales of Female Desire in Jane Bark-

er's *A Patchwork Screen for the Ladies*," *Eighteenth Century: Theory and Interpretation* 35.2 (Summer 1994): 155–172, Kathryn R. King speculates, "It is possible that the term 'unaccountable' in the early eighteenth century is a coded word" for lesbianism, as it seems to be in the Barker text that King discusses (172). However, the only other instance she cites for the code is Charke's *Narrative*, in which, as I argue, the autobiographer's sexuality is somewhat more ambiguous. I quote the word here not as evidence that Charke was a lesbian but instead as evidence that she preferred to leave her gender and sexuality undefinable and unaccounted for. See also Katherine Binhammer, "Accounting for the Unaccountable: Lesbianism and the History of Sexuality in Eighteenth-Century Britain," *Literature Compass* 7.1 (January 2010): 1–15.

40. Charke, *Narrative*, 56.

41. Ibid., 56–57.

42. Ibid., 59.

43. Ibid., 90.

44. Quoted in Morgan, *The Well-Known Troublemaker*, 64. *The Biographical Dictionary* does not mention the playbill that Morgan quotes but does list, among the roles that Charke's Punch puppet played, "the madame of a Covent Garden brothel," which suggests that Punch did assume feminine dress in at least one of Charke's productions. Phillip H. Highfill Jr., Kalman A. Burnim, and Edward A. Langhans, *A Biographical Dictionary of Actors, Actresses, Musicians, Dancers, Managers, and Other Stage Personnel in London, 1660–1800, 16 vols. (Carbondale: Southern Illinois University Press, 1975), 3:171.* See also Scott Cutler Shershow, *Puppets and "Popular" Culture* (Ithaca, NY: Cornell University Press, 1995), 152.

45. Charke, *Narrative*, 95.

46. Ibid., 82.

47. Ibid.

48. Ibid., 207.

49. Morgan, *The Well-Known Troublemaker*, 142n.

50. Colley Cibber, "To the Reader," in Colley Cibber and John Vanbrugh, *The Provok'd Husband; or, A Journey to London* (London: J. Watts, 1728), n.p.

51. Cibber's particular misspelling is also interesting. "Para*phon*alia" reinforces Cibber's preference for language grounded in performance over print, *phon*ic over standardized spellings, the individuated *Harse* over the depersonalized *horse*.

52. Fielding, *Author's Farce*, 1818.

53. Morgan, *The Well-Known Troublemaker*, 143n; Cibber and Vanbrugh, *Provok'd Husband*, 58.

54. The relationship that Fielding establishes between Cibber's deformed language and an overtly performed (and thus suspect) sexuality is evident as well in Fielding's use of the word "vartue" in *Shamela*. Such deformed language is also evident in the barely legible letter written as an expression of love from Loveman, the

queered molly who propositions the hero Henry Dumont, in Charke's novel *The History of Henry Dumont*.

55. Campbell, *Natural Masques: Gender Identity in Fielding's Plays and Novels* (Stanford, CA: Stanford University Press, 1995), 24–25.

56. Charke, *Narrative*, 13, 90.

57. Ibid., 18.

58. Straub, *Sexual Suspects*, 136. Other critics to describe the passage as an example of Charke's struggle to express herself in language that is necessarily sexist and heteronormative include Erin Mackie ("Desperate Measures"), Felicity Nussbaum (*Autobiographical Subject*), Sidonie Smith (*Poetics of Women's Autobiography*) and Cheryl Wanko (*Roles of Authority*).

59. Charke, *Narrative*, 19.

60. Marjorie Garber describes transvestitism as a "third term" that is neither masculine nor feminine but simply Other. Often, she argues, this Otherness is represented as a racial Otherness. Garber, *Vested Interests: Cross-Dressing and Cultural Anxiety* (New York: Routledge, 1992), 304–352. Although I see a similar Othering happening in Charke's description, I wish to distinguish it from the queer theory on which Garber bases her argument by suggesting that it originates not from the inadequacy but rather (like Sterne's black page) from the abundance and obviousness of identifying signifiers.

61. Thomas Davies, *Memoirs of the Life of David Garrick, Esq.*, 4th ed., 2 vols. (London, 1784), *Eighteenth-Century Collections Online* (Farmington Hills: Thomas Gage, 2003), 1.17.

62. *Laureat*, 2.

63. *The Gentleman's Magazine* (October 1755), in *Eighteenth-Century Collections Online*, 457.

64. Charlotte Charke, *The Art of Management; or, Tragedy Expell'd* (London, 1735), n.p.

CHAPTER 3

1. Laurence Sterne, *The Florida Edition of the Works of Laurence Sterne*, vol. 1, ed. Melvyn New and Joan New (Gainesville: University of Florida Press, 1978), 116.

2. Ibid., 242; Keymer, *Sterne*, 155.

3. Sterne, *Tristram Shandy*, 8.

4. Ibid., 181.

5. Stevens, *Celebrated Lecture on Heads* (Dublin, 1765), 56.

6. Sterne, *Tristram Shandy*, 33, 181.

7. Colley Cibber, *A Letter from Mr. Cibber to Mr. Pope* (Dublin: A. Reilly, 1742), in *Eighteenth Century Collections Online*, 5.

8. Sterne, *Tristram Shandy*, 26.

9. *The Clockmakers Outcry against the author of The life and opinions of Tristram Shandy* (London: J. Burd, 1760), in *Eighteenth-Century Collections Online*, vii–viii.

10. Sterne, *Works*, 155.

11. For all biographical information on Sterne, I am indebted to Arthur H. Cash's two-volume biography. Ross's *Laurence Sterne: A Life* focuses more specifically on Sterne's literary career and has been invaluable in detailing Sterne's public persona and life as a celebrity.

12. Sterne, *Works*, 242.

13. Ibid., 261.

14. Ibid., 302.

15. After Sterne's death, the books in his library were combined with those of several of his neighbors' libraries, making it impossible to separate which books were his and which belonged to his neighbors. However, as Arthur H. Cash points out, a note on the flyleaf of a volume containing both Cibber's *Letter to Mr. Pope* and Bishop Berkeley's *Querist* marks it as belonging to Sterne. Cash, *Laurence Sterne: The Early and Middle Years* (London: Methuen, 1975), 199.

16. These include George Stayley's 1762 *Life and Opinions of an Actor*, which Rene Bosch (*Labyrinth of Digressions: "Tristram Shandy" as Perceived and Influenced by Sterne's Early Imitators* [Amsterdam: Rodopi, 2007]), discusses on pages 49–50; as well as George Anne Bellamy's *An Apology for the Life of George Anne Bellamy* (1785) and Tate Wilkinson's *Memoirs of His Own Life* (1790) and *The Wandering Patentee; or a History of the Yorkshire Theatres* (1795).

17. *A Supplement to the Life and Opinions of Tristram Shandy, Gent., Serving to Elucidate That Work* (London, 1760), in *Eighteenth-Century Collections Online*, 71. The allusions include a story about Tristram's bullying at the hands of his school fellows and his adoption of the "school-boy's stile," a possible evocation of Cibber's complaint in the *Apology* that, after completing an assignment that his classmates refused, "I was so jeer'd, laugh'd at, and hated as a pragmatical Bastard (School-boys Language) who had betray'd the whole Form, that scarce any of 'em wou'd keep me company." *Supplement*, 64; Cibber, *Apology*, 22.

18. Sterne, *Works*, 238.

19. Sterne, *Tristram Shandy*, 19.

20. Ibid., 26.

21. Ibid., 25.

22. Ibid., 22.

23. *Clockmakers Outcry*, vii–viii.

24. Sterne, *Tristram Shandy*, 181.

25. Ibid., 28.

26. Ibid., 26.

27. Ibid., 257.

28. Ibid., 57.

29. Ibid., 227.

30. Lynch, *The Economy of Character*, 23.

31. Melvyn New, "The Dunce Revisited," *South Atlantic Quarterly* 72 (1973): 551.

32. Viktor Schlovsky, "A Parodying Novel: Sterne's *Tristram Shandy*," in *Laurence Sterne: A Collection of Critical Essays*, ed. John Traugott (Englewood Cliffs, NJ: Prentice-Hall, 1968), 89, 66.

33. Watt, *Rise of the Novel,* 21. This school dominates the 1968 critical anthology, edited by Traugott, which contains Schlovsky's essay; other prominent scholars in this school include Booth, Keymer, and Virginia Woolf. Also related are those, like Dennis Allen, who describe Sterne's work as the deconstruction of a novel. See also Mikhail Bakhtin's brief discussion of Sterne as practicing a "subjective" version of the carnivalesque style Bakhtin associates with Rabelais. Bakhtin, *Rabelais and His World*, trans. Helen Iswolsky (Bloomington: University of Indiana Press, 1984), 36. In *The Dialogic Imagination*, Bakhtin disqualifies *Tristram Shandy* from the category of novel due to its incomplete mastery of the dialogic form. Bakhtin, *The Dialogic Imagination: Four Essays*, ed. Michael Holquist, trans. Caryl Emerson and Michael Holquist (Austin: University of Texas Press, 1981, 2004), 226–227.

34. See Melvyn New's *Laurence Sterne as Satirist: A Reading of* Tristram Shandy (Gainesville: University of Florida Press, 1969) and his introduction to the Penguin edition of *Tristram Shandy*; as well as articles by D. W. Jefferson, "Tristram Shandy and the Tradition of Learned Wit," in Traugott, *Laurence Sterne*, and J. T. Parnell, "Swift, Sterne, and the Skeptical Tradition," *Studies in Eighteenth-Century Culture* 23 (1993): 220–242. Ronald Paulson provides a lengthier and more nuanced discussion of the distinctions between satire and the novel than I can accommodate within the scope of this chapter in his *Satire and the Novel in Eighteenth-Century England* (New Haven: Yale University Press, 1967).

35. Sterne, *Tristram Shandy*, 65.

36. Ibid., 65–66.

37. Ibid., 67.

38. Cibber, *Apology*, 7.

39. Sterne, *Tristram Shandy*, 67.

40. Ibid., 28.

41. Ibid., 16.

42. Jonathan Lamb, *Sterne's Fiction and the Double Principle* (Cambridge: Cambridge University Press, 1989), 4; Wayne Booth, "Did Sterne Complete *Tristram Shandy*?," *Modern Philology* 48 (1951): 172.

43. *Miss C——Y's Cabinet of Curiosities; Or, the Green-Room Broke Open. By Tristram Shandy, Gentleman* (Utopia: Whirligig's, 1765), 21.

44. Sterne, *Works*, 144.

45. Ibid., 154.

46. Samuel Johnson, "Preface" to *A Dictionary of the English Language* (1755),

Samuel Johnson: The Major Works, ed. Donald Greene (Oxford: Oxford University Press, 1984, 2000), 307.

47. Ibid., 310.

48. Johnson, "Preface," 324; James Boswell, *The Life of Samuel Johnson* (1791), ed. John Wilson Croker (London: J. Murray, 1848), xxiii.

49. Sterne, *Tristram Shandy*, 285.

50. Ibid., 154.

51. Ibid., 285.

52. John Hill, "Review of *Tristram Shandy*," *Royal Female Magazine* (February 1760), in *Eighteenth-Century Collections Online*, 56.

53. Also contributing to this tendency to read Yorick's description as Sterne's self-description is the fact that Sterne had already encouraged his readers to mix up his sermons with Yorick's, not only by attributing to Yorick the sermon that he inserted into Volume I but also by publishing a collection of his sermons as *The Sermons of Parson Yorick* in 1760.

54. Sterne, *Tristram Shandy*, 286.

55. Ibid., 288.

56. Ibid.

57. In a letter to Garrick written in March 1760, Sterne explicitly compares the rumors of his parody of Warburton to "one of the number of those which so unfairly brought poor Yorick to his grave." Continuing, he allies himself with his apparent enemy, portraying the two of them as united against a nosy and censorious public: "The report might draw blood of the author of Tristram Shandy—but could not harm such a man as the author of the Divine Legation [i.e. Warburton]." Sterne, *Works*, 123.

58. Sterne, *Tristram Shandy*, 292.

59. Ibid., 22–23.

60. Ibid., 24.

61. See, for instance, Dennis Allen, "Sexuality/Textuality in Tristram Shandy," *SEL* 25.3 (1985): 651–670; the essays included in David Pierce and Peter de Voogd's edited anthology, *Laurence Sterne in Modernism and Postmodernism* (Amsterdam: Rodopi, 1996); and the debate between Lamb and New, summarized in Melvyn New, "Sterne and the Narrative of Determinateness," *Eighteenth-Century Fiction* 4 (1992): 315–329.

62. Donoghue, *The Fame Machine: Book Reviewing and Eighteenth-Century Literary Careers* (Stanford, CA: Stanford University Press, 1996), 58. Alexis Tadie (*Sterne's Whimsical Theatres of Language: Orality, Gesture, Literacy* [Aldershot, UK: Ashgate, 2003]) explores how Sterne uses performance as a metaphor in his text, but does not discuss Sterne's actual performances around and outside of his text.

63. Laurence Sterne, *A Sentimental Journey to France and Italy*, ed. Tim Parnell (Oxford: Oxford University Press, 2003), 72.

64. Owen Ruffhead, *Monthly Review* 24 (February 1761), in *Eighteenth-Century Collections Online*, 102.

65. *Critical Review* 9 (January 1760), in *Eighteenth-Century Collections Online*, 73.
66. Sterne, *Tristram Shandy*, 8.
67. Ibid., 204.
68. Ibid.
69. Ibid., 16.
70. Ibid., 204.
71. Keymer, *Sterne*, 80.
72. John Croft, "Anecdotes of Sterne Vulgarly Tristram Shandy," in *The Whiteford Papers*, ed. W. A. S. Hewins (Oxford, 1898), 227.
73. Sterne, *Works*, 140.
74. Gallagher, *Nobody's Story*, 22.
75. Sterne, *Tristram Shandy*, 422.
76. William Kenrick, appendix to *Monthly Review* 21 (July–December 1759), in Laurence Sterne, *Tristram Shandy: A Norton Critical Edition*, ed. Howard Anderson (New York: W.W. Norton, 1980), 571.
77. Sterne, *Tristram Shandy*, 346.
78. Ibid., 336.
79. Ibid., 67.
80. Cibber, *Apology*, 7.
81. Sterne, *Tristram Shandy*, 340.
82. Ibid., 346.
83. Ibid.
84. Sterne, *Works*, 116.
85. Sterne, *Tristram Shandy*, 337.
86. Ibid., 339.
87. Ibid., 345–346.
88. Ibid., 258.
89. *The Life and Opinions of Jeremiah Kunastrokius* (London: E. Cabe, 1760), 67–68.
90. Sterne, *Works*, 116.
91. Carr's Volume III was identified as spurious relatively quickly, but Sterne's contemporaries were much less sure about the authorship of a spurious Volume IX, and some who recognized it as a fraud nonetheless praised it as superior to Sterne's actual volumes. Bosch notes that "some foreign publishers of *Tristram Shandy* have accidentally used the spurious *Vol. IX* for their editions." Bosch, *Labyrinth of Digressions*, 13. See also Anne Bandry, "The Publication of the Spurious Volumes of 'Tristram Shandy,'" *Shandean* 3 (1991): 126–135. Richard Griffith's *Posthumous Works of a Late Celebrated Author* was also accepted as genuine upon its publication in 1770; and scholars are still debating whether *The Clockmakers Outcry* is a parody by an especially clever imitator or a self-promotional puff of Sterne's. Bosch, 16–17.
92. *Critical Review* 9, 73.
93. *Critical Review* 19 (January 1765), in *Eighteenth-Century Collections Online*, 65–66.

94. *Critical Review* 19, 66.
95. *Clockmakers Outcry*, 40–42.

CHAPTER 4

1. King, *The Gendering of Men*, 248. Other scholars who have noted Garrick's professionalization of the stage include George Winchester Stone Jr. and George M. Kahrl, Kristina Straub, Jean Benedetti, and Heather McPherson.

2. It is possible to map my terms "earnest" and "mimetic" performance onto Erving Goffman's distinction between "sincere" and "cynical" performance. Goffman explains: "When the individual has no belief in his own act and no ultimate concern with the beliefs of his audience, we may call him cynical, reserving the term 'sincere' for individuals who believe in the impression fostered by their own performance." I have avoided the term "cynical," however, because of its negative connotations; all artists, performing plays that they know aren't real, might fall under Goffman's term "cynical." For me, "mimetic" is to "cynical" as "fiction" is to "lie": a term that recognizes the creative potential of delusion. Goffman, The *Presentation of Self in Everyday Life* (Woodstock, NY: Overlook Press, 1973), 18.

3. Todd Andrew Borlik, "'Painting of a Sorrow': Visual Culture and the Performance of Stasis in David Garrick's Hamlet," *Shakespeare Bulletin* 25.1 (2007): 7.

4. John Mullan, *Sentiment and Sociability: The Language of Feeling in the Eighteenth Century* (Oxford: Oxford University Press, 1988), 201.

5. George Anne Bellamy, *An Apology for the Life of George Anne Bellamy*, 3rd ed., 5 vols. (London: J. Bell, 1785) in *Eighteenth Century Collections Online*, 2:14.

6. Arthur Murphy, *The Life of David Garrick*, (London: J. Wright, 1801), 250.

7. Garrick, *The Sick Monkey: A Fable* (London: J. Fletcher, 1765), in *Eighteenth Century Collections Online*, 14.

8. Barbara Benedict, *Framing Feeling: Sentiment and Style in English Prose Fiction, 1745–1800* (New York: AMS, 1994), 6.

9. Ibid., 214.

10. Davies, *Memoirs*, 1:143.

11. Both Straub (*Sexual Suspects*) and Nussbaum (*Rival Queens*) read this scene in relationship to the tropes of the sentimental novel.

12. Bellamy, *Apology*, 5:60.

13. Ibid., 5:61.

14. Ibid.

15. Ibid., 5:61–62.

16. Ibid., 5:62.

17. Leigh Woods, *Garrick Claims the Stage: Acting as Social Emblem in Eighteenth-Century England* (Westport, CT: Greenwood, 1984), 98–99. The *Biographical Dictionary* notes that, though the 1741 production of *Richard III* at Goodman's Fields was Garrick's first appearance in a London playbill (as "a GENTLEMAN (*who never ap-*

pear'd on any Stage)" (6:5), Garrick had appeared on a London stage the preceding winter, when he filled in for a suddenly ill Richard Yates in the pantomime *Harlequin Student* (6:5). Highfill et al., *Biographical Dictionary*, 6, 5. "Nobody knew it," Garrick wrote later to his brother Peter, "but [Yates] and Giffard." Quoted in Highfill et al., *Biographical Dictionary*, 6:5. Between these two appearances, Garrick played Aboan in *Oroonoko*—and probably a few other roles—at a provincial theater in Ipswich. Highfill et al., *Biographical Dictionary*, 6:4.

18. The notable exceptions here are Kalman A. Burnim's book, *David Garrick: Director* (Pittsburgh: University of Pittsburgh Press, 1961); Peter Holland's article "David Garrick: '3dly, as an Author,'" *Studies in Eighteenth-Century Culture* 25 (1996): 39–62; and Stuart Sherman's article "Garrick Among the Media." As Holland points out, Garrick's contemporaries often praised his writing. "It is certain that his merit as an Author is not of the first magnitude," admitted a writer for the *Westminster Magazine*, eulogizing Garrick just after his death, in February 1779; "but his great knowledge of men and manners, of stage effect, and his happy turn for lively and striking satire, made him generally successful; and his Prologues and Epilogues in particular, which are almost innumerable, possess such a degree of happiness, both in the conception and execution, as to stand unequalled." "Memoirs of the Life of David Garrick," *Westminster Magazine* (February 1779): 58.

19. Murphy, *Life of David Garrick*, 260.

20. Garrick, *The Meeting of the Company*, in *Three Plays by David Garrick*, ed. Elizabeth Stein (New York: W.E. Rudge, 1926), 130.

21. Ibid., 139–140.

22. One of the first clues that Bayes is a representation of Garrick is the play's cast list: in the original 1774 production, the role of Bayes was taken by Thomas King, who had played the playwright Glib in another of Garrick's backstage dramas, *A Peep Behind the Curtain*. (The latter opened seven years before *The Meeting of the Company*; but King had played Glib as recently as May 14, 1774, four months before he assumed the role of Bayes.) Van Lennep et al., *London Stage, 1660–1800*, 4.1812. King's lines in the prologue to *A Peep Behind the Curtain* capitalize upon the confusion between Garrick, the actor who actually wrote the play; Glib, the character who wrote the play within the play; and King, the actor playing the character who wrote the play within the play. In addition to these casting choices, Garrick signaled Bayes as a self-portrait through Bayes's determination to train young actors in his style. Garrick was both celebrated and chastised for the rigorous training he offered to new actors in his company: "Mr. Garrick has been ever remarkably fond of teaching," jeers "Nicholas Nipclose" (a pseudonym of Francis Gentleman) in a 1772 pamphlet. And in a jab at Garrick's famously short stature, he adds, "We wonder he does not equip every male performer with cloaths of his own size, they would mostly fit as well as his manner." Nipclose (Francis Gentleman, pseudo.), *The Theatres: A Poetical Dissection* (London: John Bell, 1772), 41n.

23. Garrick, *Meeting of the Company*, 141.

24. Thomas Davies, *Dramatic Miscellanies* (London, 1783–1784), in *Eighteenth-Century Collections Online*, 96.

25. Ibid., 96–97.

26. Quoted in Burnim, *David Garrick*, 113.

27. Garrick, *Meeting of the Company*, 140.

28. Davies, *Dramatic Miscellanies*, 96–97.

29. Garrick, *The Letters of David Garrick*, ed. David M. Little and George M. Kahrl (Cambridge, MA: Belknap Press of Harvard University Press, 1963), 87–88, 1079.

30. Quoted in Roach, *Player's Passion*, 95. James Gray offers the most detailed discussion of the probable relationship between Diderot's *Paradoxe* and Garrick's performances in "Diderot, Garrick, and the Art of Acting," *Age of Johnson* 18 (2007): 243–272. See also Roach, *Player's Passion*, 95–99; and Woods, *Garrick Claims the Stage*, 120–123.

31. Garrick, *Meeting of the Company*, 140.

32. Davies, *Dramatic Miscellanies*, 97.

33. Diderot, *Paradoxe sur le Comedien*, in *Diderot: Selected Writings on Art and Literature*, ed. and trans. Geoffrey Bremner (London: Penguin, 1994), 114. Diderot's praise of the actor who "has a cool head" helps to explain, I think, one of the most perplexing statements in the *Paradoxe*: its suggestion that the best actors are those who, being "without character, excel in playing all characters" (134). Diderot is not describing actors as vapid; he is instead emphasizing that the audience should forget or at least disregard what they know of an actor's offstage activities (or what they think they know of an actor's interior "character") in order fully to appreciate his appearance in multiple roles. He is criticizing not the characters of actors, in other words, but rather the cult of celebrity, which dictates that audiences recall during an actor's performance of one role the previous roles (both onstage and offstage roles) with which his appearance is ghosted. In order to enjoy a play, according to Diderot, we must resist seeing Garrick as Garrick, and instead enjoy him as Macbeth.

34. Ibid., 105.

35. Ibid., 107–108.

36. Ibid., 154.

37. Davies, *Memoirs*, 1:163.

38. David Garrick, *An Essay on Acting* (London: Dryden Leach, 1762), in *Eighteenth-Century Collections Online*, 2.

39. Garrick, *Sick Monkey*, 14.

40. Garrick, *Essay on Acting*, n.p.

41. Vanessa Cunningham, *Shakespeare and Garrick* (Cambridge: Cambridge University Press, 2008), 53.

42. In addition to Cunningham and Davies (*Memoirs* 1:163), see George Winchester Stone Jr.'s "Garrick's Handling of Macbeth," *Studies in Philology* 38.4 (October 1941): 610; and Burnim, *David Garrick*, 105.

43. Sterne, *Works*, 116.

44. William Shakespeare, *The Tragedy of Macbeth*, ed. Stephen Greenblatt, in Greenblatt, *The Norton Shakespeare*, 2nd ed. (New York: W.W. Norton, 2008), 5.2.20–22. Paul Prescott notes that Garrick cut this line from his performance, speculating that "'dwarfish thief' was not an image Garrick, anxious of physicality and legitimacy, wanted to implant in his audience's imagination." Prescott, "Doing All that Becomes a Man: The Reception and Afterlife of the Macbeth Actor, 1744–1889," in *"Macbeth" and Its Afterlife*, ed. Peter Holland (Cambridge: Cambridge University Press, 2004), 84. The fact that Garrick included a version of the line in his *Essay*, however, suggests that his self-representations depend on a more complex relationship between self-celebration and self-deprecation than previous scholars have presumed.

45. Garrick, *Essay*, 2.

46. Ibid.

47. Quoted in Woods, *Garrick Claims the Stage*, 79.

48. Garrick, prologue to *Much Ado about Nothing*, rpt. in Murphy, *Life of David Garrick*, 454.

49. The issues of *The Craftsman* have been lost, but fortunately Fitzpatrick collected his essays on Garrick into a single pamphlet that has survived: *An Enquiry into the Real Merit of a Certain Popular Performer* (London: M. Thrush, 1760; Cambridge: Chadwyck-Healey, 1996).

50. Garrick, *The Fribbleriad* (London: J. Coote, 1761), in *Eighteenth-Century Collections Online*, 16.

51. Frederick Reynolds, *The Life and Times of Frederick Reynolds, Written by Himself* vol. 1 (Philadelphia, H.C. Carey, 1826), 62.

52. Samuel Pratt, *Garrick's Looking-Glass: or, the Art of Rising on the Stage: A Poem in Three Cantos* (London: T. Evans, 1776), in *Eighteenth-Century Collections Online*, 11.

53. Ibid.

54. Ibid., 12.

55. Murphy, *Life of David Garrick*, 82.

56. Burnim, *David Garrick*, 113.

57. William Shirley, *A Bone for the Chroniclers to Pick; or, A Take-off Scene from Behind the Curtain: A Poem* (London: J. Coote and J. Scott, 1758), 2–3.

58. *Theatrical Examiner: An Enquiry into the Merits and Demerits of the Present English Performers in General* (London: J. Doughty, 1757), 31.

59. There is some skepticism about whether or not Bellamy herself actually wrote the book that claims to be her "autobiography." Straub speculates that the sentences were actually composed by Alexander Bicknell, though in close consultation with Bellamy. Nussbaum implies the same level of involvement when she discusses the work as "ghostwrit[ten]" by Bicknell. Nussbaum, *Autobiographical Subject*, 115. Despite the question about Bellamy's authorship, I am regarding the *Apology* as an autobiographical performance for, even if Bellamy did not actually "hold the pen"

(Straub, *Sexual Suspects*, 114), she seems to have worked closely with Bicknell and to have provided much of the material for the *Apology*.

60. Bellamy, *Apology*, 1:2.

61. Ibid., 1:47.

62. "Review of *Romeo and Juliet*," *Gentleman's Magazine* 30 (October 1750): 438.

63. Ibid., 437.

64. Bellamy, *Apology*, 2:143. The allusion refers to a moment in *Tristram Shandy* when Uncle Toby's emotional (and uncharacteristically profane) oath that the suffering Le Fever "shall not die, by G——" is forgiven by "the recording angel [who] as he wrote it down, dropp'd a tear upon the word, and blotted it out forever." Sterne, *Tristram Shandy*, 383.

65. Bellamy, *Apology*, 1:154.

66. Ibid.

67. See Burnim, *David Garrick*, 62–82; and Brian Dobbs, *Drury Lane: Three Centuries of the Theatre Royal, 1663–1971* (London: Cassell, 1972), 71–72.

68. Bellamy, *Apology*, 1:154–155.

69. Ibid., 1:156.

70. Ibid., 1:159–160.

71. Ibid., 1:160.

72. *OED Online*, 3rd ed., s.v. "toilette."

73. Bellamy, *Apology*, 5:37.

74. Ibid., 5:42–43.

75. Ibid., 5:43–44.

76. Ibid., 5:44.

77. Cibber, *Apology*, 6.

78. Bellamy, *Apology*, 2:143.

CHAPTER 5

1. Cibber, *Apology*, 7.

2. Emily Hodgson Anderson, "A Shakespearean Character on the Eighteenth-Century Stage: Recognizing Perdita," *Literature Compass* 7 (2010): 274.

3. Sterne, *Tristram Shandy*, 422.

4. David Brewer, *The Afterlife of Character, 1726–1825* (Philadelphia: University of Pennsylvania Press, 2005), 174.

5. Recent work on Robinson that focuses in particular on her *Sylphid* essays include Sharon Setzer's "Mary Robinson's Self: The End of Feminine Self-Fashioning," *Philological Quarterly* 75 (1996): 501–520; as well as Judith Pascoe's *Romantic Theatricality: Gender, Poetry and Spectatorship* (Ithaca: Cornell University Press, 1997), esp. 159–162; and Martha Jane Musgrove's "The Semi-detached Flaneuse: Feminine Diversity in Romantic London," *European Romantic Review* 20 (2009): 159–166.

6. See also Linda H. Peterson, "Female Autobiographer, Narrative Duplicity,"

Studies in the Literary Imagination 23 (1990): 165-176; Stuart Curran, "Romantic Poetry: The I Altered," *Romanticism and Feminism*, ed. Anne K. Mellor (Bloomington: Indiana University Press, 1988); and Yopie Prins, *Victorian Sappho* (Princeton: Princeton University Press, 1999).

7. Marjorie Levinson, *Keats's Life of Allegory: The Origins of a Style* (Oxford: Basil Blackwell, 1988), 16.

8. In defining Robinson as *both* spectacular and disappeared, I differ from Tom Mole's recent reading of her performances as attempts to eschew spectacle and reclaim modesty. Mole, "Mary Robinson's Conflicted Celebrity," *Romanticism and Celebrity Culture, 1750-1850*, ed. Tom Mole (Cambridge: Cambridge University Press, 2009).

9. Jerome McGann identifies Sterne as "the immediate (and acknowledged) precursor of the Della Cruscan movement" and cites Peter Andrews's "Elegy on the Death of Mr. Sterne" (published under the pseudonym "Arley") as only the most explicit example of Sterne's influence. McGann, *The Poetics of Sensibility: A Revolution in Literary Style* (Oxford: Clarendon, 1996), 80, 80n.

10. West, *Image of the Actor*, 2.

11. *The Memoirs of Perdita* (London: G. Lister, 1784), in *Eighteenth-Century Collections Online*, 1.

12. Ibid., 29–30.

13. I do not mean to suggest here that Craven intended this association in her original script, which, according to the "Advertisement" prefacing the 1781 version, was originally written some time before it appeared on the stage and thus before Robinson's affair with the prince was made public. However, there is some evidence that Sheridan chose the play for its fortuitous connections to Robinson's personal life. I have found no mention of the prince's miniature in the periodicals of this time, but in her biography of the actress Paula Byrne indicates that, by the time *The Miniature Picture* debuted, the portrait was already the subject of gossip and perhaps even an accessory in Robinson's costume. "*The Miniature Picture* was no doubt chosen not only to show off Mary's legs in breeches," writes Byrne, "but also because she wore her own miniature of the Prince around her neck." Paula Byrne, *Perdita: The Life of Mary Robinson* (London: HarperCollins, 2004), 126.

14. Van Lennep et al., *London Stage, 1660–1800*, 5:347.

15. Horace Walpole, *The Yale Edition of Horace Walpole's Correspondence*, vol. 29 (New Haven: Yale University Press, 1937–1983), 44.

16. Quoted in Byrne, *Perdita*, 114.

17. Robinson, *Memoirs of the Late Mrs. Mary Robinson, Written by Herself*, 4 vols. (London: Wilks and Taylor, 1801), 2:65; rpt. in *Women's Theatrical Memoirs*, vol. 1, ed. Sharon Setzer (London: Pickering and Chatto, 2007), 271. Van Lennep et al., *London Stage, 1660–1800*, list Robinson's performance as Eliza Camply / Sir Harry Revel on May 31, 1780, as her "last appearance on the stage" (5:347), but the *Biographical Dictionary* corrects: "Though the *Memoirs* make no mention of it, not long after

the separation from her Prince, Mrs Robinson had returned to the stage—though where and when is uncertain" (13:35).

18. Elizabeth Craven, Baroness, *The Miniature Picture: A Comedy, in Three Acts: Performed at the Theatre-Royal, Drury-Lane* (London: G. Riley, 1781), *Eighteenth-Century Collections Online*, 44.

19. Though it is clear that Sheridan staged Craven's play to take advantage of Robinson's celebrity, there is no evidence that Craven wrote the part for Robinson. Nonetheless, the script evinces a generalized anxiety about celebrity that Robinson in particular seemed to embody.

20. Craven, *The Miniature Picture*, 44.

21. Ibid., 46.

22. Ibid., 52.

23. Ibid., 44.

24. Walpole, *Correspondence*, 44.

25. Craven, *The Miniature Picture*, n.p.

26. Mary Robinson, *Mary Robinson: Selected Poems*, ed. Judith Pascoe (Peterborough: Broadview, 2000), 139.

27. Joseph Roach, *It* (Ann Arbor: University of Michigan Press, 2007), 3.

28. Lynda M. Thompson, *The Scandalous Memoirists: Constantia Phillips, Laetitia Pilkington and the Shame of Public Fame* (Manchester: Manchester University Press, 2000), 172; Claire Brock, *The Feminization of Fame, 1750–1830* (New York: Palgrave Macmillan, 2006), 100.

29. Robinson, *Selected Poems*, 140.

30. Ibid.

31. Ibid., 142.

32. Ibid., 139.

33. Ibid., 140, 142.

34. Ibid., 142.

35. Sterne, *Tristram Shandy*, 1.9.16.

36. Robinson, *Memoirs*, 1:2 (original pagination).

37. Ibid., 1:185 o.p.

38. Ibid., 1:14 o.p.

39. Ibid., 1:169 o.p.

40. Ibid., 2:54 o.p.

41. Ibid., 2:59 o.p.

42. Ibid.

43. For Hester Davenport's explanation for why the letter seems more likely a continuation of the *Memoirs*, see her introduction to *The Works of Mary Robinson*, vol. 7, ed. Davenport (London: Pickering and Chatto, 2010), xix–xx. Pascoe also presents a convincing argument for the note from Robinson's editor as spurious: "Given the fact that Robinson was a very prolific writer, it seems unlikely that she was unable to finish the text by herself," she writes. "Possibly she did finish it, writ-

ing in the third person as a distancing strategy" (Pascoe, *Romantic Theatricality*, 117n).

44. I have borrowed this term from Andrew Bennett, who discusses the Romantic age as a culture interested in publishing and preserving individual subjectivities in *Romantic Poets and the Culture of Posterity* (Cambridge: Cambridge University Press, 1999).

45. Robinson, *Memoirs*, 2:71 o.p.

46. Bellamy, *Apology*, 2:152.

47. See, for instance, the debate between Anne K. Mellor ("Mary Robinson and the Scripts of Female Sexuality," in Coleman, Lewis, and Kowalik, *Representations of the Self*) and Anca Munteanu ("Confessional Texts versus Visual Representation: The Portraits of Mary Darby Robinson," *Journal for Early Modern Cultural Studies* 9 [2009]: 124–152).

48. Beverly Lemire, "Developing Consumerism and the Ready-Made Clothing Trade in Britain, 1750–1800," *Textile History* 15.1 (1984), rpt. in *Fashion: Critical and Primary Sources*, vol. 2, ed. Peter McNeil (Oxford: Berg, 2009), 244.

49. Gallagher, *Nobody's Story*.

50. Quoted in Lemire, "Developing Consumerism," 244.

51. Sterne, *Tristram Shandy*, 422.

52. For a recent exploration of the relationship between celebrity and fashion, see Laura Engel, *Fashioning Celebrity: Eighteenth-Century British Actresses and Strategies for Image-Making* (Columbus: Ohio State University Press, 2011).

53. Robinson, *Memoirs*, 1:97–98 o.p.

54. Ibid., 1:115 o.p.

55. Eleanor Ty, *Empowering the Feminine: The Narratives of Mary Robinson, Jane West, and Amelia Opie, 1796–1812* (Toronto: University of Toronto Press, 1999), 26.

56. Robinson, *Memoirs*, 2:47 o.p.

57. Robin Bernstein, "Dances with Things: Material Culture and the Performance of Race," *Social Text* 27 (2009), 69.

CODA

1. Roach, *It*, 1.

2. See Jason King, *Michael Jackson Treasures: Celebrating the King of Pop in Memorabilia and Photos* (London: Simon and Schuster, 2009), 73–74.

3. The autopsy was performed on June 26, 2009, but it was not released to the public until February 10, 2010, when it was admitted as evidence in the homicide trial against Jackson's doctor, Conrad Murray. Its immediate coverage in tabloids such as the *New York Daily News*, *New York Post*, and *Daily Mail* suggests the public demand for it. See Corky Siemaszko, "Michael Jackson Autopsy Report Confirms Singer Suffered from Vitiligo, Wore Wig, had Tattooed Makeup," *New York Daily News*, February 10, 2010: n.p., Web (June 21, 2014).

4. "Michael Jackson 'Chemically Castrated' as Child: Doctor," *Independent*, March 4, 2011: n.p., Web (July 10, 2014).

5. Margo Jefferson, *On Michael Jackson* (New York: Vintage, 2007), 7.

6. Michael Jackson, *Moonwalk* (New York: Random House, 1988, 2009), 270, 271–272.

7. *Thriller*, dir. John Landis, perf. Michael Jackson, Ola Ray, Vincent Price (MJJ Productions, 1982).

8. Cibber, *Apology*, 137.

9. King, *Michael Jackson Treasures*, 74.

10. Oprah Winfrey, interview with Michael Jackson, February 10, 1993.

11. "Tales of a Third-Grade Nothing," *Family Guy*, season 7, ep. 6, writ. Alex Carter, dir. Jerry Langford (Fox: November 16, 2008).

12. M. Jefferson, *On Michael Jackson*, 15.

13. Jackson is, of course, not the only late twentieth- or early twenty-first-century celebrity who fits this description. Consider Lady Gaga, who calls her fans "monsters" after her album *Fame Monster*, and who capitalizes on *Thriller*'s Gothic aesthetic and gender ambiguity to create her own aura of mystery and monstrousness. "Lady Gaga is, by her own admission, a fame 'monster,'" writes J. Jack Halberstam. "She is positively Warholesque in her love of attention and absolutely masterful in her use of celebrity, fashion, and gender ambiguity to craft and transmit multiple messages about new matrices of race, class, gender, and sexuality, and even about the meaning of the human" (Halberstam, *Gaga Feminism: Sex, Gender, and the End of Normal* [Boston: Beacon Press, 2012], xii). Philip Auslander suggests a history for this gender ambiguity in *Performing Glam Rock*, although I would argue that the "phoniness" that Halberstam identifies as a trademark of Gaga's brand of feminism and the "personae" that Auslander's glam rockers betray encourage us to read for the star's sincere self as much as they seem to resist a culture of sincerity.

14. *Laureat*, 75; *Clockmakers Outcry*, 40–42.

15. See Richard Chang, "Irvine Dancers Join Worldwide 'Thriller' Event," *Orange County Register*, October 28, 2007: n.p., Web (July 10, 2014); and *Thrill the World* website (thrilltheworld.com), n.d., Web (July 10, 2014).

16. Sterne, *Works*, 154.

17. Sterne, *Works*, 155; for examples of modern privacy debates, see, for instance, Vindu Goel, "Some Privacy, Please? Facebook, under Pressure, Gets the Message," *New York Times*, May 22, 2014: n.p., Web (June 21, 2014); and "Is the NSA Surveillance Threat Real or Imagined?" *New York Times*, June 9, 2013: n.p., Web (June 21, 2014).

18. Harvey, *CVDazzle*, n.d., Web, July 10, 2014.

19. Julia Plevin, "Who's a Hipster?" *Huffington Post*, August 8, 2008: n.p., Web (July 14, 2014). In 2010, Mark Greif hosted the first academic panel on the cultural phenomenon of the hipster and later published its proceeds in *What Was the Hipster? A Sociological Investigation*, ed. Greif, Kathleen Ross, and Dayna Tortorici (New

York: n+1 Foundation, 2010). In the proceedings, panelists discuss several of the qualities of the hipster subculture that interest me here, including the subculture's ambivalent relationship to technology and consumerism and its reclamation of the term "irony."

20. Christian Lorentzen, "Kill the Hipster: Why the Hipster Must Die. A Modest Proposal to Save New York Cool," *Time Out New York* May 30–June 5, 2007: n.p., Web (July 10, 2014). For a full discussion of the origin of "hipster" subculture, see Greif, Ross, and Tortorici, *What Was the Hipster?*

BIBLIOGRAPHY

The Actor: or, A Treatise on the Art of Playing. London: R. Griffiths, [1750?].

Addison, Joseph. *The Spectator.* Ed. Donald F. Bond. Oxford: Oxford University Press, 1965.

Allen, Dennis. "Sexuality/Textuality in *Tristram Shandy.*" *SEL* 25.3 (1985): 651–670.

Anderson, Emily Hodgson. *Eighteenth-Century Authorship and the Play of Fiction: Novels and the Theater, Haywood to Austen.* New York: Routledge, 2009.

Anderson, Emily Hodgson. "A Shakespearean Character on the Eighteenth-Century Stage: Recognizing Perdita." *Literature Compass* 7 (2010): 266–280.

Andrews, Peter [pseudo. Arley]. "Elegy on the Death of Mr. Sterne." *The British Album: Containing the Poems of Della Crusca, Anna Matilda, Arley, Benedict, the Bard Etc.* Ed. Robert Merry and Hannah Cowley. 2nd ed. London: J. Bell, 1790.

Armstrong, Nancy. *Desire and Domestic Fiction: A Political History of the Novel.* New York: Oxford University Press, 1987.

Auslander, Philip. *Liveness: Performance in a Mediatized Culture.* London: Routledge, 1999.

Auslander, Philip. *Performing Glam Rock: Gender and Theatricality in Popular Music.* Ann Arbor: University of Michigan Press, 2006.

Backscheider, Paula R. *Spectacular Politics: Theatrical Power and Mass Culture in Early Modern England.* Baltimore: Johns Hopkins University Press, 1993.

Bakhtin, Mikhail. *The Dialogic Imagination: Four Essays.* Ed. Michael Holquist. Trans. Caryl Emerson and Michael Holquist. Austin: University of Texas Press, 1981, 2004.

Bakhtin, Mikhail. *Rabelais and His World.* 1965. Trans. Helen Iswolsky. Bloomington, IN: Indiana University Press, 1984.

Bandry, Anne. "The Publication of the Spurious Volumes of 'Tristram Shandy.'" *Shandean* 3 (1991): 126–35.

Bandry, Anne, and W. G. Day. "The Third Edition of *The Clockmakers Outcry.*" *Shandean* 4 (1992): 153–166.

Barker-Benfield, G. J. *The Culture of Sensibility: Sex and Society in Eighteenth-Century Britain.* Chicago: University of Chicago Press, 1992.

Bellamy, George Anne. *An Apology for the Life of George Anne Bellamy.* 3rd ed. 5 vols. London: J. Bell, 1785.

Bellamy, George Anne. *An Apology for the Life of George Anne Bellamy.* 4th ed. 5 vols. London: J. Bell, 1786.

Benedetti, Jean. *David Garrick and the Birth of the Modern Theatre.* London: Methuen, 2001.

Benedict, Barbara. *Framing Feeling: Sentiment and Style in English Prose Fiction, 1745–1800*. New York: AMS, 1994.

Bennett, Andrew. *Romantic Poets and the Culture of Posterity*. Cambridge: Cambridge University Press, 1999.

Betterton, Thomas [Charles Gildon]. *Life of Mr. Thomas Betterton, the Late Eminent Tragedian*. London: Robert Jeeb, 1710.

Bial, Henry. "PS: Can We Talk about Something Else?" *Theater Historiography: Critical Interventions*. Ed. Henry Bial and Scott Magelssen. Ann Arbor: University of Michigan Press, 2010.

Bial, Henry, and Scott Magelssen, eds. *Theatre Historiography: Critical Interventions*. Ann Arbor: University of Michigan Press, 2010.

Binnhammer, Katherine. "Accounting for the Unaccountable: Lesbianism and the History of Sexuality in Eighteenth-Century Britain." *Literature Compass* 7.1 (January 2010): 1–15.

Bolton, Betsy. *Women, Nationalism, and the Romantic Stage: Theatre and Politics in Britain, 1780–1800*. Cambridge: Cambridge University Press, 2001.

Booth, Wayne. "Did Sterne Complete *Tristram Shandy*?" *Modern Philology* 48 (1951): 172–183.

Booth, Wayne. *The Rhetoric of Fiction*. 2nd ed. Chicago: University of Chicago Press, 1961, 1983.

Borlik, Todd Andrew. "'Painting of a Sorrow': Visual Culture and the Performance of Stasis in David Garrick's Hamlet." *Shakespeare Bulletin: A Journal of Performance Criticism and Scholarship* 25.1 (2007): 3–31.

Bosch, Rene. *Labyrinth of Digressions: "Tristram Shandy" as Perceived and Influenced by Sterne's Early Imitators*. Amsterdam: Rodopi, 2007.

Boswell, James. *Boswell's London Journal, 1762–1763*. Ed. Frederick A. Pottle. New York: McGraw-Hill, 1950.

Boswell, James. *The Life of Samuel Johnson*. Ed. Marshall Waingrow. New Haven: Yale University Press, 1994.

Bratton, Jacqueline S. *New Readings in Theatre History*. New York: Cambridge University Press, 2003.

Braudy, Leo. *The Frenzy of Renown: Fame and Its History*. New York: Oxford University Press, 1986.

Brewer, David A. *The Afterlife of Character, 1726–1825*. Philadelphia: University of Pennsylvania Press, 2005.

Briggs, Peter M. "Laurence Sterne and Literary Celebrity in 1760." *Age of Johnson* 4 (1991): 251–280. Rpt. in *Tristram Shandy: A Casebook*. Ed. Thomas Keymer. New York: Oxford University Press, 2006.

Brock, Claire. *The Feminization of Fame, 1750–1830*. New York: Palgrave Macmillan, 2006.

Broich, Ulrich. *The Eighteenth-Century Mock-Heroic Poem*. Trans. David Henry Wilson. Cambridge: Cambridge University Press, 1990.

Brown, Laura. *Alexander Pope*. Oxford: Oxford University Press, 1984.

Brown, Laura. *English Dramatic Form, 1660–1760: An Essay in Generic History*. New Haven: Yale University Press, 1981.

Burnim, Kalman A. *David Garrick, Director.* Pittsburgh: University of Pittsburgh Press, 1961.

Byrne, Paula. *Perdita: The Life of Mary Robinson.* London: HarperCollins, 2004.

Campbell, Jill. *Natural Masques: Gender Identity in Fielding's Plays and Novels*. Stanford, CA: Stanford University Press, 1995.

Cannan, Paul D. *The Emergence of Dramatic Criticism in England: From Jonson to Pope*. New York: Palgrave, 2006.

Carlson, Marvin. *The Haunted Stage: The Theatre as Memory Machine*. Ann Arbor: University of Michigan Press, 2003.

[Carr, John.] *The Life and Opinions of Tristram Shandy, Gentleman, Volume III*. London, 1760.

Cash, Arthur H. *Laurence Sterne: The Early and Middle Years*. London: Methuen, 1975.

Cash, Arthur H. *Laurence Sterne: The Later Years*. London: Methuen, 1986.

Castle, Terry, ed. *Literature of Lesbianism: A Historical Anthology from Ariosto to Stonewall*. New York: Columbia University Press, 2003.

Castle, Terry. *Masquerade and Civilization: The Carnivalesque in Eighteenth-Century English Culture and Fiction*. Stanford: Stanford University Press, 1986.

Charke, Charlotte. *The Art of Management; or, Tragedy Expell'd*. London, 1735.

Charke, Charlotte. *The History of Henry Dumont, Esq., and Miss Charlotte Evelyn*. London: Printed for H. Slater and H. Slater, Jr., and S. White, 1756.

Charke, Charlotte. *The Lover's Treat*. London, 1758.

Charke, Charlotte. *The Mercer; or, Fatal Extravagance*. London, 1755.

Charke, Charlotte. *A Narrative of the Life of Mrs. Charlotte Charke*. London: Printed for W. Reeve, A. Dodd, and E. Cook, 1755.

Cibber, Colley. *Another Occasional Letter from Mr. Cibber to Mr. Pope*. London, 1743.

Cibber, Colley. *An Apology for the Life of Colley Cibber, with an Historical View of the Stage during His Own Time, Written by Himself*. Ed. B. R. S. Fone. Mineola, NY: Dover, 1968.

Cibber, Colley. *The Careless Husband*. 1704. *Three Sentimental Comedies*. Ed. Maureen Sullivan. New Haven: Yale University Press, 1973.

Cibber, Colley. *A Letter from Mr. Cibber to Mr. Pope*. Dublin: A. Reilly, 1742.

Cibber, Colley. *Love's Last Shift; or, The Fool in Fashion*. 1696. *Three Sentimental Comedies*. Ed. Maureen Sullivan. New Haven: Yale University Press, 1973.

Cibber, Colley. *The Rival Fools*. 1709. *The Dramatic Works of Colley Cibber, Esq. in Five Volumes*. Vol. 2. London, 1777.

Cibber, Colley. "To the Reader." Colley Cibber and John Vanbrugh. *The Provok'd Husband; or, A Journey to London*. London: J. Watts, 1728.

Cibber, Colley. *The Tragical History of King Richard III*. 1718. *Dramatic Works of Colley Cibber.* Vol. 2. London: Printed for J. Rivington and Sons, 1777.

Cibber, Colley and John Vanbrugh. *The Provok'd Husband; or, A Journey to London.* London: J. Watts, 1728.

Cibber, Theophilus. *Four Original Letters, Viz. Two from a Husband to a Gentleman: and Two from a Husband to a Wife.* London: Printed for T. Read, 1739.

Cibber, Theophilus. *Romeo and Juliet, a Tragedy, Revis'd, And alter'd, from Shakespeare . . . to Which Is Added, A Serio-Comic Apology for Part of the Life of Mr. Theophilus Cibber, Comedian.* London: Printed for C. Corbett and G. Woodfall, 1748. Online. Cambridge: Chadwyck-Healy, 1994.

Cibber, Theophilus. *Theophilus Cibber to David Garrick, Esq.; with Dissertations on Theatrical Subjects*. London: W. Reeves and J. Phipps, 1759.

Clive, Catherine. *The Case of Mrs. Clive, Submitted to the Publick.* London: B. Dodsley, 1744.

The Clockmakers Outcry against the author of The life and opinions of Tristram Shandy. London: Printed for J. Burd, 1760.

Close, Anne. "Mary Robinson and the Gothic." *Gothic Studies* 6 (2004): 172–191.

Colley, Linda. *Britons: Forging the Nation, 1707–1837.* New Haven: Yale University Press, 1992.

Colley, Scott. *Richard's Himself Again: A Stage History of Richard III.* New York: Greenwood Press, 1992.

Colomb, Gregory C. *Designs on Truth: The Poetics of the Augustan Mock-Epic*. University Park: Pennsylvania State University Press, 1992.

Conaway, Charles. "Thou'rt the Man": David Garrick, William Shakespeare, and the Masculinization of the Eighteenth-Century Stage." *Restoration and Eighteenth-Century Theater Research* 19.1 (Summer 2004): 22–42.

Conrad, Peter. *Shandyism: The Character of Romantic Irony.* Oxford: Blackwell, 1978.

Craven, Elizabeth Craven, Baroness. *The Miniature Picture.* 1781. Online. Cambridge: Chadwyck-Healey, 1994.

Critical Review 9 (January 1760): 73.

Critical Review 19 (January 1765): 65–66.

Croft, John. "Anecdotes of Sterne Vulgarly Tristram Shandy." *The Whitefoord Papers*. Ed. W. A. S. Hewins. Oxford, 1898.

Cross, Ashley. "Coleridge and Robinson: Harping on Lyrical Exchange." *Fellow Romantics: Male and Female British Writers*. Ed. Beth Lau. Surrey: Ashgate, 2009.

Cross, Ashley. "From Lyrical Ballads to Lyrical Tales: Mary Robinson's Reputation and the Problem of Literary Debt." *Studies in Romanticism* 40 (2001): 571–605.

Cunningham, Vanessa. *Shakespeare and Garrick.* Cambridge: Cambridge University Press, 2008.

Curll, Edmund. *The Life of that Eminent Comedian Robert Wilks, Esq*. London: Edmund Curll, 1733.

Curran, Stuart. "Romantic Poetry: The I Altered." *Romanticism and Feminism*. Ed. Anne K. Mellor. Bloomington, IN: Indiana University Press, 1988.

Davies, Thomas. *Dramatic Miscellanies*. 3 vols. London, 1783–1784. Online. *Eighteenth-Century Collections Online*. Farmington Hills, MI: Thomas Gage, 2003.

Davies, Thomas. *Memoirs of the Life of David Garrick, Esq*. 4th ed. London, 1784. Online. *Eighteenth-Century Collections Online*. Farmington Hills, MI: Thomas Gage, 2003.

Davis, Leonard. *Bending Over Backwards: Disability, Dismodernism, and Other Difficult Positions*. New York: New York University Press, 2002.

Davis, Leonard. "Dr. Johnson, Amelia, and the Discourse of Disability in the Eighteenth Century." *Defects: Engendering the Modern Body*. Ed. Helen Deutsch and Felicity Nussbaum. Ann Arbor: University of Michigan Press, 2000.

Deutsch, Helen. *Resemblance and Disgrace: Alexander Pope and the Deformation of Culture*. Cambridge, MA: Harvard University Press, 1996.

de Voogd, Peter J. "*Tristram Shandy* as Aesthetic Object." *Word and Image* 4 (1988): 383–392. Rpt. in *Tristram Shandy: A Casebook*. Ed. Thomas Keymer. New York: Oxford University Press, 2006.

Diderot, Denis. *Paradoxe sur le Comedien*. 1830. *Diderot: Selected Writings on Art and Literature*. Trans. Geoffrey Bremner. London: Penguin, 1994.

Dobbs, Brian. *Drury Lane: Three Centuries of the Theatre Royal, 1663–1971*. London: Cassell, 1972.

Dobson, Michael. *The Making of the National Poet: Shakespeare, Adaptation and Authorship, 1660–1769*. Oxford: Clarendon, 1992.

Donoghue, Frank. *The Fame Machine: Book Reviewing and Eighteenth-Century Literary Careers*. Stanford, CA: Stanford University Press, 1996.

Eisenstein, Elizabeth. *The Printing Press as an Agent of Change: Communications and Cultural Transformations in Early Modern Europe*. Cambridge: Cambridge University Press, 1979.

Engel, Laura. *Fashioning Celebrity: Eighteenth-Century British Actresses and Strategies for Image-Making*. Columbus: Ohio State University Press, 2011.

Festa, Lynn. "Personal Effects: Wigs and Possessive Individualism in the Long Eighteenth Century." *Eighteenth-Century Life* 29.2 (2005): 47–90.

Festa, Lynn. *Sentimental Figures of Empire in Eighteenth-Century Britain and France*. Baltimore: Johns Hopkins University Press, 2006.

Fielding, Henry. *An Apology for the Life of Mrs. Shamela Andrews*. 1741. *Joseph Andrews and Shamela*. Ed. Judith Hawley. London: Penguin, 1999.

Fielding, Henry. *Apology for the Life of Mr. The' Cibber, Comedian*. London: Printed for J. Mechell, 1740.

Fielding, Henry. *The Author's Farce*. 1730. Ed. Jill Campbell. *Broadview Anthology of Restoration and Eighteenth-Century Drama*. Ed. J. Douglas Canfield. Toronto: Broadview, 2001.

Fielding, Henry. *Contributions to "The Champion" and Related Writings*. Ed. W. B. Coley. Oxford: Clarendon, 2003.

Fielding, Henry. *Tom Thumb: A Tragedy*. London: J. Roberts, 1730.

Fields, Polly S. "Charlotte Charke and the Liminality of Bi-genderings: A Study of Her Canonical Works." *Pilgrimage for Love: Essays in Early Modern Literature in Honor of Josephine A. Roberts*. Ed. Sigrid King. Tempe: Arizona Center for Medieval and Renaissance Studies, 1999.

Fitzpatrick, Thaddeus. *An Enquiry into the Real Merit of a Certain Popular Performer*. London: M. Thrush, 1760. Online. Cambridge: Chadwyck-Healey, 1996.

Folkenflik, Robert. "Gender, Genre, and Theatricality in the Autobiography of Charlotte Charke." *Representations of the Self from the Renaissance to Romanticism*. Ed. Patrick Coleman, Jayne Lewis, and Jill Kowalik. Cambridge: Cambridge University Press, 2000.

Folkenflik, Robert. Introduction to *The Culture of Autobiography: Constructions of Self-Representation*. Ed. Robert Folkenflik. Stanford, CA: Stanford University Press, 1993.

Fone, B. R. S. Introduction to *An Apology for the Life of Colley Cibber*. Ed. B. R. S. Fone. Mineola, NY: Dover, 1968.

Foucault, Michel. *Discipline and Punish: The Birth of the Prison*. Trans. Alan Sheridan. New York: Vintage, 1995.

Foucault, Michel. *The History of Sexuality: An Introduction*. Trans. Robert Hurley. New York: Vintage, 1988.

Freeman, Lisa. *Character's Theater: Genre and Identity on the Eighteenth-Century English Stage*. Philadelphia: University of Pennsylvania Press, 2002.

Fried, Michael. *Absorption and Theatricality: Painting and Beholder in the Age of Diderot*. Berkeley: University of California Press, 1980.

Gallagher, Catherine. *Nobody's Story: The Vanishing Acts of Women Writers in the Marketplace, 1670–1820*. Berkeley: University of California Press, 1994.

Gamer, Michael, and Terry F. Robinson. "Mary Robinson and the Dramatic Art of the Comeback." *Studies in Romanticism* 48 (2009): 219–256.

Garber, Marjorie. *Vested Interests: Cross-Dressing and Cultural Anxiety*. New York: Routledge, 1992.

Garrick, David. *An Essay on Acting*. London: Printed for Dryden Leach, 1762. Online. Cambridge: Chadwyck-Healey, 1994.

Garrick, David. *The Farmer's Return from London*. London: Printed for Dryden Leach, 1762. Online. Cambridge: Chadwyck-Healey, 1994.

Garrick, David. *Florizel and Perdita*. 1758. Online. Cambridge: Chadwyck-Healey, 1994.

Garrick, David. *The Fribbleriad*. London: J. Coote, 1761. Online. Cambridge: Chadwyck-Healey, 1996.

Garrick, David. *Lethe: A Dramatic Satire*. London: Paul Vaillant, 1749. Online. Cambridge: Chadwyck-Healey, 1996.

Garrick, David. *The Letters of David Garrick*. 3 vols. Ed. David M. Little and George M. Kahrl. Cambridge, MA: Belknap Press of Harvard University Press, 1963.

Garrick, David. *The Meeting of the Company. Three Plays by David Garrick*. Ed. Elizabeth Stein. New York: W.E. Rudge, 1926.

Garrick, David. *Miss in Her Teens; or, The Medley of Lovers*. 1747. Online. Cambridge: Chadwyck-Healey, 1996.

Garrick, David. *A Peep Behind the Curtain*. 3rd ed. London: T. Beckett and P. A. de Hondt, 1767. Online. Cambridge: Chadwyck-Healey, 1994.

Garrick, David. Prologue to *Much Ado about Nothing*. 1745. Rpt. in Arthur Murphy, *Life of David Garrick*. London: J. Wright, 1801.

Garrick, David. *The Sick Monkey: A Fable*. London: Printed for J. Fletcher, 1765.

Garth, Samuel. *The Dispensary: A poem. In Six Cantos*. 1699. London: Printed by John Nutt, 1706.

Gentleman, Francis. *The Dramatic Censor*. London: Printed for J. Bell and C. Etherington, 1770.

Gissinger, Danielle. "'The Oddity of My Appearance Soon Assembled a Croud': The Performative Bodies of Charlotte Charke and Cindy Sherman." *The Public's Open to Us All: Essays on Women and Performance in Eighteenth-Century England*. Ed. Laura Engel. Newcastle: Cambridge Scholars, 2009.

Glover, Brian. "Charlotte Charke Is Not Her Job: The Visual Imagery of Class and Profession in Charke's *Narrative*." *Mapping the Self: Space, Identity, Discourse in British Auto/Biography*. Ed. Frederic Regard. Saint-Etienne, France: Publications de l'Université de Saint-Etienne, 2003.

Glover, Brian. "Nobility, Visibility, and Publicity in Colley Cibber's *Apology*." *SEL* 42 (2002): 523–539.

Goffman, Erving. *The Presentation of Self in Everyday Life*. Woodstock, NY: Overlook Press, 1973.

Gordon, Scott Paul. "Voyeuristic Dreams: Mr. Spectator and the Power of Spectacle." *Eighteenth Century* 56 (1995): 3–23.

Gray, James. "Diderot, Garrick, and the Art of Acting." *Age of Johnson* 18 (2007): 243–272.

Greenblatt, Stephen. "Introduction to *Richard III*." *Norton Shakespeare*. Ed. Stephen Greenblatt et al. 2nd ed. New York: W.W. Norton, 2008.

Greenblatt, Stephen. *Renaissance Self-Fashioning: From More to Shakespeare*. Chicago: University of Chicago Press, 1980.

Greenblatt, Stephen, et al., eds. *The Norton Shakespeare*. 2nd ed. New York: W.W. Norton, 1997, 2008.

Greene, Jody. *The Trouble with Ownership: Literary Property and Authorial Liability in England, 1660–1730*. Philadelphia: University of Pennsylvania Press, 2005.

Greif, Mark. "Positions." *What Was the Hipster? A Sociological Investigation*. Ed. Mark Greif, Kathleen Ross, and Dayna Tortorici. New York: n+1 Foundation, 2010.

Greif, Mark. "What Was the Hipster?" *New York Magazine*. October 24, 2010. Web. July 10, 2010.

Greif, Mark, Kathleen Ross, and Dayna Tortorici, eds. *What Was the Hipster? A Sociological Investigation*. New York: n+1 Foundation, 2010.

Griffin, Dustin H. *Alexander Pope: The Poet in the Poems*. Princeton, NJ: Princeton University Press, 1978.

Habermas, Jürgen. *The Structural Transformation of the Public Sphere: An Inquiry into a Category of Bourgeois Society*. Trans. Thomas Burger and Frederick Lawrence. Cambridge, MA: MIT Press, 1989.

Halberstam, J. Jack. *Gaga Feminism: Sex, Gender, and the End of Normal*. Boston: Beacon Press, 2012.

Harding, John Anthony. "Wordsworth's *Prelude*, Tracey Emin, and Romantic Autobiography." *Wordsworth Circle* 34 (2003): 59–65.

Hartman, Saidiya. *Scenes of Subjection: Terror, Slavery, and Self-Making in Nineteenth-Century America*. New York: Oxford University Press, 1997.

Harvey, Adam. *CVDazzle*. ahprojects.com. N.d. Web. July 10, 2014.

Harvey, Adam. *Stealth Wear: New Designs for Countersurveillance*. ahprojects.com. N.d. Web. July 10, 2014.

Hawley, Judith and Cora Kaplan. "Romantic Patronage: Mary Robinson and Coleridge Revisited." *British Women's Writing in the Long Eighteenth Century: Authorship, Politics and History*. Ed. Jennie Batchelor. New York: Palgrave Macmillan, 2005.

Highfill, Phillip H., Jr., Kalman A. Burnim, and Edward A. Langhans. *A Biographical Dictionary of Actors, Actresses, Musicians, Dancers, Managers, and Other Stage Personnel in London, 1660–1800*. 16 vols. Carbondale, IL: Southern Illinois University Press, 1975.

Hill, Aaron. *The Art of Acting: Part 1*. London: J. Osborn, 1746.

[Hill, John.] "Review of *Tristram Shandy*." *Royal Female Magazine* (February 1760): 56.

Hill, John. *To David Garrick, Esq.: The Petition of I in Behalf of Herself and Her Sisters*. London: M. Cooper and J. Jackson, 1759.

Holland, Peter. "The Age of Garrick." *Shakespeare: An Illustrated Stage History*. Ed. Jonathan Bate and Russell Jackson. Oxford: Oxford University Press, 1996.

Holland, Peter. "David Garrick: '3dly, as an Author.'" *Studies in Eighteenth-Century Culture* 25 (1996): 39–62.

Holland, Peter. "Hearing the Dead: The Sound of David Garrick." *Players, Playwrights, Playhouses: Investigating Performance, 1660–1800*. Ed. Michael Cordner and Peter Holland. Basingstoke, UK: Palgrave Macmillan, 2007.

Holtz, William V. *Image and Immortality: A Study of "Tristram Shandy"*. Providence: Brown University Press, 1970.

Howes, Alan B. *Yorick and the Critics: Sterne's Reputation in England, 1760–1868*. New Haven: Yale University Press, 1958.

Hunter, J. Paul. "Form as Meaning: Pope and the Ideology of the Couplet." *Ideology and Form in Eighteenth-Century Literature*. Ed. David H. Richter. Lubbock: Texas Tech University Press, 1999.

Hunter, J. Paul. "Formalism and History: Binarism and the Anglophone Couplet." *Modern Language Quarterly* 61.1 (March 2000): 109–129.

Hunter, J. Paul. "Manliness and Poetry." *Imagining Selves: Essays in Honor of Patricia*

Meyer Spacks. Ed. Rivka Swenson and Elise Lauterbach. Newark: University of Delaware Press, 2008.

Hunter, J. Paul. "The World as Stage and Closet." *British Theatre and Other Arts, 1660–1800*. Ed. Shirley Strum Kenny. Washington, DC: Folger Shakespeare Library, 1983.

Ingamells, John. *Mrs. Robinson and Her Portraits*. London: Trustees of the Wallace Collection, 1978.

Jackson, Michael. *Moonwalk*. New York: Random House, 1988, 2009.

Jefferson, D. W. "*Tristram Shandy* and the Tradition of Learned Wit." *Laurence Sterne: A Collection of Critical Essays*. Ed. John Traugott. Englewood Cliffs, NJ: Prentice-Hall, 1968.

Jefferson, Margo. *On Michael Jackson*. New York: Vintage, 2007.

Johnson, Samuel. Preface to *A Dictionary of the English Language*. 1755. Rpt. in *Samuel Johnson: The Major Works*. Ed. Donald Greene. Oxford: Oxford University Press, 1984.

Johnson, T. [Henry Fielding]. *The Tryal of Colley Cibber, Comedian*. London: Printed for W. Lewis and E. Curll, 1740.

Jonson, Ben. *Bartholomew Fair*. 1614. *The Norton Anthology of English Restoration Drama*. Ed. David Bevington. New York: W.W. Norton, 2002.

Kelly, Hugh. *Thespis, or, a Critical Examination into the Merits of All the Principal Performers Belonging to Drury-Lane Theatre*. London: Printed for G. Kearsly, 1765.

Kenrick, William. *Love in the Suds*. London: J. Whebble, 1772.

[Kenrick, William.] *Monthly Review*. Appendix to 21 (July–December, 1759): 561–571. Rpt. in *Tristram Shandy: A Norton Critical Edition*. Ed. Howard Anderson. New York: W.W. Norton, 1980.

Keymer, Thomas. *Sterne, the Moderns, and the Novel*. Oxford: Oxford University Press, 2002.

Keymer, Thomas, ed. *Tristram Shandy: A Casebook*. New York: Oxford University Press, 2006.

King, Jason. *Michael Jackson Treasures: Celebrating the King of Pop in Memorabilia and Photos*. London: Simon and Schuster, 2009.

King, Kathryn R. "The Unaccountable Wife and Other Tales of Female Desire in Jane Barker's *A Patchwork Screen for the Ladies*." *Eighteenth Century* 35.2 (Summer 1994): 155–172.

King, Thomas. *The Gendering of Men*. Vol. 1: *The English Phallus*. Madison: University of Wisconsin Press, 2004.

Koon, Helene. *Colley Cibber: A Biography*. Lexington: University Press of Kentucky, 1986.

Kriegel, Leonard. "The Cripple in Literature." *Images of the Disabled, Disabling Images*. Ed. Alan Gartner and Tom Joe. New York: Praeger, 1987.

Labbe, Jacquelyn. "Mary Robinson's Bicentennial." *Women's Writing* 9.1 (2002): 3–8.

Labbe, Jacquelyn. "Romance and Violence in Mary Robinson's *Lyrical Tales* and Other Gothic Poetry." *A Natural Delineation of the Human Passions: The Historic Moment of "Lyrical Ballads"*. Ed. C. C. Barfoot. Amsterdam: Rodopi, 2004.

Lamb, Jonathan. *Sterne's Fiction and the Double Principle*. Cambridge: Cambridge University Press, 1989.

Laqueur, Thomas. *Making Sex: Body and Gender from the Greeks to Freud*. Cambridge, MA: Harvard University Press, 1990.

The Laureat: or, the Right Side of Colley Cibber, Esq. London: Printed for J. Roberts, 1740.

Levinson, Marjorie. *Keats's Life of Allegory: The Origins of a Style*. Oxford: Basil Blackwell, 1988.

Lichtenberg, Georg Christoph. *Lichtenberg's Visits to England*. Trans. Margaret L. Mare and W. H. Quarrell. New York: Benjamin Bloom, 1938, 1969.

The Life and Opinions of Jeremiah Kunastrokius. London: Printed for E. Cabe, 1760.

Lorentzen, Christian. "Kill the Hipster: Why the Hipster Must Die. A Modest Proposal to Save New York Cool." *Time Out New York*. May 30–June 5, 2007. Web. July 10, 2014.

Lynch, Deidre. *The Economy of Character: Novels, Market Culture, and the Business of Inner Meaning*. Chicago: University of Chicago Press, 1998.

Mackie, Erin. "Desperate Measures: The Narratives of the Life of Mrs. Charlotte Charke." *ELH* 58 (1991): 841–865.

Macpherson, C. B. *The Political Theory of Possessive Individualism: Hobbes to Locke*. Oxford: Oxford University Press, 1962.

Marshall, P. David. *Celebrity and Power: Fame in Contemporary Culture*. Minneapolis: University of Minnesota Press, 1997.

McGann, Jerome. *The Poetics of Sensibility: A Revolution in Literary Style*. Oxford: Clarendon Press, 1996.

McKeon, Michael. *The Origins of the English Novel*. Baltimore: Johns Hopkins University Press, 1987.

McKeon, Michael. *The Secret History of Domesticity: Public, Private, and the Division of Knowledge*. Baltimore: Johns Hopkins University Press, 2005.

McPherson, Heather. "Garrickomania: Art, Celebrity and the Imaging of Garrick." *Folger Shakespeare Library Online*. April 6, 2010.

Mellor, Anne K. "Mary Robinson and the Scripts of Female Sexuality." *Representations of the Self from the Renaissance to Romanticism*. Ed. Patrick Coleman et al. Cambridge: Cambridge University Press, 2000.

The Memoirs of Perdita. London: G. Lister, 1784. Online. *Eighteenth-Century Collections Online*. Farmington Hills, MI: Thomas Gage, 2003.

"Memoirs of the Life of David Garrick." *Westminster Magazine*. February 1779.

Merry, Robert, and Hannah Cowley, eds. *The British Album: Containing the Poems of Della Crusca, Anna Matilda, Arley, Benedict, the Bard, &c.* 2nd ed. London: J. Bell, 1790.

Milhous, Judith. "The First Production of Rowe's *Jane Shore*." *Theatre Journal* 38 (October 1986): 309–321.

Miss C——Y's Cabinet of Curiosities; Or, the Green-Room Broke Open. By Tristram Shandy, Gentleman. "Utopia": "Whirligig's," 1765.

Mitchell, David T., and Sharon L. Snyder, eds. *The Body and Physical Difference: Discourses of Disability.* Ann Arbor: University of Michigan Press, 1997.

Mitchell, David T., and Sharon L. Snyder. *Narrative Prosthesis: Disability and the Dependencies of Discourse.* Ann Arbor: University of Michigan Press, 2000.

Mole, Tom. "Mary Robinson's Conflicted Celebrity." *Romanticism and Celebrity Culture: 1750–1850.* Cambridge: Cambridge University Press, 2009.

Mole, Tom, ed. *Romanticism and Celebrity Culture, 1750–1850.* Cambridge: Cambridge University Press, 2009.

Morgan, Fidelis. *The Well-Known Troublemaker: A Life of Charlotte Charke.* London: Faber and Faber, 1980.

Mullan, John. *Sentiment and Sociability: The Language of Feeling in the Eighteenth Century.* Oxford: Oxford University Press, 1988.

Munteanu, Anca. "Confessional Texts versus Visual Representation: The Portraits of Mary Darby Robinson." *Journal for Early Modern Cultural Studies* 9 (2009): 124–152.

Murphy, Arthur. *The Life of David Garrick.* London: J. Wright, 1801.

Musgrove, Martha Jane. "The Semi-detached Flaneuse: Feminine Diversity in Romantic London." *European Romantic Review* 20 (2009): 159–166.

New, Melvyn. "The Dunce Revisited." *South Atlantic Quarterly* 72 (1973): 547–559.

New, Melvyn. "Editor's Introduction." Laurence Sterne, *The Life and Opinions of Tristram Shandy, Gentleman.* Ed. Melvyn New and Joan New. London: Penguin, 1978, 2003.

New, Melvyn. *Laurence Sterne as Satirist: A Reading of "Tristram Shandy".* Gainesville: University of Florida Press, 1969.

New, Melvyn. "Sterne and the Narrative of Determinateness." *Eighteenth-Century Fiction* 4 (1992): 315–329.

Nipclose, Nicholas. [Francis Gentleman, pseudo.] *The Theatres: A Poetical Dissection.* London: Printed for John Bell, 1772.

Nussbaum, Felicity. *The Autobiographical Subject: Gender and Ideology in Eighteenth-Century England.* Baltimore: Johns Hopkins University Press, 1989.

Nussbaum, Felicity. *The Rival Queens: Actresses, Performance, and the Eighteenth-Century British Theater.* Philadelphia: University of Pennsylvania Press, 2010.

Oates, J. C. T. *Shandyism and Sentiment, 1760–1800.* Cambridge: Cambridge Bibliographical Society, 1968.

Orgel, Stephen. *The Illusion of Power: Political Theatre in the Renaissance.* Berkeley: University of California Press, 1975.

Parnell, J. T. "Swift, Sterne, and the Skeptical Tradition." *Studies in Eighteenth-Century Culture* 23 (1993): 220–242.

Pascal, Roy. *Design and Truth in Autobiography*. Cambridge, MA: Harvard University Press, 1989.

Pascoe, Judith. Introduction to *Mary Robinson: Selected Poems*. Ed. Judith Pascoe. Peterborough, Ontario: Broadview, 2000.

Pascoe, Judith. *Romantic Theatricality: Gender, Poetry, and Spectatorship*. Ithaca, NY: Cornell University Press, 1997.

Pascoe, Judith. *The Sarah Siddons Audio Files: Romanticism and the Lost Voice*. Ann Arbor: University of Michigan Press, 2011.

Patrick, Duncan. "Tristram's Dialogue with Death and Thomas Patch's 'Sterne and Death.'" *Shandean* 16 (November 2005): 119–36.

Paulson, Ronald. *Satire and the Novel in Eighteenth-Century England*. New Haven: Yale University Press, 1967.

Peavy, Charles D. "The Chimerical Career of Charlotte Charke." *Restoration and Eighteenth-Century Theatre Research* 8.1 (1969): 1–12.

Peters, Julie Stone. *The Theatre of the Book, 1480–1880: Print, Text, and Performance in Europe*. Oxford: Oxford University Press, 2000.

Peterson, Linda H. "Female Autobiographer, Narrative Duplicity." *Studies in the Literary Imagination* 23 (1990): 165–176.

Phelan, Peggy. "'Just Want to Say': Performance and Literature, Jackson and Poirier." *PMLA* 125 (2010): 942–947.

Phelan, Peggy. *Unmarked: The Politics of Performance*. New York: Routledge, 1993.

Pierce, David, and Peter de Voogd, eds. *Laurence Sterne in Modernism and Postmodernism*. Amsterdam: Rodopi, 1996.

Plevin, Julia. "Who's a Hipster?" *Huffington Post*. August 8, 2008. Web. July 14, 2014.

The Poetical Epistle from Florizel to Perdita: With Perdita's Answer. London: J. Stockdale, 1781.

Pointon, Marcia. *Hanging the Head: Portraiture and Social Formation in Eighteenth-Century England*. New Haven: Yale University Press, 1993.

Pope, Alexander. *The Dunciad in Four Books*. 1743. *Poems of Alexander Pope*. Ed. John Butt. New Haven: Yale University Press, 1963.

Pope, Alexander. *The Dunciad Variorum*. 1729. *Poems of Alexander Pope*. Ed. John Butt. New Haven: Yale University Press, 1963.

Pope, Alexander. *Epigram. On Cibber's Declaration that he will have the Last Word with Mr. Pope*. 1742. *Poems of Alexander Pope*. Ed. John Butt. New Haven: Yale University Press, 1963.

Pope, Alexander. *The Poems of Alexander Pope*. Ed. John Butt. New Haven: Yale University Press, 1963.

Pope, Alexander. *The Rape of the Lock*. 1714. *Poems of Alexander Pope*. Ed. John Butt. New Haven: Yale University Press, 1963.

Pope, Alexander. *The Temple of Fame*. *The Poems of Alexander Pope*, ed. John Butt. New Haven: Yale University Press, 1963.

Porter, James I. Foreword to *The Body and Physical Difference: Discourses of Disability*. Ed. David T. Mitchell and Sharon L. Snyder. Ann Arbor: University of Michigan Press, 1997.

Postlewait, Thomas. *Cambridge Introduction to Theatre Historiography*. New York: Cambridge University Press, 2009.

Potter, Lois. "Colley Cibber: The Fop as Hero." *Augustan Worlds*. Ed. J. C. Hilson, M. M. B. Jones, and J. R. Watson. Leicester: Leicester University Press, 1978.

Powell, Margaret K., and Joseph Roach. "Big Hair." *Eighteenth-Century Studies* 38.1 (Fall 2004): 79–99.

Pratt, Samuel. *Garrick's Looking-Glass: or, the Art of Rising on the Stage: A Poem in Three Cantos*. London: T. Evans, 1776.

Prescott, Paul. "Doing All that Becomes a Man: The Reception and Afterlife of the Macbeth Actor, 1744–1889." *"Macbeth" and Its Afterlife*. Ed. Peter Holland. Cambridge: Cambridge University Press, 2004.

The Pretty Gentleman; or Softness of Manners Vindicated. London, 1747.

Prins, Yopie. *Victorian Sappho*. Princeton, NJ: Princeton University Press, 1999.

Rawson, Claude J. "Poetry of the First Half of the Eighteenth Century: Pope, Johnson and the Couplet." *The Cambridge History of English Poetry*. Ed. Michael O'Neill. Cambridge: Cambridge University Press, 2010.

Rawson, Claude J. *Satire and Sentiment, 1660–1830*. Cambridge: Cambridge University Press, 1993.

"Review of *Romeo and Juliet*." *Gentleman's Magazine* 30 (October 1750): 437–438.

Reynolds, Frederick. *The Life and Times of Frederick Reynolds, Written by Himself*. 2 vols. Philadelphia: H.C. Carey, 1826.

Roach, Joseph R. *Cities of the Dead: Circum-Atlantic Performance*. New York: Columbia University Press, 1996.

Roach, Joseph R. *It*. Ann Arbor: University of Michigan Press, 2007.

Roach, Joseph R. "Performance: The Blunders of Orpheus." *PMLA* 125 (2010): 1078–1086.

Roach, Joseph R. *The Player's Passion: Studies in the Science of Acting*. Ann Arbor: University of Michigan Press, 1993.

Robinson, Mary. *A Letter to the Women of England* and *The Natural Daughter*. Ed. Sharon Setzer. Peterborough, Ontario: Broadview, 2003.

Robinson, Mary. *Mary Robinson: Selected Poems*. Ed. Judith Pascoe. Peterborough, Ontario: Broadview, 2000.

Robinson, Mary. *Memoirs of Mary Robinson, "Perdita," from the Edition Edited by Her Daughter*. Ed. J. Fitzgerald Malloy. London: Gibbings, 1894.

Robinson, Mary. *The Memoirs of the Late Mrs. Mary Robinson, Written by Herself*. 4 vols. London: Wilks and Taylor, 1801. Rpt. in *Women's Theatrical Memoirs*, vol. 1. Ed. Sharon Setzer. London: Pickering and Chatto, 2007.

Rojek, Chris. *Celebrity*. London: Reaktion Books, 2001.

Rosenthal, Laura. *Playwrights and Plagiarists in Early Modern England: Gender, Authorship, Literary Property*. Ithaca, NY: Cornell University Press, 1996.

Rosenthal, Laura. "Trials of Manhood: Cibber, *The Dunciad*, and the Masculine Self." *"More Solid Learning": New Perspectives on Alexander Pope's "Dunciad"*. Ed. Catherine Ingrassia and Claudia Thomas. Lewisburg, PA: Bucknell University Press, 2000.

Ross, Ian Campbell. *Laurence Sterne: A Life*. New York: Oxford University Press, 2001.

Rousseau, G. S. "*Et in Arcadia homo*": Opera, Gender, and Sexual Politics in *The Dunciad*." *"More Solid Learning": New Perspectives on Alexander Pope's "Dunciad"*. Ed. Catherine Ingrassia and Claudia Thomas. Lewisburg, PA: Bucknell University Press, 2000.

Rousseau, Jean-Jacques. *The Confessions of J. Rousseau, Complete*. Echo Library, 2007.

Rowe, Nicholas. *Jane Shore: A Tragedy*. London: John Bell, 1791.

[Ruffhead, Owen.] *Monthly Review* 24 (February 1761): 101–116.

Rumbold, Valerie. "Ideology and Opportunism: The Role of Handel in Pope's *The Dunciad in Four Books*." *"More Solid Learning": New Perspectives on Alexander Pope's "Dunciad"*. Ed. Catherine Ingrassia and Claudia Thomas. Lewisburg, PA: Bucknell University Press, 2000.

Sandahl, Carrie, and Philip Auslander. "Introduction: Disability Studies in Commotion with Performance Studies." *Bodies in Commotion: Disability and Performance*. Ann Arbor: University of Michigan Press, 2005.

Sandahl, Carrie, and Philip Auslander, eds. *Bodies in Commotion: Disability and Performance*. Ann Arbor: University of Michigan Press, 2005.

Schechner, Richard. *Between Theater and Anthropology*. Philadelphia: University of Pennsylvania Press, 1985.

Schlovsky, Viktor. "A Parodying Novel: Sterne's *Tristram Shandy*." *Laurence Sterne: A Collection of Critical Essays*. Ed. John Traugott. Englewood Cliffs, NJ: Prentice-Hall, 1968

Senelick, Laurence. "Mollies or Men of Mode? Sodomy and the Eighteenth-Century London Stage" *Journal of the History of Sexuality* 1.1 (1990): 33–67.

Sennett, Richard. *The Fall of Public Man*. New York: Alfred A. Knopf, 1977.

Setzer, Sharon. "The Dying Game: Crossdressing in Mary Robinson's *Walsingham*." *Nineteenth-Century Contexts* 22 (2000): 305–328.

Setzer, Sharon. Introduction to *A Letter to the Women of England* and *The Natural Daughter*. Ed. Sharon Setzer. Peterborough, Ontario: Broadview, 2003.

Setzer, Sharon. "Mary Robinson's Sylphid Self: The End of Feminine Self-Fashioning." *Philological Quarterly* 75 (1996): 501–520.

Shadwell, Thomas. *A True Widow*. 1678. Ed. Christopher J. Wheatley. *Broadview Anthology of Restoration and Eighteenth-Century Drama*. Ed. J. Douglas Canfield. Toronto: Broadview, 2001.

Shakespeare, William. *Richard III. Norton Shakespeare*. Ed. Stephen Greenblatt et al. 2nd ed. New York: W.W. Norton, 1997, 2008.

Shakespeare, William. *Richard Duke of York. Norton Shakespeare*. Ed. Stephen Greenblatt et al. 2nd ed. New York: W.W. Norton, 1997, 2008.

Shakespeare, William. *The Second Part of Henry the Fourth*. Ed. Stephen Greenblatt et al. 2nd ed. New York: W.W. Norton, 1997, 2008.

Shakespeare, William. *The Tragedy of Macbeth. Norton Shakespeare*. Ed. Stephen Greenblatt et al. 2nd ed. New York: W.W. Norton, 1997, 2008.

Shakespeare, William. *The Winter's Tale*. Ed. Frances E. Dolan. New York: Penguin, 1999.

Shakespeare, William. *The Works of William Shakespear*. Ed. Nicholas Rowe. London: Jacob Tonson, 1709.

Shershow, Scott Cutler. *Puppets and "Popular" Culture*. Ithaca, NY: Cornell University Press, 1995.

Sherman, Stuart. "Garrick among Media: The '*Now* Performer' Navigates the News." *PMLA* 126.4 (October 2011): 966–982.

Shirley, William. *A Bone for the Chroniclers to Pick; or, A Take-off Scene from Behind the Curtain: A Poem*. London: Printed for J. Coote and J. Scott, 1758.

Smith, Sidonie. *A Poetics of Women's Autobiography: Marginality and the Fictions of Self-Representation*. Bloomington: Indiana University Press, 1987.

Smith, William, ed. *Dictionary of Greek and Roman Antiquities*. Vol. 2. Boston: Little, Brown, 1870.

Snyder, Sharon L. "Unfixing Disability in Lord Byron's *The Deformed Transformed*." *Bodies in Commotion*. Ed. Carrie Sandahl and Philip Auslander. Ann Arbor: University of Michigan Press, 2005.

Sofer, Andrew. *The Stage Life of Props*. Ann Arbor: University of Michigan Press, 2003.

Some Reflections on the Management of a Theatre. London: J. Cooke, 1760.

Sontag, Susan. "Notes on 'Camp.'" *Against Interpretation and Other Essays*. New York: Farrar, Straus and Giroux, 1961.

Spacks, Patricia Meyer. *Imagining a Self: Autobiography and Novel in Eighteenth-Century England*. Cambridge, MA: Harvard University Press, 1976.

Spengemann, William. *The Forms of Autobiography: Episodes in the History of a Literary Genre*. New Haven: Yale University Press, 1980.

Stallybrass, Peter and Allon White. *The Politics and Poetics of Transgression*. Ithaca, NY: Cornell University Press, 1986.

Staves, Susan. "A Few Kind Words for the Fop." *SEL* 22 (1982): 413–28.

Stayley, George. *Life and Opinions of an Actor*. Dublin, 1762.

Sterne, Laurence. *The Florida Edition of the Works of Laurence Sterne*. 8 vols. Ed. Melvyn New and Joan New. Gainesville: University of Florida Press, 1978.

Sterne, Laurence. *The Life and Opinions of Tristram Shandy, Gentleman*. 1759–1767. Ed. Melvyn New and Joan New. London: Penguin, 1978, 2003.

Sterne, Laurence. *The Life and Opinions of Tristram Shandy, Gentleman: A Norton Critical Edition*. Ed. Howard Anderson. New York: W.W. Norton, 1980.

Sterne, Laurence. *A Sentimental Journey to France and Italy*. 1768. *A Sentimental Journey and Other Writings*. Ed. Tim Parnell. Oxford: Oxford University Press, 2003.

Stevens, George Alexander. *Celebrated Lecture on Heads*. Dublin, 1765.

Stone, George Winchester, Jr. "Garrick's Handling of 'Macbeth.'" *Studies in Philology* 38.4 (October 1941): 609–628.

Stone, George Winchester, Jr., and George M. Kahrl. *David Garrick: A Critical Biography*. Carbondale: Southern Illinois University Press, 1979.

Strange, Sally Minter. "Charlotte Charke: Transvestite or Conjuror?" *Restoration and Eighteenth-Century Theatre Research* 15.2 (1976): 54–59.

Straub, Kristina. *Sexual Suspects: Eighteenth-Century Players and Sexual Ideology*. Princeton: Princeton University Press, 1992.

Suard, Jean Baptiste. *London Chronicle* XVII: 1299 (April 10–18,1765): 373. *Laurence Sterne: The Critical Heritage*. Ed. Alan B. Howes. London: Routledge and Kegan Paul, 1974.

Sullivan, Maureen. Preface to Colley Cibber, *Three Sentimental Comedies*. Ed. Maureen Sullivan. New Haven: Yale University Press, 1973.

A Supplement to the Life and Opinions of Tristram Shandy, Gent. Serving to elucidate that work. London, 1760.

Tadie, Alexis. *Sterne's Whimsical Theatres of Language: Orality, Gesture, Literacy*. Aldershot, UK: Ashgate, 2003.

Taylor, Diana. *The Archive and the Repertoire: Performing Cultural Memory in the Americas*. Durham, NC: Duke University Press, 2003.

Terry, Richard. *Mock-Heroic from Butler to Cowper: An English Genre and Discourse*. Aldershot, UK: Ashgate, 2005.

Theatrical Biography: or, Memoirs of the Principal Performers of the Three Theatres Royal. 2 vols. London: S. Bladon, 1772.

Theatrical Examiner: An Enquiry into the Merits and Demerits of the Present English Performers in General. London: Printed for J. Doughty, 1757.

Thompson, Lynda M. *The Scandalous Memoirists: Constantia Phillips, Laetitia Pilkington and the Shame of Public Fame*. Manchester, UK: Manchester University Press, 2000.

Tillyard, Stella. "Celebrity in 18th-Century London." *History Today* 55 (June 2005): 20–27.

Tortorici, Dayna. "You Know It When You See It." *What Was the Hipster*? Ed. Mark Greif, Kathleen Ross, and Dayna Tortorici. New York: n+1 Foundation, 2010.

Tosi, Laura. "Then Rose the Seed of Chaos": Masque and Antimasque in *The Dunciad in Four Books*." *Studies in the Literary Imagination* 38.1 (2005): 198–218.

Traugott, John, ed. *Laurence Sterne: A Collection of Critical Essays*. Englewood Cliffs, NJ: Prentice-Hall, 1968.

Trumbach, Randolph. *The Rise of the Egalitarian Family: Aristocratic Kinship and Domestic Relations in Eighteenth-Century England*. New York: Harcourt Brace Jovanovich, 1978.

Ty, Eleanor. *Empowering the Feminine: The Narratives of Mary Robinson, Jane West, and Amelia Opie, 1796–1812*. Toronto: University of Toronto Press, 1999.

Vanbrugh, John. *The Relapse; or, Virtue in Danger, Being the Sequel of The Fool in Fashion*. Ed. James E. Gill. *Broadview Anthology of Restoration and Eighteenth-Century Drama*. Ed. J. Douglas Canfield. Toronto: Broadview, 2001.

van Lennep, W., E. L. Avery, A. H. Scouten, G. W. Stone, and C. B. Hogan, eds. *The London Stage, 1660–1800: A Calendar of Plays, Entertainments & Afterpieces, together with Casts, Box-Receipts and Contemporary Comment*. 5 vols. Carbondale: Southern Illinois University Press, 1960–68.

Veni, Vidi, Vici, Ivi: or, He's Gone! Who? Yorick! Grim Death Appears! London: Printed for L. Tomlinson, 1768.

[Victor, Benjamin.] *Memoirs of the Life of Barton Booth, Esq., with His Character*. London: published for John Watts, 1733.

Vila, Anne. *Enlightenment and Pathology: Sensibility in the Literature and Medicine of Eighteenth-Century France*. Baltimore: Johns Hopkins University Press, 1998.

Wahrman, Dror. *The Making of the Modern Self: Identity and Culture in Eighteenth-Century England*. New Haven: Yale University Press, 2004.

Wanko, Cheryl. *Roles of Authority: Thespian Biography and Celebrity in Eighteenth-Century Britain*. Lubbock: Texas Tech University Press, 2003.

Warner, Michael. "The Mass Public and the Mass Subject." *Habermas and the Public Sphere*. Ed. Craig Calhoun. Cambridge, MA: MIT Press, 1992.

Warner, Michael. *Publics and Counterpublics*. New York: Zone Books, 2005.

Watt, Ian. *The Rise of the Novel: Studies in Defoe, Richardson, and Fielding*. Berkeley: University of California Press, 1957, 2000.

West, Shearer. *The Image of the Actor: Verbal and Visual Representation in the Age of Garrick and Kemble*. London: Pinter, 1991.

Wheeler, Richard Press. "History, Character and Conscience in *Richard III*." *Comparative Drama* 5 (1971–1972): 301–321.

Whyte, Samuel. "Anecdote of Mrs. Charke." *Monthly Mirror*. June 1796. 94–95.

Wilkinson, Tate. *Memoirs of His Own Life*. 4 vols. York: Wilson, Spence and Mawman, 1790.

Wilkinson, Tate. *The Wandering Patentee; or, a History of the Yorkshire Theatres, from 1770 to the Present Time*. 4 vols. York: Wilson, Spence and Mawman, 1795.

Williams, Aubrey L. *"The Dunciad": A Study of Its Meaning*. London: Methuen, 1955.

Wilson, Lisa. "From Actress to Authoress: Mary Robinson's Pseudonymous Celebrity." *The Public's Open to Us All*: Essays on Women and Performance in Eighteenth-Century England. Ed. Laura Engel. Newcastle: Cambridge Scholars, 2009.

Wimsatt, W. K. "One Relation of Rhyme to Reason: Alexander Pope." *Modern Language Quarterly* 5 (1944): 323–338.

Woods, Leigh. *Garrick Claims the Stage: Acting as Social Emblem in Eighteenth-Century England*. Westport, CT: Greenwood, 1984.

Woolf, Virginia. "The Sentimental Journey." *The Common Reader: Second Series*. New York: Harcourt, Brace, and World, 1932, 1960.

Wordsworth, William. Preface to Samuel Taylor Coleridge and William Wordsworth, *Lyrical Ballads*. 1798. Ed. W. J. B. Owen. London: Oxford University Press, 1967.

INDEX